Resentment and the "Feminine"
in Nietzsche's Politico-Aesthetics

Resentment and the "Feminine" in Nietzsche's Politico-Aesthetics

Caroline Joan Picart

The Pennsylvania State University Press
University Park, Pennsylvania

Library of Congress Cataloging-in-Publication Data

Picart, Caroline Joan S., 1966–
    Resentment and the "feminine" in Nietzsche's politico-aesthetics / Caroline Joan S. Picart.
    p.   cm.
    Includes bibliographical references and index.
    ISBN 0-271-01888-7 (cloth: alk. paper)
    ISBN 0-271-01889-5 (pbk.: alk. paper)
    1. Nietzsche, Friedrich Wilhelm, 1844–1900. 2. Femininity (Philosophy)—History—19th century. 3. Woman (Philosophy)—History—19th century.   I. Title.
B3318.F45P53   1999
193—de21
                98-39331
                      CIP

Copyright © 1999 The Pennsylvania State University
All rights reserved
Printed in the United States of America
Published by The Pennsylvania State University Press,
University Park, PA 16802-1003

It is the policy of The Pennsylvania State University Press to use acid-free paper for the first printing of all clothbound books. Publications on uncoated stock satisfy the minimum requirements of American National Standard for Information Sciences—Permanence of Paper for Printed Library Materials, ANSI Z39.48-1992.

Contents

Acknowledgments	vii
Introduction: The Problem of the "Feminine" in Nietzsche	1
1 Genealogies of the "Feminine" and "Woman"	15
2 The Pre-Zarathustran Phase: Exca/Elevating the Mother	39
3 The Zarathustran Phase: The Phallic Mother	81
4 The Post-Zarathustran Phase: Emasculate Conception	111
5 Looking Back, Looking Forward	147
Bibliography	181
Index	187

Acknowledgments

I wish to thank the Office of University Research of the University of Wisconsin-Eau Claire for a research grant that enabled me to acquire recently published material, as well as bring this manuscript to completion. Chris Lind's and Don Zeutschel's efficiency and helpfulness have been both enabling and encouraging, and have made the process of integrating research and teaching less arduous and more enjoyable.

I wish to thank those who have read and critically contributed to various sections of this manuscript. In particular, I wish to thank Stanley Rosen, Dan Conway, and Ray Fleming for many thought-provoking discussions on Nietzsche, and encouragement in pursuing what had initially been intended as a project leading to a double Ph.D. in Philosophy and Comparative Literature. My gratitude also extends to Joe Kockelmans, Carl Hausman, Irene Harvey, Doug Anderson, Nancy Love, Veronique Foti, Pierre Kerszberg, John Stuhr, Peter Lipton, Earl Fitz, and Tom Beebee, whose support in my venturing forth in interdisciplinary pursuits has been invaluable. I also wish to thank Kelly Oliver and Leslie Paul Thiele for their insightful and constructive comments, which have enabled me to refine my thoughts even further. I also wish to acknowledge a debt to David Owen, then the editor of the *Journal of Nietzsche Studies*, for granting copyright permission to reprint selections from an article, "Classic and Romantic Mythology in the (Re)birthing of Nietzsche's Zarathustra," which were incorporated into Chapter 3 of this book. I also wish to give due credit to *Research/Penn State*, which featured a section from my then-dissertation, in an article, "Inside from the Outside"; this subsequently has been modified and incorporated into Chapter 5. Finally, I also wish to thank the Media

Development Center of the University of Wisconsin-Eau Claire for their efficiency in producing a camera-ready image of "Nurturance?".

I warmly thank my colleagues and friends at the Department of Philosophy and Religious Studies, University of Wisconsin-Eau Claire: Jim Brummer, Ron Koshoshek, Dick Behling, Richard deGrood, Ned Beach, Lisa Wersal, Lori Rowlett, Martin Webb, Jonathan Paradise, Joyce Hageness, and Joanne Erickson. Their collegial and stimulating engagement as well as emotional support have helped keep this manuscript on track. My friends at the Eau Claire School of Dance, the Lynn Dance Company, the Arthur Murray Studio, and Two to Tango also deserve mention: Jerry Danielson, Barry Lynn, Michael Doran, John Speros, Stacy Nicolai, Kelly Smith, Rob Salli, Jace Smith, Ida Hinz, and many others, whose friendship and shared love of dance have provided many hours of fun that have helped me to return with renewed vigor to refining this manuscript. I would also like to thank Frank Smoot, whose sense of humor and professionalism have made the process of producing an index a fun and manageable, rather than quixotic, exercise.

I am also very much indebted to the director of Penn State University Press, Sandy Thatcher. Sandy's candid straightforwardness, helpfulness, and pragmatism have been crucial to making work on this manuscript both enjoyable and efficient. The editorial staff of Penn State University Press, notably Cherene Holland, also deserve mention for their impeccable cheerfulness and unflagging willingness to assist in every way possible.

Finally, I wish to the thank the Picart and Houck families for their affection, devotion, and irrepressible sense of humor. I wish to dedicate this manuscript to them, and to my husband, Davis, whose love, support, and belief in me have helped me continually to grow.

Introduction: The Problem of the "Feminine" in Nietzsche

> Did ancient thinking about gender difference simply reflect male dominance, or was it also an attempt by males to lay claim to a small part of what females possessed?
> —Nicole Loraux, *"What is a Goddess?"*

> At the root of this investigation, then, is a desire to set myth in the context of the city. Our choice falls on Athens, which, in Greek studies, is the city that represents the true homeland of the national concept of identity. But we should not be misled: Athens is the obvious choice in any attempt to draw up a precise list of variations on a myth, and to take into account the varying positions and sites where myth is exposed. Such a choice is essential, also, to the task of identifying the effects of myth on representations produced by the city.
> —Nicole Loraux, *The Children of Athena:*
> *Athenian Ideas About Citizenship and the Division Between the Sexes*

Peter Burgard's introductory paragraph to *Nietzsche and the Feminine* clearly outlines the basic questions haunting the topic of Nietzsche's philosophy in relation to issues of feminism:

> "You are going to women? Do not forget the whip!" What college student has not read or at least heard of this, one of the most familiar lines from one of the most familiar books of Western philosophy, *Thus Spoke Zarathustra*? . . . In studying Nietzsche, there are two basic responses to the assault perpetrated on the reader by such statements. One is to say Nietzsche was a misogynist and leave it at that. The other is to wonder what place such statements, pervasive as they are, might have in his philosophy, to recognize that their very pervasiveness demands attention.[1]

---

1. Peter J. Burgard, introduction to *Nietzsche and the Feminine*, ed. Peter J. Burgard (Charlottesville: University Press of Virginia, 1994), 1–2.

2   Introduction

As Kelly Oliver[2] corroborates, for the most part, discussions on Nietzsche's relation to the "feminine"/"woman" range from Ofelia Schutte's vehemence that Nietzsche "maintains what can be characterized fundamentally as an antifeminist position both on gender difference and on the issue of social and political equality"[3] to David Farrell Krell's attempt at a more sympathetic reading of Nietzsche as someone who "writes with the hand of woman."[4] For schematic purposes, four general warring camps of readers seem to emerge: (1) those who believe Nietzsche's writings are essentially feminist; (2) those who believe Nietzsche's writings are at least potentially useful to feminism[5]; (3) those who maintain that Nietzsche's writings are irredeemably misogynistic[6]; and (4) those for whom a possible connection between Nietzsche and feminism is not even a mentionable or speculative issue. The various camps that engage in debates on Nietzsche and his controversial relationship with the issue of the "feminine" often trade quotations, with the profeminist (essentialist and tactical) Nietzsche camps usually citing from pre-Zarathustran texts, such as *The Gay Science*,[7] and the antifeminist Nietzsche camps citing post-Zarathustran texts, such as *Beyond Good and Evil* and *Ecce Homo*.

As opposed to such approaches, what I do is a more genealogical or developmental approach, involving the use of a larger frame of investigation employing a horizontal (i.e., across texts) and vertical (i.e., within texts) analysis rather than an in-depth examination of only one or two specific texts, as many readers of Nietzsche have tended to do. Notwithstanding the observation that Nietzsche admittedly displays a type of misogyny, I am more concerned with interpreting his peculiar misog-

---

2. Kelly Oliver, *Womanizing Nietzsche: Philosophy's Relation to the "Feminine"* (New York: Routledge, 1995), 137.

3. Ofelia Schutte, "Nietzsche on Gender Difference: A Critique," *Newsletter on Feminism and Philosophy* (1990): 64. See also Ofelia Schutte, *Beyond Nihilism: Nietzsche Without Masks* (Chicago: University of Chicago Press, 1984), 176–85.

4. David Farrell Krell, *Postponements: Woman, Sensuality, and Death in Nietzsche* (Bloomington: Indiana University Press, 1986), 10.

5. For example, see Erik Patens, "Traces of Derrida, 'Woman,' and Politics: A Reading of Spurs," *Philosophy Today* 33 (Winter 1989): 291–301; Gayle Ormiston, "Traces of Derrida: Nietzsche's Image of Woman," *Philosophy Today* 28 (Summer 1984): 178–88; Rosalyn Diprose, "Nietzsche, Ethics, and Sexual Difference," *Radical Philosophy* 52 (Summer 1989): 27–32; Imafedia Okhamafe, "Heidegger's Nietzsche and Nietzsche's Play: The Questions of Wo(man), Christianity, Nihilism, and Humanism," *Soundings* 71 (Winter 1988): 533–53; Shari Neller Starrett, "Nietzsche, Women, and Relationships of Strength," *Southwest Philosophical Review* 6 (January 1990): 73–79; Keith Ansell-Pearson, "Who is the Übermensch? Truth, Time, and Woman in Nietzsche," *Journal of the History of Ideas* 53 (April–June 1992): 301–31; Lawrence Habib, "Nietzsche on Woman," *Southern Journal of Philosophy* 19 (Fall 1981): 333–46; Robert John Ackerman, *Nietzsche: A Frenzied Look* (Amherst: University of Massachusetts Press, 1990), 122–37.

6. For example, see Linda Singer, "Nietzschean Mythologies: The Inversion of Value and War Against Women," *Soundings* 66 (1983): 281–95.

7. Thomas Common's translation of *Die Fröhliche Wissenschaft* uses *The Joyful Wisdom* instead.

yny via symptomatological criteria that he himself establishes. While other scholars seem to have focused on classifying the degree of offensiveness of Nietzsche's ambivalent pronouncements on the "feminine" and "women," I attempt an approach that seeks to examine what this misogyny means for his political philosophy as a whole.

My interpretation therefore contrasts with, for instance, Koelb's thesis that Nietzsche suffers from "castration envy." Briefly stated, Koelb in "Castration Envy: Nietzsche and the Figure of Woman"[8] argues that the numerous crucial figures in Nietzsche's philosophy (such as the artist and the philosopher—i.e., the contemplatives, the creators of the world, the "male mothers") are all figures of castration and that all appear in the figure of "woman." More significantly and surprisingly, all of these are linked to castration not through anxiety but through desire, since they draw their power from the absence of the phallus. As the figure of castration, "woman" thus becomes the object of castration envy. From there, Koelb delineates several of the most important figurations of "woman" through which Nietzsche wrestles with key philosophical questions: the tropes of "woman" as nature, as veiled truth, and as life. In each of these tropes, castration is indispensable and itself becomes a trope for ultimate power—where potency of the phallus is seen as insignificant when compared to the power of the figures of its absence. Thus one of Nietzsche's central ideas, the will to power, instills envy for this castration/void/emptiness that represents absolute power. Fascinating as this thesis is, I think that Nietzsche's desire is directed less toward castration than it is toward pregnancy—his figure for creativity and generativity. In my view, Nietzsche suffers less from castration envy than from womb envy.

One could object to the term "womb envy" on two grounds: (1) womb envy is a term that would seem to belong within the realm of psychoanalytic theory or cultural analysis rather than philosophy; and (2) the womb is not analogous to the penis. The first objection springs from an anxiety that philosophy must be sharply delimited from psychoanalytic theory or cultural analysis. Insofar as I am attempting to do a critique of Nietzsche using the very standards of critique he set up and given that Nietzsche saw philosophy as a more porous discipline, interfacing with psychology, the critique of culture and art, rhetoric, politics, and myth, the use of such an interdisciplinary rather than strictly "philosophical" term is particularly appropriate. The second objection is rooted in a biologism that is not relevant to the aims of this book. Anatomically, the womb is not structurally homologous to the penis. Yet within the context of Nietzschean philosophy, what is at issue is power, and what are operative as symbols for "masculine" and "feminine" power. In Nietzsche's philosophy, the penis corresponds with the phallus, which is a recurrent symbol for masculine identity as

---

8. Clayton Koelb, "Castration Envy: Nietzsche and the Figure of Woman," in *Nietzsche and the Feminine*, ed. Peter J. Burgard (Charlottesville: University Press of Virginia, 1994), 71–81.

powerful and life-giving, while the womb is paradigmatically associated with the feminine trait of fecundity and generativity.

In brief therefore, I employ a Nietzschean critique of Nietzsche[9] in the sense that I use his own symptomatological "art of interpretation" to track the way his initial use of "feminine" (alongside "masculine") mythic anthropomorphisms as figures for modernity's regenerative powers, indicative of his early political optimism, gradually gives way to an increasingly pessimistic and misogynistic politic, resulting in the silencing and emasculation of his earlier figure-ations of the "feminine."[10] In other words, I employ a symptomatological approach to the problem of the "feminine," interpreting Nietzsche's (d)evolving tropes of "woman"/the "feminine" as indicative of modernity's and his own personal, gradually congealing, impotence and decline. A "symptomatology," as Nietzsche uses it, is a process of reading or interpreting an encrypted text with an eye to differentiating "health" (implying an individual's or culture's vitality, resilience, power) from "disease" (implying an individual's or culture's weakness, fragility, or impotence, as evidenced in its "secondary" nature, or separation from the realm of eternal health—nature). Hence, my approach begins, necessarily, with an interpretative bent, as this approach is an attempt to enter into and harness Nietzsche's methodology as turned against itself. Yet my method's ultimate objective is critical as it also aims to arrive at an account of modernity, which springs from and yet is radically different from Nietzsche's account. The similarity of this framework to Nietzsche's method lies in its use of the same ironic and "psychological" tools that are crucial to Nietzsche's genealogical arsenal; its difference lies in its bringing to the fore the voices of the "feminine" ambivalently repressed in Nietzsche's devolving political vision. Such a framework is different insofar as this account shows how Nietzsche's genealogy of modernity suffers from delusions, despite its ironic undercutting of itself.

---

9. In terms of strategy, this is similar to what Derrida would call an "immanent critique," yet it differs in stylistic form from Derrida's.

10. Similarly, on the issue of silencing the "feminine," Bernard Pautrat's "Nietzsche Medused" presents a reading of Nietzsche's identification of the eternal return with Medusa, which turns the eternal return itself into a fetish. Pautrat draws attention to the fact that in various drafts for *Zarathustra*, Nietzsche refers to "the great thought of Medusa's head: all features of the world harden, a frozen, mortal combat." Using this quotation from Nietzsche's notes for the fourth part of *Thus Spoke Zarathustra*, Pautrat interprets "the greatest thought" as the thought of eternal return. From there, he moves into theorizing what it could mean to call the eternal return a Medusa's head and why Nietzsche refrained from mentioning Medusa in the final version of *Thus Spoke Zarathustra*. He concludes that the thought of the eternal return has the same effect as a Medusa's head: it freezes the world in mortal combat; it is terrifying; it is impossible to look at. The absence of Medusa's head in the final version, he claims, makes it no less representative of the eternal return—which, in its naked presentation is, in his view, also eternally deferred. Cf. Bernard Pautrat, "Nietzsche Medused," in *Looking After Nietzsche*, ed. L. Richels (Albany: State University of New York Press, 1990), 162–63.

My intention therefore is to examine the notion of the "feminine" in Nietzsche's developing philosophy principally as an image or figure for procreative and regenerative power. That is, I focus on the fluctuating revaluations that Nietzsche's philosophy undergoes with respect to the (M)Other. This is because it is this particular meaning that is most fruitful in tracking Nietzsche's critique of modernity to his advancing misogyny (and vice versa). It is this particular valence of the "feminine" that Nietzsche himself draws repeated attention to, and is the key to arriving at a symptomatological account of how Nietzsche's attitude toward "woman" embodies or contours his devolving political vision—(dis)empowered and dis-eased by *ressentiment*. Nietzsche's use of the figures of the "feminine" (*weiblich*) and "woman" (*Weib/Frau*) changes as his political agenda changes. In his pre-Zarathustran and Zarathustran texts, the lines separating the "feminine" (understood principally in terms of ancient Greek deities or figures, such as Aphrodite or Helen) from "woman" (historically rooted, flesh-and-blood women) seem fairly clear. However, Nietzsche appears gradually to downplay the role of the "feminine" and replace her with the more negative "woman" in conjunction with his deepening sense of political impotence. By eventually appropriating the feminine power of birthing unto Zarathustra, as a Romantic reincarnation of the Zeus-Dionysus-Apollo myths, Nietzsche compensates for his growing sense of political impotence. His post-Zarathustran pronouncements increasingly seem figuratively to blame or attack women for his (and modernity's) own lack of generative powers. "Woman" (as opposed to the "feminine") somehow becomes the scapegoat upon whom modernity's (and Nietzsche's, as child of modernity) sins of sterility and impotence must be dumped in order to save Nietzsche's polis of esoteric readers.

Moving from his pre-Zarathustran texts, *The Birth of Tragedy* (1872), *Human, All Too Human* (1878), and *The Gay Science* (1882) to *Thus Spoke Zarathustra* (1883–85), and a few crucial post-Zarathustran works, such as *Beyond Good and Evil* (1886), *Twilight of the Idols* (1888), and *Ecce Homo* (1888), I trace the weblike ambivalences of Nietzsche's interaction with the "feminine"/"woman" in his developing politico-aesthetic framework. The attention to myth is crucial for this project because as I show, Nietzsche's use and recasting of mythic masks is reflective of his own (d)evolving (and increasingly misogynistic) political philosophy. His appropriation of Greek mythic gods and goddesses[11] is in line with his changing view of how the sickly age of modernity may be rejuvenated.[12] His use of mythic divinities as figures for his changing aims reflects his deepening pessimism regarding the looming

---

11. For purposes of limiting the scope of this study, I have focused mainly on Greek deities, though this is not to say that the mythic allusions Nietzsche draws from are all necessarily Greek.

12. Tracy B. Strong puts forth an interpretation of Nietzsche's politics that I find compelling, and convergent, to some extent, with directions I am interested in exploring. Strong depicts Nietzsche's

temptation to nihilism in the wake of the death of God. Hence, Nietzsche's use of myth (embodied in gendered figures) in relation to his philosophy of the polis, changes as he moves through the three phases I have roughly designated as "pre-Zarathustran" (roughly 1871–82), "Zarathustran" (1883–85), and "post-Zarathustran" (1886–88). His use of mythology as gendered is the key I use to understand the symptomatology of his politics as linked with his aesthetics.

During his most optimistic[13] phase, that prior to the publication of *Zarathustra*, Nietzsche appears to view myth as mediating, or illustrating and yet not resolving, the ambiguity binding the "illusory" and the "real," or the "artistic" and the "political" in the figures of Dionysus and Apollo, or Baubô and Medusa, for instance. However, *Thus Spoke Zarathustra* marks a shift in his thought: instead of simply mediating this aesthetic tension between illusion and reality, the converging myths of Dionysus, Apollo, and Zeus function as a "noble lie," employing at least two different voices for two different audiences—"a book for all and none." During the third phase, the post-Zarathustran phase, Nietzsche's voice grows increasingly shrill as he now uses myth in order to achieve his all-consuming political aim: to hasten the coming of the twilight of the idols, to catalyze modernity's descent into self-destruction. The weight of the mythic "noble lie" Nietzsche fashioned in *Thus Spoke Zarathustra* bears increasingly heavily upon him. What results is Nietzsche's outward advocacy for the value of a mythic noble lie (which functions to preserve human beings who are unable to withstand the absurd meaninglessness of the human condition), alongside his inward personal attempt to live without such a "noble lie." The strain of these opposing thrusts, coupled with and enhanced by Nietzsche's descent into madness, eventually leads him simultaneously to hyperbolize and internalize his principal politico-mythic figure, Zarathustra-Dionysus—and thus, to see himself as the divinely lacerated embodiment of humanity's necessary "noble lie": finally, "ready to rule the world."[14] Nietzsche, during his post-Zarathustran phase, appears to begin to believe in the "noble lie"—that humanity's salvation is to come through fertile beings

---

politics, drawn from the model of Greek political life, as a politics of transformation rather than domination. He argues that the essence of Nietzsche's politics may be regained only through a political aesthetics. I agree with Strong's reading of the complex interplay binding Nietzsche's politics and aesthetics. However, I think he overlooks the gendered nature of Nietzsche's political aesthetic, and does not take into account Nietzsche's later renunciation of a more predominantly aesthetic resolution in favor of a drastic political destruction of modernity. Cf. Strong, "Nietzsche's Political Aesthetics," in *Nietzsche's New Seas*, ed. Michael Gillespie and Tracy Strong (Chicago: University of Chicago Press, 1988), 153–74.

13. It is important to note that the use of "optimism" is mine, as it is used to describe Nietzsche's belief in the possibility of redeeming modernity, as well as his relatively more benign treatment of the "feminine." Nietzsche adopts Schopenhauer's view of pessimism as strength, and yet uses this pessimism for optimistic (that is, rejuvenatory/redemptive/salvific) aims.

14. Christopher Middleton, ed., *Selected Letters of Friedrich Nietzsche*, vol. 8 (Chicago: University of Chicago Press, 1969), 460.

capable of withstanding the vision of the eternal return—and to see himself as its bearer, and in turn, his attitude towards the "feminine" becomes increasingly hostile. His increasing advocacy for and frustration over the inefficacy of the "noble lie" leads him to "blame" women for modernity's decadence and impotence—a dystopia whose self-destructive roots and unauthoritative foundations become evident.

At this point, perhaps, it is best to attempt to render more clearly the interrelationships binding "woman," "womanly," and the "feminine" as I see them at work in the genealogy of Nietzsche's corpus. For purposes of clarity and convenience, the "feminine" (*weiblich*), as operative principally in Nietzsche's pre-Zarathustran texts, usually is figured or anthropomorphized into Greek mythic deities or figures, such as Demeter or Cassandra, and personified entities such as Nature or Art. By "woman" (*Weib/Frau*) Nietzsche usually means actual historical women living in nineteenth-century bourgeois German society. He eventually narrows this down, particularly in *Ecce Homo*, one of his post-Zarathustran texts, to refer specifically to his mother and sister. "Womanly" (*weiblich*) is an in-between category, elevating certain characteristics of "woman," such as the "gentleness of girls" to the more positively (e)valuated category of the "feminine," or debasing other characteristics of "woman," such as her alleged jealousy and possessiveness to the more negatively (e)valuated category of "woman."[15]

It is important, though, to point out that these delineations are simply rough approximations. Nietzsche's use of them tends to blur them together in varying concentrations. Hence, in his pre-Zarathustran phase, he elevates the "womanly" trait of "innocence" to the "feminine" ideal, alongside the figures of Demeter and Gaia, the all-powerful mother figures; in his post-Zarathustran phase, he simultaneously elevates Cosima to the position of the mythic "feminine" that Demeter and Gaia have occupied in *Birth of Tragedy*, and debases his own sister and mother to the equally mythic position of "woman-as-vermin" in *Ecce Homo*.

Ultimately, as I show, Nietzsche begins with a political aesthetic antidote to modernity's unhealthiness or lack of vitality as glimpsed in such texts as *The Birth of Tragedy*, *Human, All Too Human*, and *The Gay Science*. He then moves on to an aesthetic political inoculation in *Thus Spoke Zarathustra*, and eventually plunges into an emphasis on the overtly (and as the madness sets in, crudely) political amputation in response to the gangrenous state of modernity—which, following Nietzsche's characterization

15. The terms "sex" (anatomically based distinctions) and "gender" (socially determined categories), which form the currency of many contemporary debates, are not particularly useful in this context because Nietzsche tends to violate these borders via his recurring tropes of health and sickness, where the physical/physiological/anatomical/biological form a complex continuum with social, psychological, and genetic aspects. Thus, his explanation of the corruption of modernity is bound up with, for instance, his myth of the (genetic) mixing of noble and plebeian races, resulting in an effeminized (physical, physiological, anatomical, social) creature tormented by conflicting (psychological, physiological) impulses.

of it, is the corrupt and bankrupt state of Western society, the heir to Greek culture, from the nineteenth century onward. As specifically linked to the issue of the "feminine"/"woman," Nietzsche's texts initially reveal glimmers of sympathy for the sociopolitical plight of women (e.g., *The Gay Science* and *Human, All Too Human*), and use powerful "feminine" myths (e.g., Baubô and Medusa) alongside "masculine" ones (e.g., Dionysus and Apollo) as figures for doctrines such as the eternal recurrence and the will to power. Later, however, his writings reveal a gradually congealing trend of either silencing the "feminine" or downplaying the role of "woman." This begins with *Thus Spoke Zarathustra*, where the triad of Dionysus, Apollo, and Zeus now take center stage, alongside the ambivalent depiction of "feminine" figures such as the little old woman, Life, Wisdom, and Eternity. This shunning and banishing of the "feminine" and later replacement with the notorious "woman" eventually culminates in *Ecce Homo*, where Nietzsche simultaneously deifies and defies his "angelic" father, and reduces his mother and sister (and all figures of "woman"/the "feminine") to *canaille* ("rabble/riffraff") and a "hell machine,"[16] effectively bringing together, in his person, the figures of Dionysus (who embodies life's vitality and eternity, ever pregnant with creativity) and Zeus (who killed off or vanquished Kronos, his father).[17] Although it appears that Nietzsche attributes his continuing life to his mother (since as his father he is already dead), and thus, seems to leave open the possibility of a positive image of the "feminine," it is important to stress that the type of life Nietzsche views himself as inheriting from his mother is diseased and corrupt. He seems to underline the belief that he can only overcome this dread infection through the health he inherits from his father. The precondition for his regenerative powers is his father's celestial nobility, which he uses in order to restore himself to health. His "original health" is traced to his father, which is necessary in order to convert the "morbidity" from his mother into an "energetic stimulus for life."

The focus on the intersecting and undulating planes of myth and gender in relation to Nietzsche's political philosophy is vital to this project insofar as it brings to

---

16. Kofman follows a parallel track in her essay "A Fantastical Genealogy: Nietzsche's Family Romance." She also draws attention to Nietzsche's "murder" (i.e., denial) and elevation of his father to angelic realms, and his relegation of his mother, Franziska, and his sister, Elizabeth, to the status of venomous vermin. However, in contrast to the focus on the interplay binding gender, myth, and politics that I choose, Kofman takes a more Freudian psychoanalytic tack. Her eventual conclusion is that Nietzsche's radical ambivalence toward his mother and sister reveals a hidden, incestuous love. Interesting as this conclusion may be, Kofman's final conclusions diverge sharply from my interests in Nietzsche's gendered mytho-political aesthetics. Cf. Sarah Kofman, "A Fantastical Genealogy: Nietzsche's Family Romance," in *Nietzsche and the Feminine*, ed. Peter J. Burgard (Charlottesville: University Press of Virginia, 1994), 35–52.

17. Zeus, in Greek mythology, is also infamous for his incessant betrayals of Hera, an attribute Nietzsche significantly does not attempt to appropriate.

the fore questions of Nietzsche's authorship and authority—of how he both solidifies and undercuts his position as philosopher concerned with political questions: e.g., how to rescue decadent modern society and bring into effect a new world order and with it, a new morality; how to effect the re-empowerment of the healthy or noble versus the corrupt and resentful herd; how to tame woman, man's "most dangerous plaything," into collaborating in the project of giving birth to a star; how to bear and give birth to the *Übermenschen*, his figure for a type of humanity capable of enduring the nightmarish vision of the eternal return, via his own undertaking of the suffering of the anti-Christ(ian).

Nietzsche's relation to the "feminine" also revolves around the question of how he envisages the body[18] in general in relation to one of the binary dichotomies his philosophy never explodes: the notions of health and sickness. Eventually, I aim to show that Nietzsche's texts reveal an increasing emphasis on the "masculine" corporeal body and its physicality (especially his own) alongside ambivalent attempts to reconstruct the Greek figuration of nature as a "feminine" body that is simultaneously subject to dismemberment and yet enormously powerful, leading progressively to vehement appropriations of the "feminine" power of birthing unto himself. Eventually, the view he takes unto himself, as a "phallic mother," eternally pregnant, is essentially a "hysterical"[19] one—one that persistently announces its pregnancies rather than its births, as its births unleash essentially abortive stillbirths or disfigured monstrosities. The significance of this observation lies in its excavation of how Nietzsche's response to the "feminine"/"woman" relates to his political philosophy: his flirtation with parthenogenesis is indicative of his "revenge" against the depleted vitality and reproductivity of his age. "Woman" eventually emerges as the sacrificial beast upon whom the sins of modernity and Nietzsche must be heaped in order to purge and save Nietzsche's city of esoteric readers.

Ultimately, the questions I aim to answer are:

1. What myths does Nietzsche use as figures for his evolving political philosophy?
2. How do these mythic masks develop as Nietzsche moves through his pre-Zarathustran, Zarathustran, and post-Zarathustran texts, particularly in relation to the "feminine"/"woman" and political authority?

---

18. In a parallel move, Rudi Visker makes the following statement: "This understanding that bodies have a history, which derives from Nietzsche's genealogy of morals, forces us, in Foucault's view, into a 'microphysics of power, whose field of validity is situated in a sense between these great functionings [the apparatuses and the institutions] and the *bodies themselves* with their materiality and their forces.'" Michel Foucault, *Discipline and Punish: The Birth of the Prison,* in Rudi Visker, *Michel Foucault: Genealogy as Critique,* trans. Chris Turner (New York: Verso, 1995), 71–72.

19. I derive this use of the term from Gary Shapiro, *Alcyone: Nietzsche on Gifts, Noise, and Women* (Albany: State University of New York Press, 1991), 136.

3. What functions do these myths serve, which have political and philosophical import for Nietzsche's developing vision?
4. How do concepts of the "body" ("feminine" and "masculine") figure into the flux of Nietzsche's changing political mythologies and their assumptions regarding the nature of political authority?
5. What accounts of modernity and the "feminine"/"woman" emerge as a result of this peculiar genealogy?
6. How can one begin to move toward a post-Nietzschean politico-aesthetics?

Such a genealogical approach, in its initially descriptive rather than prescriptive focus, also aims to inoculate itself against Krell's objections to what he perceives as Irigaray's hidden phallicacy and *ressentiment* against Nietzsche.[20] Audre Lorde's[21] contention that the attempted destruction of the Master's house with his own tools ends up in the regressive rebuilding of such structures certainly challenges the facile adoption of subversion from within as a feminist tactic. Yet one of the issues I begin to explore in this project is how far the establishment of a post-Nietzschean construction of "authority" demands and can realistically effect the destruction of the old order. If destruction is intrinsically intertwined with (re)construction, as Nietzsche contends, then infection of the Master's tools is necessary alongside the (re)creation of the Mother's hearth. If health and disease are not as easily separable as Nietzsche desperately wanted to make them appear, can one use this fluctuating border between health and illness to produce a reconstructive politics of resistance, rather than a version of the liberatory or salvationist model Nietzsche soon realized to be impossible, as evidenced in his transmogrification of it to become a suicide-as-salvation politic?

In other words, as I begin to explore in Chapter 5, if the issue of authority is ultimately bound up with the eternal return of *ressentiment*, and the reawakening of the supposedly dead Author, how may a genuinely postmodern and post-Nietzschean philosophy of the future be tentatively configured? Part of the answer, I believe, lies in a critical reexamination of Nietzsche's effective use of the intertwining realms of politics and aesthetics as embodied in gendered and mythic representations. I think that the outlines of such a philosophy beyond Nietzsche may be glimpsed in an aesthetic that is critically engaged in a politics of resistance against the temptation to *ressentiment* and the appeal to Authority, and a politics that does not negate its aesthetic underpinnings, as a mediation between "truth" and "lie." Such a philosophy necessarily entails a critical and constructive revisioning of warring fictions in the attempt,

20. David Farrell Krell, "To the Orange Grove at the Edge of the Sea: Remarks on Luce Irigaray's *Amante marine*," in *Nietzsche and the Feminine*, ed. Peter Burgard (Charlottesville: University Press of Virginia, 1994), 185–209.
21. Audre Lorde, *Sister Outsider: Essays and Speeches* (Freedom, Calif.: The Crossing Press, 1984).

at least, to loosen the tyrannical dichotomies of Same/Center/"masculine" versus other/marginal/"feminine" so characteristic of modernity, and even Nietzsche's attempted proto-postmodernism. Such a genuinely postmodern philosophy must attempt to engage itself in concrete issues of social justice that are involved in the politics of re-presenting the myths of "masculinity"/"femininity" and "health"/"sickness" across a multicultural spectrum. In my view, this budding philosophy should be characterized by a critical replacement of the dream of redemption from *ressentiment* with a vigilant resistance against the ever-present temptation to the master-slave dialectic that has characterized Nietzsche's (masked) Romantic political aesthetics. As such, it must not locate itself in a neutral vantage point from which the ethical binds of Nietzsche's attempts to deconstruct and re-create modernity may be viewed, but as rooted in concrete practices of representing and revisioning the interconnections binding issues of power, myth, and gender. I see the beginnings of such a genuinely postmodern political aesthetics in Hélène Cixous's writings and Trin Minh-ha's films, in whose wake I wish to blaze my own path as both an artist and philosopher, as well as a woman of both Eastern and Western heritage. The outlines of how I see myself moving in the direction of what I preliminarily label a post-Nietzschean politico-aesthetic are carefully sketched in the final subsection of Chapter 5.

Both Sarah Kofman and Kelly Oliver attempt to link Nietzsche's relationships with actual women, such as his mother and sister, to their philosophical and psychoanalytic readings of Nietzsche. Although I see the value of such scholarship, this interpretative move, which comes dangerously close to psychobiography, is really not in line with the type of inquiry I am interested in. Lou Andreas-Salome voices a similar view in her portrait of Nietzsche: "Whoever wishes to view . . . Nietzsche's exterior experiences in order to grasp the inner, would at best hold only an empty shell from which the spirit has escaped."[22] In other words, I am less interested in the sundry details of his tortured relationships with his mother and sister, or his complicated (and in some cases possibly imagined) romantic liaisons with women like Salomé and Cosima Wagner, than in showing how a correspondence can be drawn between Nietzsche's remarks on the "feminine" and "woman" and Nietzsche's politics and aesthetics. In other words, it is not the microscopic view but the macroscopic dimensions of Nietzsche's gendered politics that this book is concerned with, even if the two interact. The issue of how, for instance, Elisabeth's idolatrous admiration of her brother, or Salomé's possible inspiration of Nietzsche's vision of the eternal return, *influenced* Nietzsche's philosophy is not only very difficult to prove, but would also require a very different focus from this book's.

---

22. Lou Andreas-Salomé, *Nietzsche*, ed. Siegfried Mandel (Redding Ridge, Conn.: Black Swan Books, 1988), 5.

12   Introduction

Claims of influence are particularly difficult to prove in Nietzsche's case. For example, Peter Gast, Nietzsche's only personal disciple and voluntary part-time secretary, disdainfully dismissed Salomé's account of Nietzsche on the grounds that she attempted to give an impression of longer familiarity with Nietzsche in person and correspondence than had been the case, and conveniently glossed over the violent break in their relations. Salomé's account of Nietzsche was also much maligned by Elisabeth, Nietzsche's sister, and Nietzsche's old friend, Carl von Gersdorff. The perilousness of attempting to draw clearcut conclusions regarding the connection between Nietzsche's philosophy and his relationships with women based on the accounts of these women is partially explored by Siegfried Mandel in his introduction to Salomé's *Nietzsche* (which, in itself, drapes a veil of secrecy over the intimacies Nietzsche and Salomé may have shared, and dwells instead on a psychological portrait of Nietzsche, conjecturing that his madness was simply the result of psychophysical factors evident in his writings):

> One French critic thought it a cruel irony that Nietzsche "who consistently misesteemed women was now most intimately understood by a woman." Others complained that Salomé made mythical monstrosities out of Nietzsche and his concept of the *Übermensch*, the superior man.[23]

Part of the problem with that type of inquiry is that for all of his verbosity concerning the "feminine" and "woman," with the exception of *Ecce Homo*, Nietzsche seldom writes directly and extensively about actual women he was involved with.[24] The only piece attributed to Nietzsche that deals unabashedly with this issue is controversial. *My Sister and I*, reputedly translated by Oscar Levy, editor of the authorized English translation of Nietzsche's works, was published by Seven Sirens Press in New York in 1951. The manuscript was allegedly written in secret by Nietzsche while he was confined in the Jena asylum between January 1889 and March 1890, and via a circuitous route, ended up in the hands of an American publisher of some notoriety, Samuel Roth. Walter Kaufmann[25] and Maud Rosenthal,[26] Levy's daughter, led the charge in exposing the manuscript as a fraud, pointing to anachronistic and stylistic

---

23. Siegfried Mandel, introduction to *Nietzsche*, by Lou Andreas-Salomé (Redding Ridge, Conn.: Black Swan Books, 1988), x.

24. As Mandel notes, a veil of Victorian reticence hangs over Nietzsche's sex life, and with the exception of Nietzsche's letter to Paul Deussen regarding an unexpected visit to a bordello in Cologne in February 1865 (an incident that Thomas Mann appropriated and imaginatively elaborated upon in his Nietzsche novel, *Dr. Faustus*), there is little that can be concretely established. See Mandel, *Nietzsche*, xl–xli.

25. Walter Kaufmann, "Nietzsche and the Seven Sirens," *Partisan Review* (May–June 1952).

26. Maud Rosenthal, letter to the editor, *Saturday Review of Literature*, 5 May 1952.

inconsistencies in the text. Part of the problem was that the German original, according to Roth, had been confiscated by the New York Society for the Suppression of Vice, and so there was no way of verifying whether the handwriting was indeed Nietzsche's. In addition, the printed version was based on a brittle and moth-eaten carbon copy of allegedly Levy's translation, so that mistakes, according to Roth, were inevitable. Though the manuscript has been, for the most part, regarded as a hoax, Walter Stewart argues convincingly against Kaufmann and makes a good case for the possibility that Nietzsche could have written it.[27] In any case, even if this text were authenticated as Nietzsche's last extant work, a perusal of the manuscript only overtly confirms what can be excavated from *Ecce Homo*, though some of it, such as the pornographic descriptions of lovemaking with Elisabeth, Lou, Cosima, an unknown countess, and the dark Eurasian he supposedly encountered in a brothel, yield little detail that is of direct relevance to a genealogy in relation to his politics and aesthetics. There is certainly a wealth of secondary material on the topic of Nietzsche's relationships with women,[28] but because these deviate from the focus of this study, I choose not to engage in extensive discussions of them.

27. Walter K. Stewart, "My Sister and I: The Disputed Nietzsche," in *My Sister and I*, ed. Stuart Swezey and Brian King (Los Angeles: AMOK, 1990), xxxviii–lxvi.
28. On the relationship between Lou Andreas-Salomé and Nietzsche, compare the clashing views of Elizabeth Forster-Nietzsche, *Nietzsche und die Frauen seiner Zeit* (Munich: Beck, 1935), 108ff., and Lou Andreas-Salomé, *Friedrich Nietzsche in seinen Werken* (Vienna: Konegen, 1911), 75ff. as well as Salomé's *Lebensruckblick: Grundiss einiger Lebenserinnerungen* (Frankfurt am Main: Insel Verlag, 1911). See also Biddy Martin, *Woman and Modernity: The Life(styles) of Lou Andreas-Salomé* (New York: Cornell University Press, 1991); Carol Diethe, "Lou Andreas-Salome and Female Sexuality at the Turn of the Century," in *German Women Writers 1900–1930*, ed. Brian Keith-Smith (Lampeter: Mellen, 1993); Ronald Hayman, *Nietzsche: A Critical Life* (London: Weidenfeld and Nicolson, 1980); and H. F. Peters, *Zarathustra's Sister: The Case of Elisabeth and Friedrich Nietzsche* (New York: Crown Publishers, 1977). For a more general view of the women's movement in Germany in relation to Nietzsche's writings, see Carol Diethe, *Nietzsche's Women: Beyond the Whip* (Berlin: de Gruyter, 1996), in particular, chap. 3, "Nietzsche and the New Woman," and chap. 5, "Nietzsche and the Feminists"; Carol Diethe, "Nietzsche and the Early German Feminists," *Journal of Nietzsche Studies* 12 (Autumn 1996): 69–81; and R. Hinton Thomas, *Nietzsche in German Politics and Society 1890–1918* (Manchester: Manchester University Press, 1983), especially chap. 7, "The Feminist Movement and Nietzsche."

1

Genealogies of the "Feminine" and "Woman"

> The sexless birth of Athena makes a worthy complement to the classic tale of uterus envy, the birth of Dionysus, in which the father of gods and men develops a pseudo-womb. Zeus impregnates a mortal woman, Semele; when her pregnancy is well advanced, he destroys her with his thunderbolt, removes the fetus from her body, and sews it into his thigh. . . . The choice of the thigh for the male womb, instead of the abdomen, probably reflects the practices of male homosexual life.
> —Eva Keuls, *The Reign of the Phallus: Sexual Politics in Ancient Athens*

> For Irigaray the imbalance in our social order derives from the "separation between the genders." This is a historical separation as well, since an early gynecocratic age was followed by a patriarchal one; consequently, the encounter between the two genders never really took place.
> —Luisa Muraro, *"Female Genealogies"*

Symptomatologizing the "Feminine" Versus "Woman"

Krell's *Postponements: Woman, Sensuality, and Death in Nietzsche* poses the question: "Why is Nietzsche's transition to woman always postponed and agonizing?" By moving across the figures of Ariadne, Corinna, Pana, and Calina as they appear in Nietzsche's notes, he draws attention to the need to reconceive maternity, and to bring into question the relationship between mother/nature and father/culture. Such an account is obviously important to my own attempt to unearth how Nietzsche struggles with these very questions. That it deals with Nietzsche's behind-the-scenes notes on the creation of *Thus Spoke Zarathustra* also makes it an invaluable mine of information.

Though Krell has explored similar themes, we differ radically in the style(s) we use in doing a genealogy of the relationships binding myth, politics, and gender in Nietzsche, and our emphases and conclusions differ significantly. For instance, Krell views Nietzsche as one who "writes with the hand of woman"; I disagree, and trace the ambivalences that mark Nietzsche's attempts at resentfully appropriating the style of the "feminine." In addition, while Krell stops with a critique of Irigaray's project as itself riddled with resentment (and chooses not to propose an alternative to escaping the cycle of resentment), in the final chapter I attempt to take a parallel approach to projects begun by feminists such as Irigaray, Cixous, and Minh-ha. Nevertheless, I undertake sketching the rough outlines of this prolegomenon with the acknowledgment that the fall to resentment is an ever-present temptation one must struggle with rather than hope to eradicate completely.

Thus, my interpretation of several of Nietzsche's texts, which will be taken as representative of the evolution of his political philosophy, rests on reading texts in their effective contexts while, simultaneously, reading them "against the grain" or reading them with an ear for the suppressed voices of the "feminine." This second level of reading approaches historical texts from the contemporary perspective, and as such, risks the charge of anachronism. However, since every "genealogy" or even simply "interpretation" is, arguably, a violation of the "truth"—in the sense of a timeless, irrecoverable core—every "genealogy," or more loosely, "interpretation," is anachronistic in the literal sense of the term: reading backward. "Reading backwards," particularly by appropriating Nietzsche's "genealogical" approach, enables us to tease out the "warring forces *within the text itself*"[1] and more importantly, link the focus on Nietzsche's "style" to his politics as gendered.

Most other approaches to interpreting Nietzsche fail to read the "feminine" tropes as symptoms of the devolution of his thought. Such approaches, mired in either damning or salvaging Nietzsche's misogyny, fail to employ Nietzsche's "genealogical" approach—his emphasis on the gradual hardening of an all-consuming ethical system that becomes progressively "burnt in." As Tracy Strong points out, genealogy is the centerpiece of Nietzsche's destructive enterprise, and its first task is to lay bare and unmask.[2] What I aim to lay bare is how Nietzsche's own gradually congealing politico-aesthetics eventually harden into a misogyny seething with *ressentiment* against his own inability to birth the *Übermensch*—to a new culture and a new self.

The term "politico-aesthetics" is not a peculiar jargon of my own construction but rather does have some currency within the field. For example, Tracy B. Strong uses a similar construction, "Political Aesthetics," to talk about the dynamic interactions binding Nietzsche's views on artistic and political health versus sickness. In his essay,

---

1. Kathleen B. Johnson, introduction to *Dissemination*, by Jacques Derrida (Chicago: University of Chicago Press, 1981), xiv.
2. Tracy B. Strong, *Friedrich Nietzsche and the Politics of Transfiguration* (Berkeley and Los Angeles: University of California Press, 1975), 29.

"Nietzsche's Political Aesthetics,"[3] Strong presents an alternative view of Nietzsche's politics. He claims that Nietzsche is usually read in the context of traditional philosophy as advocating a politics of domination. Beginning with what he terms "Nietzsche's new aesthetics," however, Strong depicts Nietzsche's politics as a politics of transfiguration. Strong states that Nietzsche's political model is drawn from the Greeks and argues that the essence of Greek political life in Nietzsche's view cannot be recovered in our world through politics but only by means of art. In his account, what is necessary instead is a political aesthetics. Strong's developmental approach—which moves across *The Birth of Tragedy* and culminates in some of Nietzsche's final letters, outlining the extent of influence of figures like Schopenhauer, Wagner, Burckhardt, and Emerson on Nietzsche—parallels, to some extent, my own attempt at a genealogical account, which takes into consideration Nietzsche's shifting views on the interaction between politics and aesthetics. The points at which we diverge, however, are Strong's silence regarding the gendered nature of Nietzsche's political aesthetic, as well as Nietzsche's eventual abandonment of a more predominantly aesthetic resolution for a markedly political amputation of modernity. Finally, Strong seems to share Nietzsche's early nostalgia for the culture and politics of the ancient Greeks—a culture whose tyrannical politics of gender, particularly in Athens, render such nostalgia suspect.[4]

Unlike Strong, Bianca Theisen, in her essay, "Rhythms of Oblivion,"[5] regards the question of the "feminine"/"woman" as crucial to Nietzsche's politics and aesthetics. She questions whether in Nietzsche's numerous derisive remarks on "women," he is even writing about real women or the concept of "woman." Theisen argues in the first part of her paper that based on Nietzsche's treatment of the distinction between truth and lie, he excludes "woman" doubly—from both the male and the female realms, and from both truth and lie. Thus, as non-self-identical (both woman and women), "woman" figures as a simulated truth that plays on the very distinction between truth and lie—a logical third term that calls attention to this distinction as such and thus calls into question bivalent logic. As a *tertium datur*, she argues that "woman" in Nietzsche's texts reveals as distinction the very distinctions that

---

3. Strong, "Nietzsche's Political Aesthetics," 153–74.
4. For a clear and persuasive account, based upon a thorough examination of vase paintings and other figured monuments, of the socio-politico-economic boundaries that strictly separated Greek males from females in Athens, see Eva C. Keuls, *The Reign of the Phallus: Sexual Politics in Ancient Athens* (Berkeley and Los Angeles: University of California Press, 1985). See also Loreaux's description of the complex ambivalences of the Athenian Greeks' attempts to link and yet separate the "masculine" realm of war from the "feminine" realm of giving birth. Cf. Nicole Loreaux, *Tragic Ways of Killing a Woman*, trans. Anthony Forster (Cambridge: Harvard University Press, 1987).
5. Bianca Theisen, "Rhythms of Oblivion," in *Nietzsche and the Feminine*, ed. Peter Burgard (Charlottesville: University Press of Virginia, 1994), 82–103.

determine cognition. If we are to see "woman" as a figure in Nietzsche's work at all, Theisen implies, then it is not as a figure of any particular position in an opposition within a philosophical argument, but as that which moves beyond a philosophy of binary oppositions—a figure of Nietzsche's subversion of traditional philosophy, a figure of Nietzsche's philosophy itself. While I find her thesis that Ariadne's sublime experience—in the torment of thinking, the eternal return results from the movement *through* negation that *affirms negativity*—fascinating, I disagree with the way she interprets the relation binding politics, myth, and gender in the Nietzschean constellation of texts. I am more predisposed to view *Thus Spoke Zarathustra* as functioning as a Straussian (Romantic) noble lie rather than a proto-postmodernist-feminist text, at least if we are to try to ground Nietzsche within the context of his own persistent, though masked, Romanticism, rather than the context of our own times.

Still on the topic of how the question of the "feminine" in Nietzsche may be most effectively read or interpreted, Janet Lungstrum[6] begins by laying bare the problems caused for feminism by the very discussion of figuration and examines the ways in which Nietzsche's extreme statements on women have led to the kind of feminist double bind that Alice Jardine describes—a bind whereby one either rejects the "feminine" or "woman" as "mere" figurations and thus runs the risk of falling back into metaphysical and anatomical delineations of sexual identity, or accepts such figuration and thereby risks the absence of women as subjects. Lungstrum's essay attempts to create space for a third position, which approaches Nietzsche from the perspective of eroticism-as-creativity rather than gender-as-identity, in order then to show that feminist self-empowerment can be attained through the "woman" that Nietzsche writes into existence. In this view, Nietzsche sets into play a sexual agonistics in which "woman" acts as catalytic muse in self-renewing creativity. While acknowledging that, in societal terms, Nietzsche silences female sensuality, Lungstrum argues that when viewed through the lens of art, the Nietzschean corpus may be rehabilitated, since the sexual dialectic can be just as empowering for woman as for man, and, indeed, "woman" as written by Nietzsche is endowed with a potentially greater power of creative dissimulation than the "male artist." In response to what she views as a refusal to acknowledge, or a dissolution of, Nietzsche's sexual dialectics in Irigaray and Derrida, Lungstrum opposes Lou Andreas-Salomé's reading of Nietzsche as inherently bisexual,[7] and of his philosophy as fundamentally oppositional. Lungstrum con-

---

6. Janet Lungstrum, "Nietzsche Writing Woman/Woman Writing Nietzsche: The Sexual Dialectic of Palingenesis," in *Nietzsche and the Feminine*, ed. Peter Burgard (Charlottesville: University Press of Virginia, 1994), 135–57.

7. There is textual evidence for this interpretation of Salomé's impression of Nietzsche. For example in her discussion of the intersections between his life and his work, Salomé writes: "In Nietzsche's spiri-

cludes that his contradictions about "woman" form part of a more basic contradiction between "masculine" and "feminine" forces within himself. She concludes that Nietzsche's dialectical articulation of the "feminine" in his writing allows woman to (re)create herself. In her view, the feminist rewriting of Nietzsche is thus already intrinsically contained in Nietzsche.

Persuasive as Lungstrum's line of argumentation is, I disagree with her on several points. First, she neglects the fundamentally Romantic politics that animates Nietzsche's interactions with the "feminine," and she mistakes Nietzsche's "phallic motherhood" with his apparent "bi-sexuality." Second, she tends to blur the terms "woman," "Woman," and "feminine" together with little or no sensitivity to how these terms interact in Nietzsche's developing philosophy, and she does not attempt to explain how Nietzsche's account of "Woman" (which seems to function as a synonym for the "feminine" in her reading of Nietzsche) liberates "woman" to "recreate" herself.

The driving thesis of this book is that the disease that (em)powers and disempowers Nietzsche's philosophy is *ressentiment*.[8] This is strikingly revealed in the onset and progression of the clustering symptoms of his macroscopic and microscopic treatment of the "feminine"/"woman." The microcosm of Nietzsche's frustration over his political impotence parallels his own constructed or projected macrocosm of modernity's lack of generative powers. Nietzsche's advancing misogyny and increasing frustration with modernity's impotence are symptoms of the fundamental disease that ails him: that he himself is irremediably diseased and decadent, and that the fundamental dichotomy upon which he builds his political philosophy, the opposition between health and disease, is rotten at its core. A further symptom of his progressive descent into the realms of *ressentiment* and sickness is his replacement of a complex interplay between his politics and aesthetics—either as mediating

---

tual nature was something—in heightened dimension—that was feminine." See Andreas-Salomé, *Nietzsche*, 29–30. It is important to note, though, that the basis for this interpretation roots itself in *The Gay Science*, which was composed during Nietzsche's pre-Zarathustran phase, which is characterized by his ambivalent "optimism" concerning the "feminine." Thus, Salomé's original text actually lends credence to the overall schema I propose.

8. Conway arrives at a similar conclusion: "Nietzsche's decadence is thus responsible for the crowning irony of his life and career: It is only as a decadent, as the consummate man of *ressentiment*, that he commands anything like the power and influence he regularly claims for himself" (Daniel Conway, *Nietzsche's Dangerous Game: Philosophy in the Twilight of the Idols* [Cambridge: Cambridge University Press, 1997], 258). There are two significant elements differentiating this book from his work: (1) Conway focuses purely on Nietzsche's post-Zarathustran writings (1885–88), while I schematically trace the development of Nietzsche's politico-aesthetics through his pre-Zarathustran, Zarathustran, and post-Zarathustran writings (1871–88); and (2) Conway's thesis is built centrally upon a contrastive analogy between Odysseus's dangerous venture of surviving the sirens' song via taking effective innoculative measures, and Nietzsche's unsuccessful limnal confrontation with nihilism via the uncertain cultivation of an unstable readership, while this book is more concerned with doing a genealogy of Nietzsche's ambivalences toward the "feminine"/"woman" in relation to his aesthetics and politics.

dichotomies, as in his pre-Zarathustran phase, or as functioning as a mythic noble lie, as in his Zarathustran phase—with a crude and ruthless politics in his post-Zarathustran phase.

The notion of "birthing" the *Übermensch* is an aspiration to which Nietzsche repeatedly admits, and authors such as Ansell-Pearson have pointed out that "birthing the *Übermensch*" may mean cultivating readers who are capable of the art of "malicious" interpretation (or, using Straussian and Krellian terms, being able to speak in "esoteric" and "halcyon tones" to the "few"/"short-eared"). Finally, especially with a thinker like Nietzsche, who unabashedly weaves together the personal and the public, the psychological and the political, and does so with painful contortions around issues of power and gender, it is difficult to separate his personal life, triumphs, and frustrations from his intellectual pursuits. As Leslie Paul Thiele writes: "One must return to Nietzsche's life and philosophy as a whole to find their meaning. These concepts, as with Nietzsche's thought in general, were the product not merely of a sophisticated intellectual exercise, but of a lived experience."[9] It is striking that as Nietzsche's misogyny is more shrilly sounded, his nihilism grows more stridently evident; as the hopeful doctrine of the coming of the *Übermensch* disappears, it is replaced by repeated exhortations advocating modernity's self-destruction. As his doctrine of hope for the rejuvenation of modernity fades, the destructive aspects of his rhetoric become more vehement. These developments are clearly seen by focusing on how Nietzsche uses the figure of birthing in relation to his political visions.

By appropriating Nietzsche's own role as a "psychologist of the feminine," I shall attempt to excavate repressed motivations and valuations that drive Nietzsche's developing philosophy as embodied in his (d)evolving figural depiction of the "feminine." The question of piercing through Nietzsche's masks or of applying the symptomatologist's very method to himself is answered in the method I employ via an attempt to trace how Nietzsche's mythology of the "feminine" (in relation to the "masculine") shapes his political philosophy. It is via the pivot point of how Nietzsche frames the function of the myth (as gendered) in relation to the salvation (or destruction and hopeful resurrection) of the *polis* that this method finds its center.

---

9. Leslie Paul Thiele, *Friedrich Nietzsche and the Politics of the Soul: A Study of Heroic Individualism* (Princeton: Princeton University Press, 1990), 197. Thiele's reading of Nietzsche's works as a "political biography of his soul" is a fascinating thesis, and intersects with this project's attempt to plot the fluctuating relations binding the theoretical and personal in Nietzsche, without delving into the minutiae of a form of psychobiography. However, whereas Thiele is of the view that "unlike Plato, [Nietzsche] has no concern with the noble lies involved in expatiating this answer [to the question: What is the best form of political regime?]" (222), I argue that Nietzsche's rhetoric, in keeping with his "inverse Platonism," particularly during his Zarathustran and post-Zarathustran phases, frames several noble lies in order to sift his "short-eared" or rare descendants from his "long-eared" or plebeian progeny.

Justification for such a move may be found, to some extent, in the writings of both Paul Ricoeur and Luce Irigaray. For Ricoeur, myth, in its ability to manifest imaginatively and indirectly the conundrum of human beings caught in between their fractured natures and their potentialities as integrated selves, is prior to philosophy. As "prior denizens of a world of symbols and myths,"[10] it is through mythopoetic forms of expression, such as the Hebrew and Greek myths of primordial chaos, primeval fall, original defilement, exile from paradise, and tragic fate, that a surplus of meaning—unavailable to modes of intellectual inquiry that deny any truth-value concerning the human condition from such myths and symbols—may be glimpsed as well as re-envisaged. Ultimately, "the recovery of the power of myth and symbol is possible only through a self-critical, always revisable, and never certain hermeneutical wager" (2). This is a wager that this project attempts to make—a wager that traces its roots to the very point at which Western philosophy attempted to characterize itself as *philo sophia* in Plato's dialogues, where myth and the search for wisdom are inextricably intertwined. In Plato's *Republic*, for example, the attempt to build an ideal *polis* and the justification for the noble lie as the prerogative of only the philosopher-king are rooted in the myth of metals, and the myth of Er and the afterlife. Even at this earliest stage, when philosophy struggled to identify itself qua philosophy, myth remained, and, in my view, continues to remain, indispensable.

Similarly, Luce Irigaray places a great emphasis on myth in her reconception of female genealogies. Irigaray perceives the violent beginnings of patriarchal society in the *Oresteia*. According to her, myths have a historical value. Mythical narratives are not independent of history, but express history's molding in narratives that illustrate the major developmental contours of a given period. Indeed, Irigaray maintains that ancient mythology proves that a gynecocratic society existed before patriarchy. The mythic mode of narrating history, she explains, depends on the fact that at that time word and image were not separate. She concludes that "the mythical expression of history is more akin to female and matrilineal traditions."[11]

In keeping with the mythic focus that both Ricoeur and Irigaray stress, I show that Nietzsche's use of myth initially elevates the "feminine" as an equally valid or authorized symbol for the awesome vitality and enigma of life, and eventually attempts to harness the feminine power of birthing unto an increasingly phallocratic mythology. Yet this "genealogical" account aims to do more than simply unmask. What it hopes to do is to effect an explosion from within, to implode his own

---

10. Mark Wallace, introduction to *Figuring the Sacred: Religion, Narrative, and Imagination*, by Paul Ricoeur, trans. David Pellauer (Minneapolis: Fortress Press, 1995), 5.

11. Luce Irigaray, "Female Genealogies," trans. Luisa Muraro, in *Engaging with Irigaray: Feminist Philosophy and European Thought*, ed. Carolyn Burke, Naomi Schor, and Margaret Whitford (New York: Columbia University Press, 1994), 321.

account of modernity as suffering from delusion. It aims to show how a Nietzschean-all-too-Nietzschean approach bears the seeds of its own destruction within itself—and to begin that process of self-destruction. Such an approach forms a parallel strategy to Irigaray's "castrating" and "mimetic" (rather than strictly "genealogical") approach of revealing Nietzsche's hidden *ressentiment* against the "feminine," while trying to keep to a minimum the latter's vulnerability to mirror-imaging charges of *ressentiment*. Instead of trying to effect a poetic conversation with Nietzsche by constructing a language other than, yet resonant with, Nietzsche's own in which direct interrogation and confrontation comprise the main strategy (as Irigaray does), I attempt a strategic appropriation of Nietzsche's own language in order to infect and implode that very language, with its attendant political vision and implicit delineation of authority.

The notion of the "feminine" in Nietzsche is polyvalent, encompassing a diverse host of meanings, reverberating with, but never explicitly indicating, biological, sociological, political, linguistic, psychoanalytic, and theological dimensions. To demarcate more clearly, for methodological purposes, the scope of this book, I wish to stress that this project's initial focus begins more strictly with the "feminine" rather than historical women within Nietzsche's texts. In a manner analogous to a theoretical move that Nicole Loraux begins with (but ultimately, also cannot sustain), "This is not . . . about women, though well before the final chapters, devoted to the study of a few paradoxical [and mythical] feminine figures, . . . women are often discussed. . . . It is . . . about men or the feminine."[12] Correspondingly, as I shall show, as Nietzsche's politics grows increasingly misogynistic, the borders separating "woman," "womanly," and the "feminine" break down. As the visages of Helen, Baubô, and Medusa recede from his texts, they are either combined with or are replaced by the new myths of "woman-as-parasite" or "feminist-as-abortive-female."

Beyond (Effacing) Nietzsche's Misogyny

The extent and range of literature on Nietzsche is immense. Hence, I choose not to address a number of complex problems left in the wake of the corpus of notable interpreters of Nietzsche, such as Heidegger,[13] as well as a host of other eminent

---

12. Nicole Loraux, *The Experiences of Tiresias: The Feminine and the Greek Man*, trans. Paula Wissing (Princeton: Princeton University Press, 1995), 3.
13. Martin Heidegger, *Nietzsche*, vols. 1–4, trans. David Farrell Krell, Joan Stambaugh, and Frank A. Capuzzi (San Francisco: Harper and Row, 1979).

European and American commentators, because their works do not directly address the focal point of this study. Instead, I limit myself to examining the literature that specifically addresses issues of feminism in relation to Nietzsche's politics and aesthetics. Thus, in this section, which attempts a concise review and a description of the methodology I use, I limit myself first to a brief look at the context that, for so long, prevented philosophical investigation of Nietzsche in relation to the "feminine." Then I describe my own methodology, grounding it within the context of contemporary conversations regarding the links binding Nietzsche's thoughts on politics, aesthetics, and myth in relation to the intertwining issues of the "feminine" and "woman." Finally, I also draw out, in brief, how these cited texts impinge upon this book, and how my method figures in relation to theirs.

To begin, Peter Burgard traces the avoidance of the question of the "feminine" (which he does not define concretely in relation to "woman" or women) in Nietzsche studies to Walter Kaufmann. Although Burgard does praise Kaufmann highly for his rescue of the philosophical Nietzsche from his tabooed fascist image,[14] he notes that Kaufmann's facile dismissal of Nietzsche's all too human judgements concerning women as "philosophically irrelevant"[15] effectively instituted a compelling interdiction to further investigations on this topic for a long time.[16] Alison Ainley makes similar observations regarding Kaufmann's commentary on *The Gay Science*:

> Walter Kaufmann writes: "This whole sentence, like many of Nietzsche's generalizations of women, descends to a lower level—stylistically as well as in content. It seems to be intended merely to lead up to the pun that follows it."[17] Kaufmann's apology to woman may now seem not only shamefaced but misplaced, in the sense that it reduces the complexity and caution advocated elsewhere in Nietzsche to a simple equation of representation. . . . Such a reading might well engender indignation and anger, placing Nietzsche within a philosophical tradition of misogyny.[18]

---

14. For an informative account of Kaufmann's defense of Nietzsche from both right- and left-wing political associations, as well as the development of various left-wing German political trends in relation to Nietzsche's writings, see Seth Taylor, *Left-Wing Nietzscheans: The Politics of German Expressionism 1910–1920* (Berlin: de Gruyter, 1990).

15. Walter Kaufmann, *Nietzsche: Philosopher, Psychologist, Antichrist*, 3d ed. (Princeton: Princeton University Press, 1968), 84.

16. Burgard, *Nietzsche*, 3.

17. Friedrich Nietzsche, *The Gay Science*, trans. Walter Kaufmann (New York: Vintage Books, 1974), 317.

18. Alison Ainley, "'Ideal Selfishness': Nietzsche's Metaphor of Maternity," in *Exceedingly Nietzsche*, ed. David Farrell Krell and David Wood (New York: Routledge, 1988), 118.

24   Resentment and the "Feminine"

Serious scholarly attention to this problem began only in the late 1970s, with studies that originated in France: Sarah Kofman's "Baubo: Theological Perversion and Fetishism" and Jacques Derrida's *Spurs: Nietzsche's Styles*. Kofman's article was not translated into English until 1988;[19] however, Derrida's book was quickly translated in 1979[20] and as such, generated numerous responses.[21] I reserve a brief discussion of Derrida's *Spurs* for later, as his insights are best reviewed in relation to Irigaray's. Below, I outline crucial arguments in Kofman's "Baubo."

Briefly, Kofman's "Baubo" begins with unearthing Baubô's mythic roots. Baubô makes her appearance in the mysteries of Eleusis consecrated to Demeter. Grieved by the disappearance of Persephone, Demeter, goddess of fecundity, had been acting like a sterile woman.[22] For nine days and nine nights, she did not drink, eat, bathe, or adorn herself. Baubô made her laugh by pulling up her skirts and showing her belly on which a figure had been drawn. This figure is believed to be that of Iaachos, the child of Demeter, an obscure deity sometimes identified with Dionysus. Drawing from several sources, Kofman arrives at this startling interpretation:

> Reinach interprets it as a magic scene whose aim is to restore to earth the fecundity that it had lost during the sorrow of Demeter.[23] Comparison with Greek legends such as those of Bellephoron, and with Irish and Japanese ones, allows us to assert that wherever a woman raises her skirts, she provokes laughter or flight, such that this gesture can be used as apotropaic means. . . . The belly of the woman plays the role of the head of the Medusa. . . . By lifting her skirts, was not Baubo suggesting that she go and frighten Hades, or that which comes to the same, recall fecundity to herself?

---

19. Sarah Kofman, "Baubo: Theological Perversion and Fetishism," in *Nietzsche's New Seas*, ed. M. A. Gillespie and T. B. Strong (Chicago: University of Chicago Press, 1988), 175–202.

20. Jacques Derrida, *Spurs: Nietzsche's Styles*, trans. Barbara Harlow (Chicago: University of Chicago Press, 1979).

21. For example, see Alice Jardine, *Gynesis: Configurations of Woman and Modernity* (Ithaca: Cornell University Press, 1985); Kelly Oliver, "Woman as Truth in Nietzsche's Writings," *Social Theory and Practice* 10 (Summer 1984): 185–99; Kelly Oliver, "Nietzsche's 'Woman': The Poststructuralist Attempt to Do Away with Women," *Radical Philosophy* 48 (Spring 1988): 25–29; Gayatri Chakravorty Spivak, "Displacement and the Discourse of Woman," in *Displacement: Derrida and After*, ed. Mark Krupnick (Bloomington: Indiana University Press, 1983), 169–95; Gayatri Chakravorty Spivak, "Feminism and Deconstruction, Again: Negotiating with Unacknowledged Masculinism," in *Between Feminism and Psychoanalysis*, ed. Teresa Brennan (New York: Routledge, 1989), 206–22; Ackermann, *Nietzsche*; Schutte, *Beyond Nihilism*; Henry Staten, *Nietzsche's Voice* (Ithaca: Cornell University Press, 1990)—to name only a few.

22. The equation of extreme grief with sterility is Kofman's. What she effectively seems to do is hyperbolize Demeter's grief to the level of a type of death—a barrenness or inability to give birth, analogous to her daughter's descent into the underworld.

23. Salomon Reinach, *Cultes, mythes, religion*, vol. 4 (Paris: Leroux, 1912).

By displaying the figure of Dionysus on her belly, she recalls the eternal return of life.[24]

Kofman strengthens her position by recalling the etymological origins and other mythic underpinnings of the name "Baubô." *Baubo* is the equivalent of *koilia*, another of the "improper" words used in Greek to designate the female sex. *Baubon*, the symbol of the male sex, is derived from *Baubo*. Through the intermediary of *Baubon*, the story of *Baubo* intersects with that of Dionysus. There are two intersections: (1) in one myth, Dionysus is born in Nysa, at the spot where Hades carried off Persephone (thus initiating Demeter's descent into grief); and (2) in another myth, when Dionysus was looking for the road to Hades, he encountered Proshymnnos with whom he had "unspeakable relationships." After Proshymnos's death, Dionysus replaced him with a figwood phallus (*baubon*) to console himself. Thus, *Baubon* and *Baubo*, as personifications of the two sexes, appeared in these guises in the Eleusinian rites where Baubô is an animated *koilia*. Kofman clinches her argument: "In the Eleusinian mysteries, the female sexual organ is exalted as the symbol of fertility and a guarantee of the regeneration and eternal return of all things" (197).

Kofman's position, that "Baubo can appear as a female double of Dionysus" (197) effectively locates Baubô and Dionysus as eternally self-generating and protean masks for life. This thesis is of significance to my genealogy of Nietzsche's evolving view of the "feminine" in his political philosophy, as depicted in the various mythic figures, both "masculine" and "feminine," that he adopts for his purposes. However, as I show, Nietzsche's adoption of Baubô as a figure for the doctrine of eternal recurrence alongside Dionysus occurs principally during his pre-Zarathustran phase, when he is still "optimistic" enough to resort to the head of Medusa as an apotropaic medium against the wild visage of Dionysus in *The Birth of Tragedy*. Contrary to Kofman, who maintains that throughout his writings Nietzsche differentiated superiority from inferiority based purely on types of "men" and "women" (affirmative or degenerate), I believe that Nietzsche's ambivalence (admiration, fear, desire, jealousy, repulsion) towards "woman" congeals in the latter part of his life into an uncompromising ambition to harness, appropriate, and silence both the "feminine" and "woman."

In resonance with Kofman's stress on the imbricated questions of power and the "feminine" in Nietzsche, the method I use may be characterized as "political," "mythic," "gendered," and "embodied." For the purposes of clarity and brevity, I define these terms in the following way: by "political," I refer to mechanisms that delineate and maintain the boundaries separating the empowered from the disempowered; by "mythic," I refer to the implicit characterization of "authority" through

---

24. Kofman, "Baubô," 196–97.

the use of mythic figures or real people fictionalized to the extent of performing a "mythic" function (mediating between truth and lie) as either empowered or disempowered; by "gendered," I mean the construction, deconstruction, and reconstruction of "masculinity" or "femininity" as figures for either the powerful or the impotent; and by "embodied," I refer to the stress on the body, particularly its generative and regenerative powers—or conversely, its bankrupt and impotent state—which function as figures for and of empowerment or disempowerment. The string that runs through all these is the issue of how the boundaries of power and authority congeal because myth, gender, and embodiment are simply matrices within which these demarcations of power are drawn, implicitly and invisibly.

To illustrate further what I mean by "political," "mythic," "gendered," and "embodied," I draw from several sources whose most relevant features I summarize—not to follow slavishly, but to do a genealogy of my own genealogy, and to show how my study enters into the contemporary arenas of Nietzsche studies, political philosophy, and feminism. Borrowing and combining analogies from Strong[25] and Shapiro,[26] I use these various sources as signposts delineating a flow of relationships that structure the Nietzschean city of ideas (whose topography both does not possess a calculus-like system, and yet is systematic in some organic fashion), while venturing forth, listening for that faint halcyon tone which pervades Nietzsche's work.[27] Borrowing yet another analogy from Irigaray, what I attempt is an infection (simultaneously inside and outside) and innoculation against the corruption that pervades Nietzsche's construction of mater-iality and modernity.

As "political" and "embodied," my method is partially influenced by two sources: (1) Leo Strauss's *The City and Man* and (2) Eric Blondel's *Nietzsche: The Body and Culture: Philosophy as Philological Genealogy*. As "gendered" and "embodied," it draws partially from (1) Julia Kristeva's characterization of the "feminine" as characterized in Jean Graybeal's *Language and "The Feminine" in Nietzsche and Heidegger*, and (2) Luce Irigaray's *Marine Lover of Friedrich Nietzsche*, among others that constitute the current arena in which Nietzsche studies, political philosophy, and aesthetics converge.

---

25. Strong, *Nietzsche*, 4–7.
26. Shapiro, *Alcyone*, 1.
27. This is an allusion to Shapiro's *Alcyone*, where Shapiro uses the figure of the halcyon tone—associated with the myths surrounding Alcyone, a figure Nietzsche uses several times—to imply a form of encrypting that Nietzsche uses to hide his esoteric messages. "I want to suggest that beyond any such views, maxims, declarations, or anecdotes, we would do well to hear a certain tone, the one that Nietzsche calls *halcyon*, that resounds here and throughout his texts" (2). However, whereas Shapiro sees this encrypting as a completely deliberate and intentional process, I view the process to be more complicated, involving a complex interplay between the volitional/controlled and repressed. Furthermore, Shapiro brushes aside the issue of Nietzsche's misogyny in favor of salvaging what he can of Nietzsche's status as a philosopher of culture. In contrast, I see excavating the development of Nietzsche's hardening misogyny as crucial to understanding and learning from Nietzsche's fatally all-too-modern gendered politics.

In *The City and Man*, particularly in the essay, "On Plato's Republic," Strauss draws attention to two areas that are crucial to my interpretation of Nietzsche's developing political philosophy. These are (a) Strauss's focus on Platonic dialogues as involving communication with different audiences at the same time (i.e., the notion of having exoteric and esoteric messages deliberately embedded in the same text);[28] and (b) his emphasis on the noble lie. For Strauss, writings are essentially defective if they are equally accessible to all who can read. In contrast, Strauss claims, Platonic dialogue says different things to different people—not accidentally, as every writing does, but because it is consciously contrived as to say different things to different people. Platonic dialogue, if properly read, reveals itself to possess the flexibility or adaptability of oral communication, as it is deeply ironic.[29]

The polyphonous character of Platonic dialogue, for Strauss, does not stem merely from the fact that the structure of the dialogue enables a certain literary distancing of the views of the author from his characters. "If someone quoted a passage from the dialogues in order to prove that Plato held such and such a view, he acts about as reasonably as if he were to assert that according to Shakespeare life is a tale told by an idiot, full of sound and fury, signifying nothing" (50). In addition to the fact that the dialogue enables a dispersion of voices through the use of different characters, the apparently unproblematic main mouthpiece of Plato, Socrates, is an ironic character. Strauss's characterization of the ironic character of Socrates explains why Platonic dialogues are masked and dissimulating. Socrates, the penultimate "magnanimous" man, who regards himself as "un"-worthy of great things while in fact being worthy of them, is truthful and frank because he is in the habit of looking down—and yet he is ironic in his intercourse with the many. For Strauss, irony is essentially related to the fact that there is a natural order of rank among human beings; thus, irony consists in speaking differently to different kinds of people (51).

Strauss grounds his interpretation of Nietzsche's works on their similarities to Platonic dialogues: both Plato's and Nietzsche's texts are masked and dissimulating, and hence, tools in interpreting Plato are likely to be useful in reading Nietzsche. Nietzsche's fascination with irony and certain aspects of Greek culture, especially Socrates and Plato's teachings, provides clues as to how he probably wanted his writings to be read: as a reverse Platonism glorifying, nevertheless, the ancient Greek stress on irony and hierarchy. Although I am not politically inclined to the aristocracy built into a Straussian reading of Nietzsche, this interpretative strategy seems quite fruitful in reading Nietzsche, particularly with respect to teasing out how

---

28. Lampert regards Strauss's esoteric "whispering" of his understanding of both Nietzsche and Plato as a "failure in the historical sense." For an interesting analysis of Strauss's interpretation of Nietzsche in relation to Plato, see Laurence Lampert, *Leo Strauss and Nietzsche* (Chicago: University of Chicago Press, 1996), 184.
29. Leo Strauss, *The City and Man* (Chicago: Rand McNally, 1964), 52–53.

Nietzsche not only increasingly de-mater-ializes the "feminine" as a figure for his philosophical doctrines, but also, less and less seems to speak to women as a potential audience.

Nietzsche's styles of writing have been the focus of numerous studies, many of which point to its polyphonic and fragmented voices.[30] In line with this, adopting Strauss's depiction of "irony" and authorship in Plato,[31] I use an approach that attempts to listen to the babel of voices that Nietzsche orchestrates, and to discern the play of masks and the costumes that Nietzsche assumes and sheds in the numerous textual dramas he stages (or inverted Platonic dialogues he scripts). Intrinsic to this approach as well is an attention to Nietzsche's hidden ranking order, indicating hierarchies of power, particularly with respect to the issue of the "feminine"/"woman."[32]

Strauss also brings up the issue of the "noble lie" in relation to the governance of the *polis*, whose *locus classicus* lies rooted in Plato's *Republic*: "the gods possess all

---

30. As Ansell-Pearson points out, Nietzsche's response to the problem of nihilism, and the crisis of authority it spawns, is refractory. Zarathustra, who teaches the "self-overcoming of morality" and the doctrine of the *Übermensch*, presents two kinds of politics to his readers. One is a "politics of survival," which parodies and is ironic toward the ideals of humanity. The other is the "politics of cruelty" associated with Nietzsche's aristocratic radicalism, and his insistence on maintaining a "pathos of distance" in keeping with an "order of rank." See Keith Ansell-Pearson, *An Introduction to Nietzsche as a Political Thinker* (Cambridge: Cambridge University Press, 1994), 148.

31. Along a parallel track, exploring a Straussian-inspired reading of Nietzsche's politics, Pippin points out that the story of Zarathustra is that of a person unable to rest content in any one place, either alone or in community with others. As Pippin puts it, the dilemma is thus an age-old "political" one—that of the relation of the philosopher and the city. In addition, he draws out the fact that the plot of the book revolves around failures and shows that there is a substantial ironic distance between Nietzsche and his main character. Ultimately, Pippin shows that Zarathustra's fate consists of irreconcilable options, neither a final going over nor a resigned going under, and that Zarathustra's self-knowledge cannot be completed either alone or publicly. Pippin's stress on the political and the ironic, alongside his analysis of *Thus Spoke Zarathustra*, resonates with my reading of the same text, which unfolds principally in my third chapter, "The Phallic Mother." Cf. Robert Pippin, "Irony and Affirmation in Nietzsche's *Thus Spoke Zarathustra*," in *Nietzsche's New Seas*, ed. M. A. Gillespie and T. B. Strong (Chicago: University of Chicago Press, 1988), 45–71.

32. For a clear and informative review of the debates surrounding Nietzsche as a political philosopher (Hitler, Rosenburg, Mussolini, Förster-Nietzsche, Strauss, Foucault) or as an apolitical thinker (Heidegger, Kaufmann, Stern, Deleuze, Danto, Schacht), see Ike Okonta, *Nietzsche: The Politics of Power* (New York: Peter Lang, 1992), 1–28. I agree with Okonta's observation that ultimately, Nietzsche's "'grand' politics itself is fundamentally indistinguishable from a grand nihilism" (163) insofar as it is rooted in a will to power that requires no justification for its creation and destruction, advocating that no values are eternal. Dannhauser also comes to a similar conclusion when he notes that Nietzsche's notion of "spiritedness" or "courage" (*Mut*) is ultimately indistinguishable from frenzy, or "energy without focus." See Werner Dannhauser, "Spiritedness in *Thus Spoke Zarathustra*," in *Understanding the Political Spirit: Philosophical Investigations from Socrates to Nietzsche*, ed. Catherine Zuckert (New Haven: Yale University Press, 1988), 180–95. However, I limit this observation principally to Nietzsche's post-Zarathustran writings, and focus on Nietzsche's gendered politics, which Okonta does not address, and Dannhauser ironically reifies in the statement: "Man needs courage to face the truth—to pursue it—when the truth has ceased to be beautiful. Truth may be a woman but that woman may be old and gnarled and ugly" (190).

virtues, hence also justice, and justice sometimes requires lying; as Socrates makes clear, . . . rulers must lie for the benefit of their subjects."³³ The basic idea appears to be that most citizens need to be protected from certain truths concerning the nature of reality, the state, and political life. For instance, in the *Republic* Socrates cites the "myth of the metals" as one such "noble lie" whose nobility lies in its ability to mediate between the lawgiver's insight into the truths of nature and the psyche of the common citizen.

This notion of myth politically functioning as a "noble lie" has been unearthed, in Nietzsche's writings, to some extent, by Werner Dannhauser's existentialist interpretation.³⁴ Dannhauser draws attention particularly to Nietzsche's post-Zarathustran writings, in which Nietzsche explicitly advocates the need to resort to some sort of life-sustaining mythology in defense against the looming nihilistic threat. In Dannhauser's interpretation of Nietzsche, human life can only thrive within a certain horizon that human beings believe to be the absolute truth. But if in reality this supposed "absolute" is merely one of many possible horizons, then life is in need of illusions, and the truth that exposes that horizon as *mere* horizon is deadly. There is, then, a conflict between truth and life, or between life and wisdom (832).

Ultimately, Dannhauser's Nietzsche advocates the choice of life over wisdom, given such a conundrum as "there can be life without wisdom, but there can be no wisdom without life" (832–33). In other words, living demands illusions that must be mistaken for truths, for to view illusions as illusions is humanly unbearable. "Myths are useful only so long as they are mistaken for the truth. A man's horizon is his most comprehensive myth, and it enables him to live because he thinks of it as the truth" (833). "Truth" is a noble lie. As Paul de Man phrases it: "Nietzsche tells the tale of the reversed pattern: in order to survive in society, man began by lying."³⁵

Building upon these insights while simultaneously excavating further into Nietzsche's assumptions concerning power and authority, I hope to show that Nietzsche's configuration of myth within his aesthetic politics begins much earlier than his Zarathustran phase (as Dannhauser contends) and has more optimistic roots. In his pre-Zarathustran texts, Nietzsche advocates the appropriation of Greek myths as figures for his vision of overcoming decadence and recapturing the golden age. However, Nietzsche's vision of myth effectively functioning as a "noble lie" crystallizes most clearly within *Thus Spoke Zarathustra*, in which the main character, the prophet-dancer-iconoclast Zarathustra, preaches the doctrine of the coming of the *Übermensch*, and knows, even with his animals and disciples, that his teachings are

---

33. Strauss, *The City and Man*, 99.
34. Werner Dannhauser, "Friedrich Nietzsche," in *History of Political Philosophy*, 3d ed., ed. Leo Strauss and Joseph Cropsey (Chicago: University of Chicago Press, 1987), 829–50.
35. Paul de Man, *Allegories of Reading* (New Haven: Yale University Press, 1979), 112.

in constant danger of being reduced to a "hurdy-gurdy song." The fact that the doctrine of the *Übermensch* is a lie is evidenced in Zarathustra's eventual birthing of his malformed higher men and the institution of the mass of the ass; its life-sustaining nobility is revealed in its promise of an eventual overcoming of the decadence and corruption of modernity. In his post-Zarathustran phase, Nietzsche employs a twofold strategy: outwardly applauding humanity's need for a noble lie while inwardly attempting to live without such a lie (to the point of identifying with Dionysus); and advocating the recognition of modernity's illusion as illusion—of exposing her Wagnerian bursts of energy as death throes rather than explosions of renewed strength—and thus, hastening modernity's self-destruction. His political agenda moves from resuscitating modernity to encouraging its suicide—a political agenda I aim to expose as intrinsically flawed: doomed to extinction by virtue of its tyrannical repression of the "feminine," powered by Nietzschean resentful dis-ease.

The second text I draw from partially in order to arrive at a "political" and "embodied" approach is Eric Blondel's *Nietzsche: The Body and Culture: Philosophy as Philological Genealogy*.[36] For Blondel, genealogy is to be conceived as fundamentally "interstitial," operating in the lacunae between structure and reference, surface and depth, word and action (133). Similarly, philology is primarily concerned with the linguistic, while recognizing the need for reference to that which is not linguistic, the body. In Blondel's vision, therefore, genealogy is a discourse of bodies, their affiliations with others and their differences, both internally and with others. Along parallel lines, philology emerges as a genealogy of the text (33, 35); it is devoted to pluralizing it and indicating its connection with the body. Genealogy, similarly, is a philology of the body: a practice of making the body speak. As Blondel reconceives it, philosophy as a philological genealogy is concerned with that questionable category, culture—the site of the impossible but necessary intersection of body and culture. Blondel understands culture as the totality of answers given by a society or an age to the question "what are you living for?" (54) (which is the principal question the mytho-political noble lie seeks to address). As such, culture is simultaneously a bodily response, a function of vitality or weakness, for example, and a linguistic formulation. While I do not intend to use Blondel's rhetoric, the nature and focus of his method resonate with those of my own, with its stress on the genealogical, the bodily, the figural, mythic and political. Nevertheless, unlike Blondel, I aim not only to explicate the genealogical model, but also to turn it against Nietzsche, in order to deliver a Nietzschean critique of Nietzsche's own political mythology.

While Strauss's, Dannhauser's and Blondel's accounts do much to establish a manner of reading Nietzsche that pays attention to the interplay between the textual and

---

36. Eric Blondel, *Nietzsche: The Body and Culture: Philosophy as Philological Genealogy*, trans. Sean Hand (Stanford: Stanford University Press, 1991).

the bodily as sites for the encrypting of Nietzsche's political messages,[37] they do not address the question of how gender sculpts the resultant political frame. Hence, I supplement these prisms with refracted images from feminist thinkers, such as Kristeva and Irigaray, among others, whose psychoanalytic, mirroring and miming strategies serve to expose the blind spots of the earlier frames.

Jean Graybeal's adoption of the Kristevan notion of the "feminine" is a clear starting point for characterizing what I mean by the "feminine" and outlining this project's "gendered" and "embodied" approach. Weaving together and displaying how a myriad of threads come to constitute the garment of the Kristevan feminine, Graybeal shows how the "feminine" holds together complex factors of social reality (actual women's marginality and exclusion from institutions of power), psychological situation (the development of subjects in relation to parental forces distinguished by gender identifications), and language theory (the semiotic dimension as maternally connoted). In the Kristevan sense, the "feminine" also recognizes a religious or mythical dimension, a "theological temptation"—the ever-present desire to substitute in the vacant space of the old Father God a Mother Goddess with a slightly altered physiognomy and thus, to betray the challenge of a new vision of the human situation.[38]

Briefly described, Graybeal's thesis is that both Nietzsche's and Heidegger's explorations of language reveal a deep, abiding concern and fascination with "the feminine," in some of the many forms it can take. By this, she does not mean to posit that Nietzsche and Heidegger were really feminists or protofeminists. Nor does she mean to suggest that what she perceives as their fascination with a "feminine" dimension in language outweighs or subsumes their attitudes towards women. Instead, she argues that "a careful reading of certain texts of Nietzsche and Heidegger provides valuable insight into the processes of human constitution within

---

37. For a different approach to Nietzsche's politics, see David Owen, *Nietzsche, Politics, and Modernity: A Critique of Liberal Reason* (London: Sage Publications, 1995). Owen's conclusion is that Nietzsche provides a sustained critique of liberalism from an agonistic perspective, without eliding pluralism and abrogating the autonomy of citizens. Similarly, Hatab takes up the task of revising Nietzsche's reviled image as the most venomous denouncer of modernity. Hatab's Nietzschean defense of democracy capitalizes on the *agon*-istic and ironic aspects of Nietzsche's writings to argue for a path that avoids the three most common responses to Nietzsche's politics: the first deflects Nietzsche's antidemocratic passages by interpreting them in nonpolitical terms—promoting creativity, individuality, excellence, and philosophical insight; the second blatantly ignores Nietzsche's problematic politics; the third takes Nietzsche at his word and sees in his writings a quasi-fascist aristocraticism. Hatab's project consists in showing that "democracy is compatible with Nietzsche's thought, that democracy can be redescribed in a Nietzschean manner." See Lawrence Hatab, *A Nietzschean Defense of Democracy: An Experiment in Postmodern Politics* (Chicago: Open Court, 1995), 2. From a gender-neutral point of view, this type of analysis is convincing; however, since I take Nietzsche's gender politics to be at the very heart of his philosophy, I take a more critical view of his agonism.

38. Jean Graybeal, *Language and "The Feminine" in Nietzsche and Heidegger* (Bloomington: Indiana University Press, 1990), 20.

language, including a dimension that is linked in ways we shall explore with women and 'the feminine'" (1).

In order to accomplish her aims, Graybeal devotes an initial chapter to Julia Kristeva's work, arguing that her perspectives on the position of the subject in relation to language are "ethically" motivated, and that they can serve as powerful hermeneutic tools for the exegesis of literary-philosophical texts such as the works of Nietzsche and Heidegger. In particular, she draws heavily from Kristeva's notions of the "symbolic" and "semiotic" dispositions in language, and their resonances with the cultural facts of male dominance and female "marginality" in her analyses of Nietzsche's *The Gay Science*, *Thus Spoke Zarathustra*, and *Ecce Homo*.

While this project parallels Graybeal's in terms of its genealogical and stylistic method, as well as its conclusions regarding the development of Nietzsche's political philosophy in relation to the problem of the "feminine," it diverges with regard to Graybeal's principal stress on the biographical and psychoanalytic. Eventually, in her analysis of *Ecce Homo*, Graybeal uses Kristeva's notion of abjection to show how Nietzsche abjects his mother, Franziska, and speculates that Nietzsche might have retained his sanity if he had been able to articulate his relationship to his mother (138–40). Notwithstanding the intriguing quality of Graybeal's hypotheses, what I find more useful for my project would be, in the words of Kelly Oliver, to "move Graybeal's analysis from the level of personal psychology to the level of textual positionality."[39]

In other words, although the notions of the "feminine" that I attempt to explore in this project do, to a certain extent, unearth and draw from sociological, psychoanalytic, and linguistic dimensions crucial to the development of Nietzsche's thought,[40] my primary focus remains Nietzsche's repeated attempts to define and redefine the "feminine"/"woman" at the intersection of politics and myth in his evolving generation of the doctrines of the eternal return, the coming of the *Übermensch*, and the will to power. In addition, as I show, Nietzsche's notion of the "problem of 'woman'" does not preclude the Kristevan "theological temptation"—his political philosophy eventually forges the image of the phallic mother, a mirror image of the very idol Kristeva shuns.

What is unique to this project is in keeping with the "symptomatological" approach I adopt: I show how a provisional and developmental fixture of the meaning and significance of the "feminine" as fertile or regenerative is not only possible and revelatory, but also authorized by Nietzsche's own symptomatological stress on health as reproductive. Conversely, I shall also show that Nietzsche increasingly associates the realm of "woman" with disease, impotence, and death. Based upon my analysis of Nietzsche's pre-Zarathustran and Zarathustran texts, I agree with Kelly

---

39. Oliver, *Womanizing Nietzsche*, 144.
40. These are dimensions one can see at work in the texts of Kristeva and Graybeal.

Oliver's reading that Nietzsche strategically collapses the "feminine" (*weiblich*) to mean strictly the "maternal" (*mutterlich*)—and I argue that he does this in an attempt precisely to reduce the complexity of the "feminine" and thus, to harness the maternal power of birthing unto his mytho-political image of the phallic mother. Such an approach aims to trace how Nietzsche's initial political optimism crystallizes in relatively nonmisogynistic mythic configurations of the "feminine" and eventually dissolves into a pessimism that increasingly attempts to silence and appropriate the "feminine" and denigrate "woman." In my genealogy of Nietzsche's devolving[41] political philosophy, the "feminine" is initially a figure for or symptom of modernity's generative capacities; later, its repression becomes symptomatic of Nietzsche's *ressentiment* against his own and modernity's political impotence.

Finally, Luce Irigaray's *Marine Lover of Friedrich Nietzsche*[42] is another text whose conclusions resonate, to a large extent, with mine. Here, Irigaray suggests in her polemically poetic way that Nietzsche's notions of the eternal return and the *Übermensch* are designed to cover over a debt to the maternal. Nietzsche-Zarathustra exploits these concepts to give birth to himself without woman.[43] Irigaray purportedly attempts to initiate "a lover's discourse" with Nietzsche, in the course of which she attempts to listen to his muted murmurings in *Thus Spoke Zarathustra*. She thereby tries to decipher what has been silenced in his writings, namely the foundational ground upon which he erects his philosophy of will to power—the "immemorial waters" from which everything emerges, the realm of the (M)Other whom Nietzsche has sought to expel. In effect, her "lover's discourse" with Nietzsche is an attempt to use Nietzsche's very own strategies against him—in order to divine the visage that lies beneath the numerous masks.

Phrased slightly differently, Irigaray's ironic and mimetic attempt at a "lover's discourse" with Nietzsche aims to show that even though Nietzsche criticizes the metaphysical tradition that claims to have separated the man of reason from his elemental and material being, his own transvaluation of "woman's materiality" as the untruth of truth, still remains fixed within the Platonic paradigm that he ventures to explode. According to Irigaray, by projecting the concentric circle of the subject that wills power, Nietzsche's overman attempts to appropriate every being within his own perspectival subjectivity, and in so doing, he simultaneously expels the (M)Other.

41. For purposes of clarity, I use "devolving" when I am referring specifically to Nietzsche's gradually hardening misogyny; when I speak of his "evolving" political vision, I am using a more generic and neutral term to describe, in general, the changes his thoughts undergo, via reference to a historically and biographically based timeline.

42. Luce Irigaray, *Marine Lover of Friedrich Nietzsche*, trans. Gillian Gill (New York: Columbia University Press, 1991).

43. For a similar assessment of Irigaray's position, see Oliver, *Womanizing Nietzsche*, xvi.

Moreover, in his pursuit of the "higher man," Nietzsche projects an elevated and lofty world in which Zarathustra reigns. In his flight to the mountains and in his quest for the eternal return of the same, Irigaray perceives Nietzsche as being an accomplice to the denial of, and the escape from, the elemental (mother) earth that made his birth possible. What results, however, is an anemic phallic motherhood: "Something red was lacking, a hint of blood and guts to revive the will, and restore its strength."[44]

Although my conclusions concerning Nietzsche's response to the "feminine," particularly in his post-Zarathustran phase, reverberate with Irigaray's, and I also attempt to use Nietzsche's very own "symptomatogical" strategies against him, I employ a comparatively more "genealogical" and expository rather than a principally mimetic, poetic (and "castrating") approach, as Irigaray does. Naturally, the method I employ cannot be absolutely distinguished from Irigaray's, as it is partially inspired by her own method, which certainly employs strategies of immanent critique. Nevertheless, the symptomatological and genealogical method I employ attempts to trace the tensions, the fluctuations, the ambivalences that characterize Nietzsche's gradually hardening mythology of the "phallic mother." In fact, I also attempt to show that Nietzsche, at least during his pre-Zarathustran phase, did not suffer such overtly and unambiguously misogynist pangs (which Irigaray seems to assume as a constant in Nietzsche's writings), and even expressed, in some sections, a sympathy for women's socio-political victimization, and employed "feminine" figures as powerful tropes for his doctrines.

Returning to Irigaray's focus on the interrelated issues of the "feminine" and the political in Nietzsche, Derrida's *Spurs: Nietzsche's Styles* similarly focuses on the relationship between Nietzsche's style and the manner in which he figures "woman." For instance, in his commentary on section 60 of *The Gay Science*, entitled "Women and Their Action at a Distance," Derrida remarks:

> Perhaps woman is, as non-identity, non-figure, simulacrum, the *abyss* of distance, the distancing of distance; the cut [*coupe*] of spacing, distance itself if one could still say, which is impossible, distance *itself*.[45]

Nietzsche, as Derrida reads him, is concerned with opening philosophy to the marginalized/non-Platonic "others"—the body, the unconscious, nonmeaning, the "feminine." The "feminine," as that which enables distance, is the invisible "other" required by the categories of the "Same" to affirm or maintain itself. Insofar as

---

44. Irigaray, *Marine Lover*, 79.
45. Jacques Derrida, *Spurs*, 48. I draw this translation from Graybeal, *Language*, 38.

Derrida is concerned with opening up the possibility of talking about these subjects that have been traditionally excluded from philosophy, especially the issue of the philosophical "feminine," his project, at least to some degree, resonates with Irigaray's and mine.

Margaret Whitford, in "Reading Irigaray in the Nineties,"[46] points out that there has as yet been little extensive discussion of Irigaray's relation to Derrida's work, despite the intertextualities that echo in their works.[47] And indeed, the ties binding and unleashing Derrida and Irigaray are complex and manifold. For instance, Elizabeth Weed traces the Derridean resonances of Irigaray's work.[48] For Weed, both Irigaray and Derrida employ deconstructive readings that are "homeopathic"—both operate within what they are seeking to contest, and to accept that there is no position *outside* metaphysics or language from which to disrupt metaphysics or language. Similarly, Elizabeth Grosz argues that Irigaray's use of deconstruction is an exemplary feminist strategy for approaching patriarchal theory. However, more critically, Rosi Braidotti takes up the position that Derrida's work, despite its value as a critique of phallogocentric metaphysics, appropriates women's right to speak for themselves, and in a sense substitutes itself for women's voices once again. Whereas Derrida mainly aims to deconstruct identity, Irigaray's later focus argues for the construction of a new identity. From Irigaray's point of view, the charge may be leveled that Derrida's work may still be implicated in a patriarchal imaginary economy, in which woman remains the ground or condition of predication.

Plunging into the conversations regarding Nietzsche and the "feminine," Kelly Oliver's *Womanizing Nietzsche: Philosophy's Relation to the Feminine* is one of the most recent attempts to carry further this dialogue between Nietzsche, Derrida, and Irigaray. By engaging in close readings of texts by Nietzsche, Derrida, Irigaray, and others, she attempts to use the case—and figure—of Nietzsche as a way of diagnosing philosophy's relation to the "feminine." Her central thesis is that although Nietzsche

---

46. Margaret Whitford, "Reading Irigaray in the Nineties," in *Engaging with Irigaray: Feminist Philosophy and European Thought*, ed. Carolyn Burke, Naomi Schor, and Margaret Whitford (New York: Columbia University Press, 1994), 17.

47. A few schematic discussions on the relationship between Derrida and Irigaray is found in texts such as Rosi Braidotti, *Patterns of Dissonance: A Study of Women in Contemporary Philosophy*, trans. Elizabeth Guild (Cambridge: Polity, 1991); Drucilla Cornell, *Beyond Accommodation: Ethical Feminism, Deconstruction, and the Law* (New York: Routledge, 1991); Elizabeth Grosz, "Derrida, Irigaray, and Deconstruction," *Intervention* 20 (1986): 70–81; Toril Moi, *Sexual/Textual Politics: Feminist Literary Theory* (London: Methuen, 1985); Andrea Nye, *Feminist Theory and the Philosophies of Man* (London: Croom Helm, 1988); Margaret Whitford, *Luce Irigaray: Philosophy in the Feminine* (New York: Routledge, 1991).

48. Elizabeth Weed, "The Question of Style," in *Engaging with Irigaray: Feminist Philosophy and European Thought*, ed. Carolyn Burke, Naomi Schor, and Margaret Whitford (New York: Columbia University Press, 1994), 79–109.

and Derrida, in particular, attempt to open up philosophy to others, such as the body, the unconscious, nonmeaning, even the feminine, they effectively close off philosophy to any specifically feminine other. While their texts open up the possibility of talking about those subjects that traditionally have been excluded from philosophy, they continue to exclude the feminine, especially the "feminine mother." Oliver eventually argues that talk of the death of philosophy is the result of this very exclusion. "Philosophy cannot kill off its feminine other and survive."[49]

While my conclusions regarding Nietzsche's relation to the "feminine" do not differ significantly from Oliver's, our aims differ somewhat. Oliver is determined to explore the conditions of possibility of establishing an ethical ontology based on a description of the maternal body or the mother's relation to the child (186); my principal aims, in this book, lie in locating and interpreting Nietzsche's ambivalences with respect to the "feminine" in his developing political philosophy, symptomatic of his philosophico-political will-to-resentment. From there, in my concluding chapter, I begin exploring whether or not it is possible to escape this tyranny of resentment, as manifested in the eternal return of the spectre of Authority. The issue of how my genealogical interpretation of Nietzsche's interweaving system of politics, gender, and myth may be used to contribute to feminism's aspirations to a transformative politics and a critical political theory (an extended future project whose outlines I begin to sketch) ultimately depends on how I can (re)configure and embody the nature of "authority" as a concept and practice within the intertwining realms of myth and politics, after I have done this initial genealogical excavation/exhumation of several key Nietzsche texts.

Returning to the range of philosophical literature responding to the issue of the "feminine" in Nietzsche's politics, Oliver's later essay, an analysis of "Nietzsche's Abjection,"[50] like Kofman's essay, treats the philosopher's position on woman as a function of his relationship to his mother. Nevertheless, Oliver insists that we must keep in mind the difference between the feminine and the maternal. She uses Kristeva's separation of the feminine operation from the maternal function and her theory of abjection to illustrate how Nietzsche *reduces* woman and the feminine to the maternal—i.e., that he is not able to make that crucial separation, and thus that his problematic relation to "woman" derives directly from his disturbed relation to his mother. In an argument running counter to Kofman's, Oliver asserts that Nietzsche is caught at the stage of abjection, with no loving father to support his separation: that he is never able to separate the maternal function from the mother and this would split the mother into the abject and the sublime, which would in turn

---

49. Oliver, *Womanizing Nietzsche*, xi.
50. Kelly Oliver, "Nietzsche's Abjection," in *Nietzsche and the Feminine*, ed. Peter Burgard (Charlottesville: University Press of Virginia, 1994), 53–67.

enable him to develop an autonomous identity. She concludes that the three "Nietzschean women" hypostatized by Derrida—castrated woman, castrating woman, and affirming woman—are simply three faces of mother. In essence, then, for Oliver, there is no "woman" or "feminine" in Nietzsche, insofar as these "feminine figures" always remain inscribed in maternal relation. I agree with Oliver's analysis of Nietzsche's collapse of the "feminine" and "woman" into the "maternal"; however, I diverge again methodologically (and rhetorically) from her as she builds principally from Kristeva's and Derrida's insights to arrive at her conclusions, which I do not.

Finally, in "The Laugh of the Medusa,"[51] Hélène Cixous rewrites Nietzsche by abandoning his valorization of strength and casting those economies in terms of gender and intersubjective relations. She unmasks the economy grounded on the law of return as based on the notion of property and the phallocentric desire to appropriate the other. This "masculine" economy—founded on the fear of castration, of losing what one already possesses—does not allow true giving, because in order to prevent loss, it always requires something in return. A "feminine" economy, on the other hand, can bear separation—giving up what is its own—and promotes giving for the sake of establishing relationships that neither maintain the division of self and other nor effect the appropriation of the other. Such insights are important to revisioning the nexus between Nietzsche and the "feminine," as I show in Chapter 5, where I draw heavily from both Cixous's and Minh-ha's aesthetico-political attempts to break the eternal return of *ressentiment* and the Author and to sketch the outlines for a possible prolegomenon for a genuinely postmodern and post-Nietzschean philosophy.

Hence, this study attempts to trace the ambivalences of Nietzsche's textual encounters with the "feminine"—attacking and retreating, adoring and shunning, appropriating and silencing. It is an attempt to get beyond the simplistic question of whether or not Nietzsche was a misogynist by turning to a genealogical approach that attempts to plot the tensions of the development of Nietzsche's thought, via the intersecting planes of politics, gender, and myth.

Negotiating a path between Straussian and feminist readings of Nietzsche is a difficult task. Numerous potential rifts are possible: whereas for Straussians, gender is not a significant area to address, for feminists, this is central to any discussion of power. For Straussians, Nietzsche is an ironic aristocrat; for many feminists, Nietzsche is a misogynist unworthy of discussion, a secret advocate of liberal democracy, or the benevolent benefactor of feminist strategies that enable the undercutting of prevailing conditions of power. This project is an attempt to

---

51. Hélène Cixous, "The Laugh of the Medusa," trans. Keith Cohen and Paula Cohen, in *New French Feminisms*, ed. I. de Courtivron and E. Marks (New York: Shocken Books, 1981), 245–65.

negotiate a path across these rifts, while preserving many of the valuable insights these perspectives offer.

Ultimately, this study is a symptomatology of Nietzsche's subterranean gendered and political mythology—a genealogy that attempts to trace the movement of Nietzsche's devolving politics; a strategic appropriation of his own critical terms and vocabulary. It attempts to reveal how earlier interpretations of Nietzsche's attitude toward the "feminine"/"woman" have fallen into traps of either taking Nietzsche too literally or not teasing out the implications of Nietzsche's figural depictions of women in a manner sensitive to his own changing political genealogy. This study aims to reveal how the development of Nietzsche's political mythology is intimately intertwined with his devolving image of the "feminine." It illustrates how Nietzsche's initial microscopic diagnosis of his own political potency parallels his macroscopic vision of modernity's recuperative powers and manifests itself in a nonmisogynistic figuration of the "feminine"/"woman." Conversely, it displays how Nietzsche's eventual macroscopic denunciation of modernity's decadence is reflective of his own microscopic acknowledgment of his political impotence, as embodied in his resentful attempts to appropriate and eventually silence the "feminine"/"woman." Thus, this study, which claims the heritage of Nietzschean strategies, employs his own weapons against him with the aim of yielding an account that looks underneath the mask Nietzsche believed to be his own face (a mask he was neither willing nor able to take off) by virtue of his ambivalent configuring of the "feminine." One of the final aims of this approach to Nietzsche involves effecting a self-destructive implosion of Nietzsche's account of modernity, and I hope, taking steps toward re-valuing "authority" as gendered and mythic. For indeed, if gender operates as a signifier, or a mode of representation of the political, as it certainly does in Nietzsche's texts, there is a need to interrogate the nature of the political as intertwined with the aesthetic. Instead of asking whether women are written about in such texts or focusing purely on the texts' misogynistic content, there is a need to explore how Nietzsche uses the absence or appropriation of the "feminine" in order to demarcate the space of (mythic) politico-aesthetic action.

2

The Pre-Zarathustran Phase: Exca/Elevating the Mother

> There are two powers, young man, which are supreme
> In human affairs: first, Demeter—the same goddess
> Is also Earth; give her which name you please—and she
> Supplies mankind with solid food. After her came
> Dionysus, Semele's son; the blessing he procured
> And gave to men is the counterpart to that of bread:
> The clear juice of grape.
> —Euripides, *The Bacchae*

> Two grey old women, witchlike, with hanging breasts . . . were busy there, between flaming braziers, most horribly. They were dismembering a child. In dreadful silence they tore it apart with their bare hands—Hans Castorp saw the bright hair bloodsmeared—and cracked the tender bones between their jaws, their dreadful lips dripped with blood.
> —Thomas Mann, *The Magic Mountain*

Introductory Remarks

Sarah Kofman, in her attempt to unearth Nietzsche's repressed or subterranean metaphors for metaphor itself, isolates two such figures: (1) the metaphor of Chladni's sound figures, a model fashioned to depict sound vibrations visually—built upon the analogy of a sound appearing as a sand figure; an "X" initially making its appearance as a nerve stimulus, then as an image, and finally as a sound[1]—and (2) the metaphor of the blind painter using song to paint the picture he has before his eyes (41–42). Part of Kofman's project is showing that in order to describe metaphorical activity, Nietzsche supplies several complementary yet different metaphors, each describing a particular aspect of metaphor, yet never totalizing it—an act of description best illustrated in each metaphor's inadequacy for tyrannizing "metaphorical activity as a 'pure' concept" (40). Yet her ambitions aim higher; she aims to show that "the metamorphosis of the

---

1. Sarah Kofman, *Nietzsche and Metaphor*, trans. Duncan Large (Stanford: Stanford University Press, 1993), 40–41.

metaphor into a 'proper'[2] implies relations of violence, and transformations in the relations of force" (43) in Nietzsche's excavation of society's "forgetting" of metaphor in favor of concept, logic, and science. Kofman's interpretation of Nietzsche's project renders him the supreme unmasker: by deliberately transforming the world into set metaphors, he renders translucent the mask of metaphysical tatters, behind which a nihilistic will lurks—"a life which is afraid of life" (72).

Along a track parallel to Kofman, in this chapter, I excavate several of the key figures Nietzsche uses to embody his political project of curing modernity of its decadence, which he still believes is possible during his pre-Zarathustran phase. Unlike Kofman, one of the key aims of this chapter is to reveal how Nietzsche's aesthetico-political philosophy is rooted not simply in a generalized notion of metaphor as the key trope, but more essentially in personified/anthropomorphized figures of mythology as gendered.

The principal tropes in Nietzsche's political philosophy are *personifications* or *anthropomorphisms*: masks of flesh and blood through whom the drama of the eternal resurgence of life plays itself out. Relations of violence, forgetting, and sundering between "truth" and "lie," language and song, consciousness and unconsciousness, reflection/self-knowledge and naiveté become more than anemic abstractions when they are enfleshed in the battles between Plato-Socrates and Dionysus, and Aeschylus and Euripides, for instance. These anthropomorphisms may be classified into five general categories: (1) actual mythic personages, such as Dionysus, Apollo, Baubô, or the Sphinx; (2) historical personages elevated to the mythologico-historical, such as Socrates or Euripides; (3) entities granted mythic status, such as "Nature," "Tragedy," "Life," or "World;" (4) literary characters re-created as (a)kin to mythic deities, such as Hamlet or Faust; or (5) characteristics used as analogies to set up a gendered mythic ideal, such as the gentleness of young girls, the nurturance of mothers, or the virility of warriors. It is important to note that especially in *The Birth of Tragedy*, Nietzsche uses the five types fairly interchangeably. Although he is using different subtypes of anthropomorphisms, he uses them as a proverbial "mobile army of metaphors": each subtly distinguished from the other in terms of (uni)form, but fluidly uniting toward a single goal—the rescue of modernity from its decadent Christian, democratic, and Romantic influences. Whether the original subjects are mythic deities (such as Demeter), mythic personas (such as Helen), historical figures (such as Euripides), entities that have been granted mythic status (such as Nature), literary characters that have entered into the realm of the mythic (such as Hamlet), or even characteristics that Nietzsche elevates to the mythic (such as unbounded vitality), Nietzsche uses all of these levels of metaphorization or anthropomorphism fairly interchangeably. It is as if they all become actors in the grand play he orchestrates, where Hamlet is saved from his dark vision by his saving sorceress, Art, and Sacrilege is anthropomorphized either into a "masculine" form (*der Frevel*) or a "feminine" form (*die Sünde*). Despite the plurality of anthropomorphisms that surface in

Nietzsche's *The Birth of Tragedy*, there are two principal figures around whom the other figures revolve. Helen and the satyr, Antigone and Cassandra, and Homer and Archilochus are but some of the masks for these two principal anthropomorphisms: Apollo and Dionysus. As Sallis writes: "Only two gods, Apollo and Dionysus, figure primarily in the disclosure; whatever disclosive significance might accrue to other gods will prove to depend on their relation to Apollo or Dionysus, on their capacity to represent . . . Apollo or Dionysus."[3]

The aims of this chapter, therefore, are as follows:

1. To describe/articulate, in some detail, the various mythic masks Nietzsche constructs as he moves through *The Birth of Tragedy, Human, All too Human*, and *The Gay Science*.[4] I choose to examine these texts in particular because they, in comparison with others, make more overt pronouncements concerning Nietzsche's presuppositions concerning the connections binding myth, politics, philosophy, and gender.
2. To illustrate how a correspondence exists between Nietzsche's benevolent (though ambivalent) treatment of the "feminine" (that progressively becomes collapsed with "woman"), and a relatively strong optimism regarding the political project of saving modernity from its decadence. Both these aspects, his benevolence toward the "feminine" and his optimism regarding the recuperation of modernity, are distinctive attributes of his pre-Zarathustran phase, and disappear as he moves into his Zarathustran and post-Zarathustran phases, as I shall show in Chapters 3 and 4.
3. To formulate a coherent account of how Nietzsche appropriates and recasts mythic narratives to authorize his political aim of redeeming modernity via an initially aesthetic, and eventually, scientifico-aesthetic cure.

Mythic Anthropomorphisms/Personifications

Beyond Modernity: Rebirthing Apollo and Dionysus

Dionysus and Apollo are immediately introduced as the principal mythic figures in the first chapter of *The Birth of Tragedy* (hereafter *Birth*).[5] From the very start,

---

3. John Sallis, *Crossings: Nietzsche and the Space of Tragedy* (Chicago: University of Chicago Press, 1991), 17.
4. The translation of Nietzsche's *Die Fröhliche Wissenschaft* by Thomas Common, which I use, translates this title as *The Joyful Wisdom*.
5. Friedrich Nietzsche, *The Birth of Tragedy and The Case of Wagner*, trans. Walter Kaufmann (New York: Random House, 1967), 33; Friedrich Nietzsche, *Sämtliche Werke: Die Geburt der Tragödie,*

Nietzsche links the "development," "growth" or "evolution" (*Fortentwicklung*) of art with the "Apollinian" and the "Dionysian" via an analogy to sexual reproduction which requires a duality (*Zweiheit*) of the sexes—a duality involving continuous warfare (*fortwährendem Kampfe*) and periodically appearing/intervening reconciliations or appeasements (*periodisch eintretender Versöhnung*).[6] Nietzsche uses *Duplicität* to describe the relationship binding the Apollinian and the Dionysian. *Duplicität* may generally be translated to mean "duality." However, within context, it may mean not simply a duality between Apollo and Dionysus, but also a duality within the two gods.[7]

Certainly, Greek mythic depictions of Apollo and Dionysus show both gods as possessing "masculine" and "feminine" traits, or as having a gendered duality. One of their many appearances is as beautiful, effeminate looking youths. Hence, Euripides' *Bacchae* depicts one of Dionysus's forms to be that of a youth with long, flowing locks;[8] Thomas Mann's Tadzio brings together the figures of Dionysus, Apollo, Eros, and Hades in the slight figure of a boy whose beauty drives the aging Aschenbach to his maddened and plague-ridden death.[9] Yet *Duplicität* (duality) may also connote *Duplizität* (double-sidedness, duplicity), particularly against its backdrop of continuous battle and tenuous ceasefires.

A footnote from Walter Kaufmann's translation of *Birth* seems to point to Nietzsche's grappling with this very issue of the nature of the two gods and the relationship binding them. In Kaufmann's account of the first edition of *Birth*, with respect to the Apollinian and Dionysian duality, the text reads that there is "an opposition of style: two different tendencies run parallel in it, for the most part in conflict."[10] The later version reads: "*dass in der grieschen Welt ein ungeheurer Gegensatz, nach Ursprung und Zielen,*"[11] and may be translated to mean: "that in the Greek world, a tremendous opposition, in origin and aim." The earlier version seems to build a relatively more harmonious and organic model of the relationship, building upon parallel but conflicting styles, while the latter version emphasizes a striking opposition extending backwards (origin) and forwards (aim).

Unzeitgemäße Betrachtungen 1–4, Nachgelassene Schriften 1870–1873, ed. Giorgio Colli and Mazzino Montinari (Berlin: de Gruyter, 1988), 25.

6. Sallis also draws attention to the centrality of duality, yet he views the relationship between Apollo and Dionysus as one of "monstrous opposition" (*Crossings*, 14).

7. Sallis similarly notes: "the two sexes are represented, on the side of art, by two male figures" (*Crossings*, 18).

8. Euripides, *The Bacchae and Other Plays*, trans. Philip Vellacott (New York: Penguin Books, 1973), 191.

9. Thomas Mann, *Death in Venice and Seven Other Stories*, trans. H. T. Lowe-Porter (New York: Vintage Books, 1936), 3–75. See also Caroline Joan S. Picart, *Thomas Mann and Friedrich Nietzsche: Eroticism, Death, Music, and Laughter* (Dordrecht, Netherlands: Rodopi/Kluwer Academic Press, forthcoming).

10. Nietzsche, *Birth*, trans. Kaufmann, footnote 1, 33.

11. Nietzsche, *Birth*, trans. Kaufmann, 33; Nietzsche, *Die Geburt*, 25.

Yet what is even more significant is that the Apollinian and the Dionysian forces, in order to produce Greek tragic art—equally Apollinian and Dionysian—continually have to excite, stimulate, rouse, or irritate (*reizen*) each other into new births. The Dionysian and the Apollinian forces, in new births ever following and mutually augmenting or intensifying each other (47, 41) ground the Hellenic genius. What emerges, therefore, is less a reproductive model of two separate heterosexual mythic organisms who must copulate with each other in order to produce progeny bearing characteristics of both. Instead, what emerges is a more complex model of reproduction, in which both entities appear to possess a reproductive duality—possessing both "masculine" (excitatory) and "feminine" (birthing) capacities—within themselves, and yet require each other in order to effect birthing. The Apollinian and the Dionysian forces appear essentially to undergo a form of parthenogenesis—a self-birthing—yet it is an autogenesis that demands interaction with an other, as well as an autogenesis that requires an internal duality. The Apollinian and Dionysian only *appear* to be coupled or mated (*mit einander gepaart erscheinen*) (33, 25) with each other through the metaphysical miracle of the Hellenic "Will," thus generating an equally Dionysian and Apollinian form of art—Attic tragedy.[12] For Nietzsche, it is only when the Apollinian and the Dionysian forces exist in art that art is "healthy"—possessing a dynamic balance between the rational and elemental.

For Nietzsche, Apollo and Dionysus rebirth themselves and their productive opposition by donning various masks. For instance, Helen makes a brief appearance, as the appearance of the Greek gazing upon the ideal picture of his own existence, or as the apparition of the apparition "floating in sweet sensuality [*In süsser Sinnlichkeit schwebende*]" (41, 35). She is thus but one among the pantheon of masks Nietzsche fashions for Apollo, as the appearance of appearance as mere appearance—profound superficiality.

Correspondingly, Nietzsche grants the satyr the status of the Dionysian chorist, who inhabits a religiously hallowed reality under the sanction of myth and cult. The satyr is the fictitious natural being (*das fingirte Naturwesen*) (59, 55) in whose presence the Greek man of culture felt nullified, counterbalanced, lifted up, and sublated (*aufgehoben*) (60, 56). The mixture of god, goat, and man becomes the personification of what Nietzsche terms the "metaphysical comfort [*der metaphysische Trost*]" (60, 56) with which genuine tragedy leaves us—the vision of life as infinitely powerful,

---

12. There are indications that Nietzsche also grappled with the nature of this "coupling." In another footnote, Kaufman's translation of the same section of *Die Geburt* remarks that an earlier version read: "till eventually, at the moment of the flowering of the Hellenic 'will,' they appear fused to generate together the art form of Attic tragedy" (33). "Fusion" is a less overtly erotic term than "coupling" and again seems to point towards a more organic model Nietzsche seems to have abandoned in favor of a more overt and yet complex sexual one in the latter version.

pleasurable, and indestructible, at the bottom of things. The chorus of satyrs incarnates this metaphysical comfort, as a vision of natural and ineradicable beings, simultaneously hyperboreanesque and subterranean, the ground upon which civilization builds its Apollinian heights, in spite of the passing away of generations and the turbulent history of nations (60, 56).

The satyr, unlike the tender shepherd, his modern and decadent shadow, is the embodiment of the highest and most intense emotions—who is enraptured by and suffers with the god he follows. For Nietzsche, the satyr is the mouthpiece of nature, the fleshly incarnation of its tragic wisdom. The satyr, within the Greek constellation of symbols, was a powerful figure for the sexual omnipotence of nature—hence, another mask for the Dionysian force (61–62, 57–58).

For Nietzsche, the history of the unfolding of art is tied up with this amorous agonistic between Apollo and Dionysus. Hence, in his view, Attic tragedy and the dramatic dithyramb present themselves as the spontaneous yet hard-fought goals or glorious consummation of the Apollinian and the Dionysian forces: children bearing the features of both Antigone and Cassandra (47, 42). Sophocles's Antigone, in Nietzsche's account, seems to be another mask for the Apollinian force, in her embodiment of the "feminine" heroic manifestations of Greek tragedy; Aeschylus's Cassandra, on the other hand, appears another mask for the Dionysian force, in her untamed oneness with the tragic vision.[13]

Similarly, Homer bears the visage of Apollo, and Archilochus wears the mask of Dionysus in Nietzsche's account of the twofold paternity of Greek poetry. According to Nietzsche, when Archilochus proclaims both his mad love and contempt to the daughters of Lycambes, the vision of Dionysus and his Maenads dancing in orgiastic frenzy readily emerges; and it is only as Archilochus sinks into drunken stupor on a high mountain pasture in the noonday sun that Apollo approaches and touches him with the laurel—sparking off tragedies and dramatic dithyrambs. Thus, in Nietzsche's account, these two "torchbearers," Homer and Archilochus, father the highest forms of Greek art—precisely as visages for the Apollinian and Dionysian forces (49–50, 44).

As yet another micronarrative to the overall tale of the (re)productive *agon* between Apollo and Dionysus, Nietzsche uses the tale of the capture of Silenus, the satyr companion of Dionysus, by Midas, to illustrate the Greek awareness of the sacrifice underneath the Olympian magic mountain: a sacrifice Thomas Mann immortalized in his rendition of Hans Castorp's fevered dream,[14] another mask of the

---

13. Kaufmann reports that Wilamowitz, in his first polemic (1872), flung down the gauntlet, challenging anyone to attempt a coherent reading of these lines, saying such, if credible, would deserve a "suitable reward" from him. Kaufmann also adheres to the view that Antigone stands in for the Apollinian, and Cassandra stands in for the Dionysian in this context (footnote 2, 47).

14. Thomas Mann, *The Magic Mountain*, trans. H. T. Lowe-Porter (New York: Vintage Books, 1969), 494.

Dionysian force or insight into the nature of human existence. Silenus, coerced by Midas into revealing the best and most desirable thing for humanity, bursts out: "What is best of all is utterly beyond your reach: not to be born [*nicht geboren zu sein*], not to be [*nicht zu sein*], to be nothing [*nichts zu sein*]. But the second best for you is—to die soon [*bald zu sterben*]" (41, 35).

Yet Nietzsche uses the figures of Midas and Silenus as simply two masks in varied array of mythic *dramatis personae*. Facing the titanic powers of nature (*die titanischen Mächte der Natur*) (41, 35) and the inexorable reign of Moira (Fate), Prometheus must bear the nightly visitations of the vulture feasting upon his liver, Oedipus must become a blind exile, and Orestes must commit matricide. The titanic reign of terror, which one glimpses in the dark visage of Dionysus, gives way, only through the striving of the Apollinian impulse, to produce beauty, just as roses burst forth from thorny bushes (42, 36). It is in the figures of Prometheus, Oedipus, and Orestes that the Dionysian and the Apollinian lock into shadowy embrace, simultaneously producing and punishing the excessive wisdom of Oedipus, the titanic love for humanity of Prometheus, and the powerful urge for justice of Orestes. It is only via this intense coupling that Apollinian and Dionysian forces produce "healthy" art.

Finally, for an illustration of the inextricability of the Apollinian force in art from the Dionysian force in Nietzsche's pre-Zarathustran constellation, I turn to Nietzsche's examination of Raphael's *Transfiguration*.

Raphael's famous painting displays a possessed boy, mouth frothing and agape, eyes eerily averted, surrounded by his despairing companions as well as the bewildered, terrified disciples in the shadowy foreground. In the background, a mountain juts upward, above which Christ and two prophets, bathed in light, hover—ethereal and unbounded. To Nietzsche, the figure of the maddened boy blurs into the figure of Dionysus, alongside his masks of the satyr and Cassandra, in their embodiment of the "mere appearance" of eternal contradiction, the father of all things (45, 39).

The representations of Christ and the two prophets that surround him blur into the figure of Apollo, with his masks of Helen and Antigone, in their embodied revelation of the necessity of the entire world of suffering. Through their gestures and expressions, the redeeming vision, the consummation and saving of primal unity through mere appearance as mere appearance, gleams forth (45–46, 39–40).

It appears that in Nietzsche's analysis of Raphael's painting, the *Transfiguration* is a paradigmatic retelling of the primordial desire for mere appearance as pure appearance—nature's joy in the naive artist and the naive work of art. It is a compelling testimony of how nature longs ardently for salvation through illusion, and how eternally suffering and chaotic primal unity requires this rapturous vision for its continuous redemption. The Apollinian and the Dionysian are intertwined in a complex, erotic embrace at the heart of nature and genuine art.

However, Nietzsche's mytho-political casting of the birth of Tragedy through the amorous agonistic between Apollo and Dionysus moves on to a darker phase: the murder of classic Tragedy at the hands of Euripides-Socrates, and Tragedy's monstrous rebirth in Euripidean drama and the New Attic Comedy. For Nietzsche, Euripides creates a new sacrilegious category, bearing a closer resemblance to the Semitic or "feminine" version (Eve's original sin) rather than the Aryan or "masculine" version (Prometheus's original transgression), when he abandons Dionysus in favor of a new god, Socrates.

Sacrilege, for Nietzsche, may take either a "masculine" (*der Frevel*—crime, wantonness, wickedness) or "feminine" (*die Sünde*—sin, offense, transgression) form. Just as the original and more properly "sacrilegious" act was committed by a man, the original sin was fallen into by a woman. Nietzsche characterizes the "masculine" form as "Aryan" and active, the "feminine" form as "Semitic" and passive. Mythically, "masculine" sacrilege is personified in the noble suffering of Oedipus and Prometheus who must solve the riddle of nature, and yet resist her most sacred laws and violate her strictest taboos. "Feminine" sacrilege or more properly, sin, has been mythically cast into the story of "the Fall." Thus, "feminine" transgression came to imply the slide into preeminently "feminine" affects (*weiblicher Affectionen*) (71, 69)—characterized as curiosity, mendacious deception, susceptibility to seduction, and lust—and eventually became regarded as the origin of evil.

In Nietzsche's account of the death of Tragedy, the flight of Dionysus culminates in the disappearance of even Apollo, resulting in the suicide of classic Greek Tragedy. Her monstrous rebirth, performed under the ministrations of Socrates, results in the New Attic Comedy, a daughter of the Euripidean elevation of the plebeian and ignoble. Graeculus, the cunning house slave, replaces the noble Odysseus; the chorus of spectators is trained to sing in the Euripidean key. Greek cheerfulness, the trait of the cunning slave Archilochus, is the Euripidean-Socratic heritage that has outlined the rise of the decadence of modernity (82, 83).

For Nietzsche, science, like Euripidean drama, worships "the naked goddess,"[15] and views the unveiling of truth as its ultimate aim. As such, the scientific enterprise comprises the modern counterpart to the Euripidean delight in logic and argumentation. In Nietzsche's view, the theoretical man, a son of science, is radically opposed to the Dionysian man. As such, the theoretical man is a clumsy lover of nature who operates via the principle: "I desire you; you are worth knowing" (109, 115). Nietzsche views faith in science—which he characterizes as essentially a belief in the total explicability of nature and the unbounded powers of scientific knowledge as a panacea—as simply a phase modernity must undergo in order to rebirth Tragedy.

---

15. By this, Nietzsche means "she who must be bared/seen/known," a pun upon the Greek word, "*aletheia*."

Nietzsche claims that once science gives in to the plague that ravages her innards, the music-practicing Socrates, bringer of new health, may be born. This music-practicing Socrates, savior of modernity, appears, on one level, to be Richard Wagner (as evidenced in the paean of praise that makes up sections 16–25 of the *Birth*) or Nietzsche himself (as evidenced in his aspirations to be both a musician and philosopher of his time) (106, 111). Nevertheless, what is clear is that Nietzsche thinks that the redemption of modernity, through the leadership and guidance of a musical Socrates is possible. In order to try to explain how such a recovery is possible, Nietzsche resorts to an unusual mytho-historical model that seems to bears some kinship to Plato's myth of the reversed cosmos.

Nietzsche seems to construct a version of Plato's myth of the reversed cosmos for his own purposes in the final sections of *Birth*. In Plato's version of the myth, there are two time periods—the period of Zeus, when generation runs its normal course from infancy to senescence, and the time of Kronos, when, through the mediation of a demigod, the spokes of heaven are pushed to rotate the other way, so that autochthonous warriors spring from the earth and living organisms regress backwards till they disappear. Nietzsche's version appropriates the idea of regression, of moving backwards through the various developmental stages, from the Alexandrian to the Hellenic, or the scientific to the tragic. Yet unlike Plato's version, where the inversion of the developmental stages leads to the loss of the normal reproductive process (either as autochthony or disappearance into nothingness), Nietzsche's mythic account envisages the vigorous rebirth of Tragedy, as teeming with fertile, reproductive powers. Nietzsche's vision of historical regression is actually a mythical evolution from the death of modern science to a resurrection of classical tragedy, and through that, a rebirthing of classical society, morals, and politics (121, 128).

Robert Eden arrives at a similar conclusion:

> To imagine the scope of Nietzsche's politics, one might compare the myth of the cycles in Plato's *Statesman*. Like Plato, Nietzsche assigns a long but finite career to the cycle of human generation and nurture: the biological and erotic foundations of human life can be shaken by great cataclysms.... The task of philosophic leadership is to seize the opportunity of a most comprehensive crisis. At the moment in Plato's myth when the *demiourgos* releases the helm and allows the world to reverse its cyclic motion, Nietzsche's philosopher must seize the helm, take advantage of the most unprecedented interplay of contingency and necessity, and swing the world and man into its most beautiful motion.[16]

---

16. Robert Eden, *Political Leadership and Nihilism: A Study of Weber and Nietzsche* (Tampa: University Presses of Florida, 1983), 124–25.

Hence, for Nietzsche, it is during Hamlet's hour of greatest temptation—the moment of blackest despair for the modern Dionysian man—that Art approaches as a saving sorceress, skilled in the healing art of medicine (*rettende, heilkundige Zauberin*) (60, 57). It is she who transforms the nightmarish glimpse into the horror and absurdity of existence into notions with which he can embrace life with a passion. Through her ministrations, the horrible is artistically tamed into the sublime, and the nausea of the absurd is cathartically discharged as the comic. For Nietzsche at this stage, it is principally Art that sa(l)ves the modern Dionysian man, by making him drink deeply of the draught of artistic illusion.

In keeping with the redemptive thrust of Nietzsche's aesthetico-political project, I close with Nietzsche's analysis of Faust. For Nietzsche, Faust symbolizes the modern man who begins to become aware of the limits of the Socratic worship of the "nude goddess"—the obsession with scientific truth. Like the aging Socrates who obeys his *daimonion*'s exhortations for him to practice music, Faust strains his eye for a coast in the unremitting expanse of the ocean of knowledge (111, 116). Faust is born from the Socratic womb, yet in him lie the seeds of a new culture uncorrupted by Euripidean optimism or Graeculean cheerfulness. It is upon this salvation via Art that Nietzsche's gendered politics is hung: a thread running through his pre-Zarathustran phase.

Fettered, All Too Fettered

Nietzsche continues with his myth-theme of attempting to save (or salvage) decadent modernity in *Human, All Too Human I* (hereafter *Human I*). Yet this time, the principal anthropomorphisms are not Apollo-Dionysus versus Socrates-Euripides. They are the "free spirit" versus the "fettered spirit." Hence, his use and realignment of mythic figures revolves around this polarity. Nietzsche aligns the figures of Janus, Aphrodite, Achilles, and the centaur with the "free spirit;" he consigns Pandora and Homer to an alliance with the "fettered spirit."

In his preface to *Human I*, Nietzsche freely admits to inventing the "free spirits" (*freie Geister*)[17] as companions for him, to cheer him on in his loneliness, besieged by various ills (sickness, solitude, unfamiliar places, inactivity). Despite the fact that he admits that they are but phantoms and hermit's phantasmagoria (*Schemen und Einsiedler-Schattenspiel*) (6, 9), he dedicates the book to them, and attempts to has-

---

17. Friedrich Nietzsche, *Human, All Too Human*, trans. R. J. Hollingdale (Cambridge: Cambridge University Press, 1994), 6; Friedrich Nietzsche, *Nietzsche Werke: Kritische Gesamtausgabe: Menschliches, Allzumenschliches I; Nachgelassene Fragmente 1876 bis Winter 1877–1878*, ed. Giorgio Colli and Mazzino Montinari (Berlin: de Gruyter, 1967), 9.

ten their arrival, so vivid in his mind's eye, by describing the paths they must take in order to come into being, and with that, bring into fruition Nietzsche's vision of great health (*grosse Gesundheit*).

Nietzsche sees himself and his kindred spirits as infected with pessimism, brought about by the supposedly now-recognized virus of Romanticism, and transmitted by its hosts, Wagner and Schopenhauer. In order to regain health, Nietzsche prescribes two methods: (1) a step deeper into convalescence, so as to emerge, mistrustfully, into life (13, 13); and (2) the homeopathic application of small doses of health, so as to become gradually healthier (13, 13).

The principal existential dilemma that faces the free spirit is the problem of the order of rank, for it is an undeniable phenomenon, for Nietzsche, that where life has been circumscribed to its meanest, narrowest, and neediest manifestations, in its self-preservative drive, the lower form of life has sought to take itself as the goal and measure of things, insidiously and venomously crumbling away the higher, greater, and richer (9, 14–15).

In contrast to the free spirit, Nietzsche molds the image of the "fettered spirit" (*gebundenen Geister*) (109, 195) who unknowingly infuses the corrupt societal order and institutions with his force and endurance, solely through his belief in these institutions. Among the masks of the fettered spirit that Nietzsche fashions are the Christian believer, the ascetic priest or saint, and the most ardent believer and priestess of *pudendum* Christianity, "woman" (*Weib*).

Nietzsche does not draw a detailed portrait of either the Christian believer or the priest/saint. He tries his hand at quick, aphoristic sketches of them, such as that of the saint's burning eye in a body half-destroyed, the last pleasure-horror that antiquity had invented (76–77, 136–37); the hermit-saint's secret lust for power (78, 137–38); and the ascetic's need to worship a part of himself as God in order to diabolize the other part (74, 131).

Yet of "woman," Nietzsche does not seem to be able to resist numerous ambivalent attempts at portraiture, as if she were a subject whose features were so fearful and fascinating that such repeated attempts were not only merited but necessary. For Nietzsche, "woman" is to be feared as she is the custodian of the ancient ways, the priestess of that ruder stage of culture in which a visible synechdoche of savagery is substituted for a physical assault, as is evidenced in her perfection of the art of the k/chilling look (143–44, 77).

Along the same lines, in Nietzsche's eye, the beauty of a modern building is like the beauty of a mindless "woman"—masklike and dead, rather than the veiled Greek and early Christian architectural creations that inspired dread (101, 180–81). And indeed, he claims that like such veiled creatures, the more beautiful a "woman" is, the more modest she is (152, 277). Yet he does not hesitate to write that there are always "women" who have no content and are purely masks—the perfect snare for a man who seeks after her supposed soul and keeps searching in vain (152, 278).

It is equally important to draw out how Nietzsche views "women" in comparison to "men." For Nietzsche, "men," unlike "women," wield their assertions as if they were weapons—like marksmen taking aim, or warriors drawing their swords, or men of great strength flailing about with clubs. "Women," on the other hand, speak as creatures who have done nothing but sit at the loom, plied the needle, or have been childish with children (141, 255). Nietzsche claims that even in modern manners of speaking, one hears the echo of the primal origins of "woman" as a "fettered spirit." Even more striking in Nietzsche's view is the fact that "intelligent women," in their attempt to break from their origins, overcompensate, and often leave an alienating and forbidding impression upon a male public audience, while becoming "female" (*Weibern*) again only in smaller company, in whose presence they amiably recovering their charms (147–48, 267–68). Finally, "men" (and more "excusably," "women," due to historical reasons, as Nietzsche puts it) who live in total dependence upon others are but ignoble, blood-sucking parasites, who harbor a secret and deadly animosity toward their hosts (143, 259).

Nietzsche's views concerning the "perfect" or "clever" woman are just as derogatory. In Nietzsche's view, the "perfect woman" is higher than even the "perfect man," and is even rarer—as attested to by science (150, 273). For the "male" ailment of self-contempt, Nietzsche prescribes his foolproof cure: the love of a clever "woman" (150, 274), for such a love makes the "male" realize his own natural elevation over even the cleverest "female."

Yet, Nietzsche's attitude toward the "maternal" is refractory. One one hand, he claims, in a salutary tone, that it is the eternal and indelible portrait of his "mother" that a "man" bears within him that determines whether he respects, despises, or is indifferent to "women" (150, 274). Yet in his cynical voice, he also claims that a "mother" is jealous of her son's friends, as they threaten the bond between herself and herself in her son (150, 274). This same ambivalence continues in his observation that some "mothers" require happy, respected children in order to be happy; others require unhappy ones. Either way, he claims that what ensures a "mother's" happiness is her ability to display her goodness as a "mother" (151, 275). All this ambivalence toward the "maternal" is eventually grafted on to "woman" as Nietzsche claims that "womanly" love always has an element of "motherly" love (151, 275).

From the purely "maternal," Nietzsche moves on to a discussion of marriage. Love-marriages are "fathered" by error and "mothered" by need, Nietzsche quips (151, 275). Since marriages reduce "men" and elevate "women," it is not surprising, Nietzsche claims, that extremely intellectual "men" have a great need for marriage and yet they resist it as if it were foul-tasting medicine (151, 276). Stable marriages, for Nietzsche, form only when each uses the other for his or her own ends—the wife seeks to become known through her husband; the husband, to be liked through his wife (152, 277). The battle of the sexes is stayed in an uneasy and selfish truce in such cases.

Nietzsche elevates to the realm of the mythic the "womanly" traits of possessiveness and jealousy. Unsurpassable in their jealousy and possessiveness, he claims, "women" are remarkable in their skill at assessing whether a "man's" soul is inhabited by other passions, such as his ambition, political activities, arts, and sciences (153, 279–80). Correlatively, they are capable of a love that would keep a "man" of consequence under lock and key, if only their desire that he appear a "man" of consequence to others as well were not stronger (152, 277).

For Nietzsche, "love" is the counterpart of "woman's" jealousy and possessiveness. Nietzsche conjectures that the idolization of love was originally a product of "woman's" shrewdness. However, since he claims that tables have now turned, it is she who stands to suffer more intensely than the "man" when the inevitable disillusionment comes—provided, of course, that "she" has sufficient intelligence and imagination to be deceived and disillusioned at all (154, 282).

Given the natures of "man" and "woman," Nietzsche recommends that a "man" marry twice: (1) at the age of twenty-two, he should marry a "girl" who is older than him who is his intellectual and moral superior, so as to guide him through the perils of the twenties, such as ambition, hatred, self-contempt, and various passions; and (2) in his thirties, as the "first wife's" love matures into "motherly" love, he should again marry, naturally, at his "wife-mother's" own prompting, this time to educate a "woman" younger than himself (419, 284–85). Along similar lines, Nietzsche advocates a system of concubinage based on the reasoning that to require a "woman" to be friend, assistant, mother, family head, housekeeper, and head- and heart-satisfying companion (for which a concubine, represented in the personage of Aspasia, an Athenian courtesan and mistress of Pericles,[18] is best) would be to require too much of her.[19]

Despite Nietzsche's more negative characterization of "woman" (as opposed to the "feminine") as the most fettered spirit-less being of them all, there seems to be a sense in which Nietzsche seems to want to distinguish between the "ignoble/slavish woman" and the "noble woman," and between the "ignoble/slavish man" and "noble man." In one instance, he writes that the superiority of "noble men and women" lies in their mastery of the arts of commanding and proud obedience.[20]

If this interpretative strategy were taken, one could then attempt to try to distinguish between Nietzsche's use of *Weib* (which is predominantly derogatory) and *Frau*

---

18. Nietzsche, *Human, All Too Human*, 157.
19. Nietzsche, *Nietzsche Werke*, 286.
20. Nietzsche, *Human, All Too Human*, 167; Nietzsche, *Nietzsche Werke*, 297.

(which, at least in the instance above, is positive in its assessment). However, a problem I find with this particular interpretation, a version of which Kofman puts forth, for instance, is that there is no or little other mention of "noble women" in the entire book, and that "women" (*Weib*) and one of their most primordial masks, "Mother" (*Mutter*), are predominantly set up as foils to the free spirits.

There are also indications that Nietzsche pokes fun at some types of "men"—particularly "married men," who are the comical and detestable male counterparts of the "women" they marry. So, for instance, Nietzsche states that in affairs of the highest philosophical kind, all "married men" are suspect (160, 291–92). With a sarcastic wit similar to Oscar Wilde's, he goes on to write that some husbands have sighed over the abduction of their wives, but most have sighed over the fact that no one has wanted to abduct their wives (151, 275). And even more strategically, he begins with first assigning "reason" (*der Verstand*) (153–54, 280) to "woman" and "passion and temperament" (*das Gemüth und die Leidenschaft*) (153–54, 280) to man; moves on to showing that "man" actually makes better use of his reason than "woman," and yet is somehow initially more passive, owing to his deeper, more powerful drives (*die tieferen, gewaltigeren Antriebe*) (153–54, 280); and ends by saying that in their choice of a marriage partner, "men" and "women" are actually seeking idealized versions of themselves (153–54, 280).

Nevertheless, although Nietzsche depicts "women" (*Weibe*) implicitly as the most dangerous parasites, capable of weakening even the best of "men," there are several ambiguous passages in which he seems almost to lay part of the blame for their decadence on "men." To name one instance, Nietzsche, employing the figure of Proteus, states that "women" in love come to possess the visage their beloveds project onto them (152, 277).

Yet ultimately, it is the image of "women" as the ultimate poison, the hemlock even Socrates demanded Criton take away, on account of their wailing and weeping (160, 292), that predominates Nietzsche's treatment of the nature of *Weib*. And it is in her image as the supreme embodiment of the fettered spirit, seething with secret hostility (if she is intelligent), and vacuous (if she is devoid of intelligence), that Nietzsche's portrait of "woman" is clearest. However, Nietzsche's treatment of the "feminine" (as opposed to "woman"), at this point, is still refractory. "Feminine" figures may either be aligned with the free spirit (such as Aphrodite or "good" Eris) or the fettered spirit (such as Pandora).

To illustrate, Nietzsche appropriates much of the Pandora myth, and yet strategically recasts it. His version of the myth begins similarly: Pandora unleashes all the evils onto humankind. Yet instead of allowing hope, the last entity to escape from the box to counter all the suffering she had unleashed upon humanity, Nietzsche's Pandora maliciously shuts the box, in keeping with Zeus's will, in order to prolong the torment of humanity. Zeus desires that humanity, despite the torments it suffers, should not choose death—in order that the divine infliction of pain may be extended further.[21]

Here Pandora, unlike in the Greek mythic version, becomes the willing advocate of Zeus's toying with human frailty; in Nietzsche's retelling of the myth, both she and Hope are but weapons in Zeus's arsenal against the mortal race of humanity. Pandora's myth therefore becomes, through Nietzsche's skillful maneuvering, simply another mask for the boisterous and sneering proclamation that is wrenched from Silenus by Midas in *Birth*.

However, another "feminine" figure, Aphrodite, figures more positively in his new opposition between the free/healthy and the fettered/sick. Nietzsche, in one of his diatribes against Christian taboos associated with sexuality, enlists Empedocles's Aphrodite in his battle against Christian morality. To Empedocles (and Nietzsche), Aphrodite is the figure of hope and salvation—the guarantee that strife will not rule forever, and that one day, a gentler daemon shall rule in strife's stead (76, 135). Unlike Pandora, therefore, Aphrodite is a "feminine" figure positively valorized.

Nietzsche's attitude toward Aphrodite shifts, however, when he begins to address the issues of concrete love, passion, or commitment in relation to modern "women." The fair visage of the goddess transmogrifies into a creature whose members seem to wage battle against each other. Aphrodite becomes a swamplike creature, spawned in the morass of ironic and conflicting needs and demands between the ideal "man" (or the "free spirit") and "woman," thus necessitating their total separation.

Another "feminine" mythic figure Nietzsche uses is "good" Eris. Nietzsche borrows Hesiod's distinction of "good" Eris, a goddess of peaceable competition, from "terrible" Eris, a bringer of war and strife.[22] For Nietzsche, good Eris is the mask for the type of genius that the Greek tragedians (among whom are not only Aeschylus, but also Euripides, the much-maligned murderer of Attic tragedy in *Birth*) possessed by virtue of the type of ambition they cultivated—an ambition that demanded excellence and superiority in their own eyes. Within the classic Greek context, honor meant both making oneself superior and advocating that that superiority be accorded public recognition; its modern and decadent counterparts split into two: vanity and pride. Vanity exists when one does not possess superiority and yet wishes to be acknowledged as such; pride manifests itself when one is not given recognition and yet does not regret the lack of public recognition (90, 160–61). In Nietzsche's account, good Eris, a "feminine" mythic mask, becomes the figure for the classic (and "masculine") virtue of "honor" or "ambition."

---

21. Nietzsche, *Human, All Too Human*, 45; Nietzsche, *Nietzsche Werke*, 80.
22. Hollingdale explains this in a footnote (90).

Nietzsche continues the dichotomy between fettered and free spirits by using Achilles versus Homer as additional masks for these two main players. Homer makes another entrance in *Human I*, not as the enlightened poet of Apollo, as he appeared in *Birth*, but now as the decadent shadow of Achilles. Nietzsche reasons that unlike Achilles, the supremely passionate man who allows himself to be ravaged by his experiences, Homer simply describes such experiences. For Nietzsche, the modern artist, for whom Homer is now a mask, simply pretends to be a man of great passion. Actually, Nietzsche claims, it is only when this modern/Romantic artist contrives not to contrive—when he acts not as an "artist"—that he becomes an unbridled and genuine man of passion (97–98, 174–75); a genuinely unfettered man. The reference seems to be to Wagner, the "actor."

Similarly, Janus makes another appearance, this time in Nietzsche's *Human I*, where he becomes the mask for all great perceptions, having a simultaneously fruitful and fearful visage. Paul Rée is the priest of Janus to whom Nietzsche pays homage. From Rée's book, *On the Origin of Moral Sensations*, Nietzsche lifts the proclamation that moral man occupies no privileged spot, and does not stand closer to the intelligible or metaphysical world than does physical man.[23] Nietzsche thus reenlists Janus, his ally in the earlier *Birth*, in his new battle against Wagner, Christianity, and at least ostensibly, Romantic art.

Finally, the centaur—half-beast, half-man, and with angel's wings attached to his head—becomes Nietzsche's mask for the genius of culture, one of the most striking illustrations of Nietzsche's myth-theme of the free spirit. This genius of culture, for Nietzsche, should be a melding of demon and angel, insofar as this type of being should be capable of manipulating falsehood, force, and unrelenting self-interest to suit his ends, yet whose effects would somehow radiate forth as great and good (115, 206). Freedom from traditional distinctions of "truth" and "lie" seem to be among the attributes of the genuinely free spirit. Yet it is evident that Nietzsche's desire to grant his genius this freedom is spurred by the desire to re-create rather than to destroy modernity.

Womanly, All Too Womanly

Nietzsche intensifies his attack on both Christianity and "woman" (*Weib*) in the second part of *Human, All Too Human*. For instance, he enlists the figure of Pilate into his cause of laying siege upon Christianity by depicting Pilate as having been gleefully coerced, with his statement, "What is Truth?," to become an advocate of Christ.

23. Hollingdale provides this biographical fact in a footnote (33).

For Nietzsche, through such a treacherous tactic, Pilate becomes the means through which the known or knowable becomes mere appearance, and the Cross is erected against the Golgothic backdrop of the Impossibility of Knowledge (216, 19–20).

Furthermore, in a witty parody of John, Nietzsche writes that the most serious parody he had ever heard was "In the beginning was the nonsense, and the nonsense was with God, and the nonsense was God" (218, 24). Finally, for Nietzsche, the two greatest judicial murders, those of Christ and Socrates, were simply well-concealed suicides: in both cases, Christ and Socrates willed death (233, 50).

Yet Nietzsche reserves his full scale attacks for "woman" (*Weib*), for it is she who best embodies the imperfect artist and the most ardent Christian believer. Among the imperfect artists—those who are led to art by virtue of self-disgust, as opposed to the Greeks, who were motivated by delight in themselves—Nietzsche lists (1) the cultured, who are not free enough to dispense with the consolations of religion, even if they are not satisfied by its fragrance; (2) the highly gifted, who think themselves too dignified to be of service by modest activity, but in reality are too lazy for genuine, self-sacrificing labor; (3) "girls" who cannot create for themselves a satisfactory scheme of duties; (4) "women" who are both tied, but not securely enough, to light-hearted or nefarious marriages; and (5) scholars, physicians, merchants, and officials who have specialized too early, know their work all too well, but suffer from worms that gnaw at their hearts. Such imperfect artists narcotize themselves with art, driving away moments of discomfort, boredom, half-bad conscience, and, if possible, have their faults writ large into world-destiny (250–51, 83). Art, in this case, is no longer a healing balm but an addictive narcotic.

Nietzsche tightens the decadent alliance binding "woman" and imperfect/sick artist by classing them as two types who go against the few who take pleasure in untying the knot of things and unravelling its woof. Unlike these "few," the "many" (such as "woman" and the [imperfect] artist) insist upon weaving the woof together again so as to entangle everything, thus rendering the conceived into the unconceived or even inconceivable (221, 29).

On the link between "woman" and Christianity, Nietzsche remarks that only the cleverest type of "woman" and the lowest type of "man" find comfort in the Christian notion of "love," because their lives have never been touched by Eros (233, 51). For Nietzsche, Christian love, the palliative of unhealthy creatures, is a watered-down and sick version of Eros.

Nietzsche returns to the topic of differentiating between the natures of "man" and "woman." For Nietzsche, Nature shows what she has done so far through the figure of "woman;" through the figure of "man," she reveals what she has had to overcome, and what she still proposes to accomplish for humankind (278, 131). He argues further that "woman's" nature is undeniably base; how and when she laughs reveals the level of her culture, but the ring in her laughter reveals her treacherous nature (278, 131). As further proof, he contends that "women" and misguided youths (i.e., youths lacking "manly" characteristics), tormented by boredom and lacking work, require the art of barbaric disorder—quite unlike the art that streams out of Homer, Sophocles, Theocritus, Calderon, Racine, and Goethe, containing superabundant illustrations of a wise and harmonious conduct of life (254–55, 89).

Nietzsche attempts to sketch a clearer picture of "woman's" decadence by comparing her with "man" (*Mensch*). For example, the old soldier, in one of Nietzsche's haikuesque narratives, approvingly remarked, upon hearing the story of Faust, "One should behave as a man of honour even toward the devil and pay his debts. . . . Hell is the right place for Faust!" His wife protested, saying, "His only fault was having no ink in his ink-stand! It is indeed a sin to write with blood, but certainly, for that such a handsome man ought not to burn in Hell-fire?" (321, 210). In thus caricaturing the old soldier and his wife, Nietzsche attempts to depict "man's" preoccupation with matters of honor and "woman's" obsession with sin and superficiality.

Nietzsche also returns to the topic of "woman's" innate intellect. In several aphorisms, Nietzsche depicts "woman's" desire to appear unintellectual so as not to scare off men (375–76, 308). One of these aphorisms uses the very form of aphorism within it to play off levels of meaning against each other. "Stupid as a man," say the women; "cowardly as a woman," say the men—but stupidity in a "woman" is "unfeminine," leaving the reader to wonder which is the greatest lie: that "woman" is stupid or unfeminine? (376, 309).

Of "woman's" intellect, Nietzsche does not tire in his tirades. In one excerpt, he speaks of how "woman" offers her intellect as a love sacrifice to her "man," and yet, consequently, is impelled toward a foreign aftergrowth of a second intellect that is antithetical to her nature (a decadent inversion of the Zeus-Athena model of birthing) (277, 130). He exhorts the "friends of music" (*Freunde der Musik*) to laugh at the "man in the moon" (*Man im Monde*) and the "woman in music" (*Weib in der Musik*) (349, 261)—both of whom, like whimsical nursery rhymes, are entertaining but should not be taken seriously.

As Ellen Kennedy points out, although Nietzsche concedes that women have intellect, this does not matter because what matters for genuine citizenship is will.

> Women have reason, but it doesn't count; women have passion, but the wrong kind; men have less reason and less passion than women—but mysteriously, their combination of both is just the right one.[24]

---

24. Ellen Kennedy, "Nietzsche: Women as *Untermensch*," in *Women in Western Political Philosophy*, ed. Ellen Kennedy and Susan Mendus (New York: St. Martin's Press, 1987), 197. I agree for the most

Regarding "manly" and "womanly" fashion, Nietzsche draws a stark picture. "Men's" fashion is indicative of intellectual pursuit, wishes to be neither individual nor universal, and is not subject to fervid fluctuations. "Women's" fashion, on the other hand, is indicative of their main goal—the pursuit of men. As such, it is possessed by the desire to appear as individual and as young as possible, and is subject to extreme fluctuations. Dandies and dawdlers, "effeminate men" who dress like "women," are in between and have not yet reached manly maturity (363–65, 285–88). Proof of this, Nietzsche contends, is the youth's bitter resentment toward the old man because of the elder's advice to the younger that in order to be fruitful, he must lose those buds, and dispense with their fragrance: two all too "womanish" traits! (280, 135).

Despite all these unflattering images of "woman," there is a sense in which Nietzsche displays flashes of sympathy and understanding for the socio-political plight of women. For instance, the saddest error, he writes, is that of discovering that one was convinced of being loved, when, all along, one has been regarded purely as a household utensil and decoration, whereby the master of the house may further display his vanity before his guests (229, 44). While this may be simply an allusion to his break with Wagner, there is also a sense in which he is aware of women's repression, and the preceding aphorism could be read in conjunction with Nietzsche's observation concerning elevation and debasement in the sexual domain. For Nietzsche, "men," in the sexual realm, may be elevated to such a height that even desire is silent, whereas "women" often climb down to succumb to desire and thus lower themselves in their own eyes—one of the most "pathetic" (*Herzbewegsten*) sensations that the idea of a "good marriage" entails (277–78, 130).

In addition, Nietzsche observes that "woman," unlike "man," cannot deny herself the triumph of setting her heel upon the neck of the vanquished when she is conceded to as being right, precisely because she is unaccustomed to victory. Such a statement may be read in at least a twofold sense: as a dramatic testimony to woman's unvalorous behavior, and as a peek/apologia at why she is so lacking in chivalric behavior (280, 135). Even more compelling is Nietzsche's use of the young bride's radiant gaze upon her husband as a figure for the greatness and transitoriness of human happiness (376, 308). Yet perhaps the most revealing portrait Nietzsche draws is that of the "woman" who enjoys the *intelletto del sacrifizio*, the intellect of sacrifice,[25] with her

---

part with Kennedy's insightful analysis, except for her statement that the "outline of Nietzsche's view of women appeared first in *Menschliches Allzumenschliches* (1878) and remained constant throughout his works" (185). In contrast, I argue that Nietzsche's philosophy grows increasingly misogynist, rather than remains obstinately opposed to all that is "feminine" from the very start.

25. This is a pun upon the Jesuitic *sacrifizio dell'intelletto*, as noted in a footnote by Cohn. Cf. Friedrich Nietzsche, *Human, All Too Human II*, trans. Paul V. Cohn (New York: Gordon Press, 1974), 328.

husband until her husband refuses to sacrifice with her. Then, unwittingly, she is transformed, in her bitterness and disillusionment, from sacrificial victim to sacrificial priest (376, 308).

Both *Frau* and *Weib* now blur into each other—both masks of the plebeian, and yet there are indications that Nietzsche does not lay all of the blame upon "woman"/women for being what they are: victims and priestesses of decadence. In line with this general ambivalence toward "woman," Nietzsche's mythic sketches of the "feminine" anthropomorphisms (in relation to the "masculine") run the gamut from the very positive (such as Io and Nature) to extremely negative (such as German Virtue).

To illustrate, when he is envisaging the possibility of an ever-growing ego (i.e., a new heroic soul for a new age), Nietzsche uses the mythic personification of the hundred-eyed Argos, traveling across vast areas, accompanying his fair Io as (his) ego: an ever-growing, ever-altering ego. In Greek mythology, Io was a woman whom Zeus secretly loved, and whom he had turned into a white cow to protect her from his wife's jealous rage.[26] In Nietzsche's retelling, Io—the eternal wanderer held prisoner by the gaze of the hundred-eyed Argus, henchman of Hera, who follows her in her frenzied flight—becomes the hundred-eyed creature's most intimate companion. Io, the eternally fleeing "feminine" of many trans-figure-ations, becomes the innermost soul of this hundred-eyed creature. As he pursues her and trains his eyes upon her, his ego, he gains the self-knowledge that is the key to glimpsing universal knowledge. As such, Argus, to Nietzsche, becomes the prototype possessing the self-direction, self-training, and foresightedness necessary for the siring/birthing of the most free of spirits (268, 114). Nietzsche's (e)valuation of Io cannot be more salutary at one level: Io, the "feminine" object of his/Argus's gaze, is the portal to this acquisition of the highest type of (self) knowledge.

Convinced that he, himself, possesses such a heroic soul, Nietzsche speaks of those noontide (*Mittag*) moments when the swell of life seems to abate a little—all grows silent around the being to whom an active and stormy life has been given, voices sound further and further in the distance, the sun's rays sit upon his shoulders. At such moments, it is as if this heroic soul/Nietzsche/Nietzsche's followers glimpse(s) the god Pan asleep with Nature, an expression of eternity upon both of their faces. Such a vision ensnares the (on)looker in a net of light and fills him with a heavy kind of happiness. Nietzsche calls this a death with waking eyes (*es ist ein Tod mit wachen Augen*) (328). In Nietzsche's mythic segment, Pan and Nature, "masculine" and "feminine" mythic personifications of the vastness of the natural, grant the seer a vision of eternity in their unguarded moment of sleep.

---

26. See, for instance, Edith Hamilton, *Mythology* (New York: Penguin, 1982), 75–78.

Contrary to Nietzsche's positive treatment (at least on one level) of the mythologized anthropomorphisms of Io and Nature, Nietzsche negatively "feminizes" German Virtue as a figure for the current of moral awakening that flowed through Europe from the eighteenth century onward. For Nietzsche, German Virtue, by regaining her power of speech and self-esteem, fashioned philosophies and poems for her own glorification. Nietzsche cites Rousseau and Stoic Rome as the principal priests of this decadent goddess (i.e., German Virtue); it is they whom Nietzsche blames for generating the second-generation priests, Kant and Beethoven. In Nietzsche's eyes, German Virtue is but another decadent muse, a siren whose lyrical song disfigures the lay of the land and prevents the recognition of bourgeois moral phenomena for what they are: womanly, all too womanly fetters (365–66, 288–90).

Separating the Healthy from the Sick: The Not-So-Gay Physician

In line with his future-oriented task of saving modernity, Nietzsche outlines several key questions for the immoralist, the student of morality and future disciple of Nietzsche. Among them are Where would one find a history of love, of avarice, of envy, of conscience, of piety, of cruelty? Where would one find a comparative history of law and punishment? How do the day's activities get pigeonholed into categories of work, feasting, and rest? Do we know the moral effects of alimentary substances? Is there a philosophy of nutrition? How does one form an account of the "conditions of existence" (*Existenz-Bedingungen*)[27]: of reason, passion, and superstition? How does one plot out the various degrees of the development of human impulses across various moral climates?

Yet the ultimate question, for Nietzsche, would be Assuming that all such questions were answerable, presumably in a scientific manner, can science furnish goals for human action after it has proven that it can take them away and annihilate them? Nietzsche uses the mask of the Cyclops to speak of this envisaged peak of the scientific spirit, this great period of moral and heroic experimentation. The Cyclopean eye, with its piercing and far-seeing ability, becomes a trope for Nietzsche's aspiration for an age in which the intertwining issues of morality and physicality will become central to the scientific adventure (43–44, 379–80).

Correspondingly, one of Nietzsche's principal myths in *The Gay Science* is the separation of the healthy from the sick, the strong from the weak, the few from the many. Not devoid of parodic allusions to the Parousia or Second Coming of Christ,

---

27. Friedrich Nietzsche, *The Joyful Wisdom*, trans. Thomas Common (New York: Gordon Press, 1974), 43. Friedrich Nietzsche, *Sämtliche Werke: Kritische Studienausgabe: Morgenröte; Idyllen aus Messina; Die Fröhliche Wissenschaft* (Berlin: de Gruyter, 1988), 379.

Nietzsche envisages a future period in which the decadent, closely associated with "woman" and Christianity, may be sifted away from the vital/"man."

For Nietzsche, the history of culture has simply been a history of narcosis, with theatre, music, hashish-smoking, and betel chewing among its most popular painkillers (122, 444). Modernity is an age of genuine, and not merely formal, savagery (84, 413) as is evidenced by its massification and slavery, conditions that are hostile and life-threatening to the "few" (183, 494).

As far as Nietzsche's cyclopean eye can see, everywhere, the savage tribes, in whom the instincts of the noble still live, are being decimated by the most insidious European narcotics: brandy and Christianity (181, 492). The imagery he uses to describe the "happiness" of modernity is that of being like a shipwrecked man who goes ashore and is surprised to find that it does not rock—the sign of a spirit so steeped in decadence that health is an inconceivable novelty (83, 412).

Nietzsche returns to a myth-theme and mythic anthropomorphism in *Birth* to illustrate better how the "new" health may be recovered from its classical roots. For Nietzsche, the origins of poetry lie in superstitious utility (*aberglaübische Nützlichkeit*) (117, 440). Via the Hermes of rhythm, the Greeks sought to offer a plea more eloquently and inexorably before a god. Rhythm was believed to function as a magic noose with which the god's favor could be captured. Music, and its counterpart, dance, by virtue of their common nature of rhythmicity, functioned as *Melos*—a soothing agent, which is not soothing in itself, but soothing in its effects (118, 441). Thus was the image of Apollo fashioned, a rhythmic formula performed to control the future, an Apollo who could command the Fates (118–19, 441–42). Ultimately, for Nietzsche, one can attain the wisdom of the ancients only by becoming a fool of rhythm, as is evidenced by philosophers lapsing into poetical sayings in order to authorize their own thoughts. Thus, Apollo, the god of poetry, music, and dance, comes to personify the visage of the science of the future: the rhythmic gay science, through whom one may dance into the age of new health.

In contrast, the three representatives or masks of sickly modernity that Nietzsche particularly castigates are Romanticism, Christianity, and "woman." Nietzsche identifies Romanticism as yet another narcotic to which those ailing from reduced vitality are addicted. For Nietzsche, every art and philosophy is an attempt to ease the pain and suffering of a growing, struggling life. Yet there are two types of suffering: suffering wrought by overflowing vitality and suffering from a lack of vitality. Those suffering from an excess of vitality need Dionysian art and require a tragic insight into life; those tormented by a deficiency in vitality require repose, quietness, calmness, and deliverance from themselves—which they acquire either through narcotizing art or philosophy, or through temporary relief provided by intoxication, spasm, bewilderment, and madness. The Romanticism in the music of Wagner, the miniaturist with grand ambitions (123, 445), and the philosophy of Schopenhauer, the grand necrophiliac (123, 445),[28] are supreme manifestations of the decadence of Romanticism as an effete and life-disabling art form (332, 620).

To paint a vivid image of Christianity's decadence, Nietzsche differentiates between the classical Greek and Jewish conceptions of sin—a topic he had already discussed in his distinction between *der Frevel* ("masculine" sacrilege) and *die Sünde* ("feminine" sacrilege) in *Birth*. For Nietzsche, the ancient Greeks would have laughed scornfully at the Christian/"womanly" notions of sin and repentance and dismissed them as the sentiments of a slave (174, 486). For unlike the Jewish notion of sin, which breeds shame and guilt, the classical Greek understanding of transgression imbues it with a certain type of pride and nobility, as in the cases of Prometheus and Ajax (175, 487).

For Nietzsche, Christianity was born from the bad weather of Yahweh's thunderous cloud, whereas elsewhere good weather was the rule (176, 488). It utilized the will to death, a sign of the widespread decadence of the times, to consolidate its power even more, by sanctioning special types of suicide, martyrdom and asceticism, as the only allowable forms of suicide (173, 485). In Nietzsche's eyes, Christ's greatest error was that he thought that men groaned from the welts wrought by the burden of their sins, while he was without blemish. Christ's resultant pity for the sinful became the cornerstone upon which the Christian religion was built—but it was a fundamental error, which Christ's followers, in Nietzsche's view, do not have problems converting into truth, the Truth of a "religion of smug ease" (176, 488). Such a religion, for Nietzsche, fails to recognize that happiness and misfortune are twins—brother (happiness) and sister (misfortune)—who either grow tall together or remain dwarfed together (267, 567).

"What if God turns out to be our most persistent lie [*wenn Gott selbst sich als unsre längste Lüge erweist*]?" (268, 577), Nietzsche asks, like the madman in the marketplace (167–69, 480–82) who draws attention to the divine putrefaction that infuses the very air of modernity, and proclaims the death of God at the hands of humanity. Yet Christianity, for Nietzsche, is not simply the worship of a dead god; it is the most refined and un-self-conscious form of the will to Nothingness, or the resentment against life. Yet the death of the Christian God, for Nietzsche, also signals not merely the preliminary descent into darkness and gloom, but also the dawning of a new day upon an ocean of boundless horizons. The annihilation of the God of error and weakness (along with the Socratic philosophy as siren's music, vampire, and disease) will birth a new and more vital age (276, 574).

---

28. For the decadent kinship Nietzsche draws between Schopenhauer and Wagner, see 132–37, 453–57.

Nietzsche's ambivalences concerning "woman" are particularly striking in *The Gay Science*. For on the one hand, he does draw a strong correspondence between the (Romantic) musical mood brought by warm and rainy winds and the amorous fantasies that visit "women" in churches filled with the same winds, implying the kinship of "woman," Christianity, and decadent Romantic music (100, 330; 425–26, 618). He does make much of "woman's" supposed skill in exaggerating weakness as a defense against the strong (101, 426) and paints an ironic portrait of a "noble woman" who, suffering from a poverty of spirit, offers her most prized possessions, her virtue and modesty to a "man," as a testament of commitment—only to find out that there has been a discrepancy of (e)valuation between the giver and the receiver (101, 426). And it is with great relish that he sketches the image of "woman" as parasite, who scents out the weakest and most underdeveloped functions of a "man," in order to maintain herself in an alien organism, and become that weak part—his purse, his politics, his social intercourse. Such parasites, according to Nietzsche, cannibalize themselves in vexation and agitation if their attempts at infiltration fail (162–63, 476).

Yet on the other hand, there is a sense in which Nietzsche, in some sections, draws up a more benign and sympathetic image of "women" as victims—of society, and supposedly, of their own nature. For instance, in fragment 68 of *The Gay Science*, Nietzsche uses a narrative structure reminiscent of both the classical dialogue between student and teacher and the Biblical parable. In this section, Nietzsche has the sage proclaim that it is "man" who corrupts "woman," and that everything deficient in "woman" should be atoned for by and in "man," for it is "man" who "creates for himself the ideal of 'woman,' and 'woman' molds herself to this ideal [*denn der Mann macht sich das Bild des Weibes, und das Weib bildet sich nach diesem Bilde*]" (102, 427). The sage continues that the "law of the sexes," which is very hard upon "woman," demands that "man's" attribute be will, and "woman's" be willingness. Hence, he claims that the better education of "man," and not "woman," is necessary, for "woman," is two times innocent for her existence (as formed by man's social rules and the iron law of nature) (102, 427).

Similarly, Nietzsche posits that "men" and "women" love differently, by virtue of the differences in their natures: "woman" surrenders totally and unconditionally, "man" demands precisely this devotion from "woman" and thus thinks himself exempt from the prerequisites of "feminine" love (321, 611). Hence, a "man" who becomes "womanish" in love becomes a slave, whereas a "woman" who loves as a "woman" should become a more perfect "woman" (322, 611). In addition, for Nietzsche, fidelity is an inescapable attribute of "womanly" love; fidelity may result from a "manly" love, but it is not the essence of his love—no social contract or desire for justice may alleviate this discrepancy between the sexes, for such is the nature of "womanly" and "manly" love, within the primordial and amoral realm of the natural (322–23, 611–12).

Even more striking is Nietzsche's analysis of "feminine" chastity, which he critiques as the imposition of erotic ignorance upon "women," burnt in with horror and shame at even the mere suggestion of sex. He reasons that this heavy yoke is made even heavier upon the marriage bed, where the young woman must suddenly confront the unexpected proximity of God and animal, experiencing, in one conflicting flash, the rapture, abandonment, duty, sympathy, and fright of that revelation. It is thus that the seeds of skepticism are sown in the "poor, unhinged soul [*in der armen aus den Fugen gerathenen Seele*]" (104, 429) and bring forth fruit in which poison is progressively more concentrated and lethal (100–101, 426).

Despite the fact that Nietzsche appears to paint the image of "woman" as victim rather than malicious parasite at this point, it is equally compelling that not one of these accounts clears Nietzsche of the charge of misogyny. For in his account, "woman" is to be pitied (the virtue of that most decadent of religions, Christianity) because she cannot help being what she is—the most concentrated repository of all that is spiteful, weak, and sickly, the most unhealthy of modernity's monstrous progeny. Her only strength, the ability to endure suffering, is a slave virtue, a strength of weakness (250, 553). Again in his ironic tone, Nietzsche speaks of a "woman" who casts a net to enslave a weak man, only to find herself his slave (201, 511).

Nietzsche's ambivalence toward "woman" is also true of his treatment of the "feminine." As proof of this, I cite Nietzsche's positive treatment of the "feminized" anthropomorphism of "Knowledge," his ambivalent characterization of "Poetry," and his negative dismissal of "Pleasantness" as the "country sister" of the classical Graces.

Sketching, in broad strokes, the context within which Nietzsche "feminizes" Knowledge, I imagine that Nietzsche envisages the coming of a more "manly" and warlike age that will give way to a higher age in which battles will be waged for the sake of ideas. In the meantime, the coming of such a lofty age requires the patient labor and sacrifice of "men" in whom cheerfulness, patience, simplicity, and contempt of the great vanities, alongside magnanimity in battle, spontaneously inhere. The means that Nietzsche advocates as the way to make this age of higher warfare come into being is to live dangerously: to build cities on the slopes of Mt. Vesuvius, that capricious fire-breathing mouth; to venture forth into unexplored realms via the dangerous and unpredictable sea; strategically to become robbers and spoilers, while the time is not yet ripe for kingship and possession. Yet Nietzsche characterizes the Muse of this coming warlike age, Knowledge, as "feminine"—and urges these warriors and spoilers to welcome her (218–19, 526–27).

As a "masculine" heroic counterpart, Prometheus also makes a brief appearance in *The Gay Science*, but one very different from those in *Birth* and *Human, All Too*

Human. Unlike in *Birth* and *Human, All Too Human*, where Prometheus-Oedipus is the mask for "masculine" transgression and the tragic awareness of art and life, Prometheus is now a figure for the hero and great man who suffers not from the enormity of his sacrifice, but from the pangs of insecurity that assail him during certain "evil moments"—an image not without its autobiographical resonances in Nietzsche's portrait as a thinker, writer, and artist. For Nietzsche, Prometheus is happy as long as he sympathizes with humanity and sacrifices for them; he is miserable when he becomes envious of Zeus and the homage mortals pay to him. Self-pity and resentment are the greatest temptations for both Nietzsche and Prometheus, the heroes of the age that is to be redeemed from the ashes of modernity (206, 516).

Moving on, Nietzsche's continuing ambivalence toward the "feminine" may still be seen in his characterization of Poetry as an amiable goddess with fine hands and delicate little ears, against whom prose is an uninterrupted, polite battle. This war, for Nietzsche, personifies the "father" of all good things, among which is good prose (125–26, 447–48). Nietzsche advocates that Poetry, the medium of ancient art, must be engaged in battle—mockingly, laughingly, confrontationally—in order to bring forth the new prose-poetry, as Giacomo Leopardi, Prosper Mérimeé, Ralph Waldo Emerson, and Walter Savage Landor have done.

Finally, the contrast Nietzsche draws between the mythic anthropomorphisms of the Graces and "Pleasantness" is far from flattering. In *The Gay Science*, the Graces make a brief appearance in Nietzsche's appraisal of German Romantic art—but only as an appearance of a disappearance. Nietzsche claims the Graces are only reluctantly allowed entry into German music because it is only with Pleasantness, the country sister of the Graces, that Germans feel morally at ease. The Graces and Pleasantness thus become "feminine" figures for the contrasting aesthetic and moral standards of the two different periods (140, 459).

The only constant in Nietzsche's pre-Zarathustran response to the "feminine"/"woman" is his inconsistency—his rapid and ambivalent shifts across positive and negative poles. How this contours his gendered political philosophy is the subject of the rest of this chapter.

Political Philosophy

The Midwife

In *Birth*, Nietzsche's political agenda, the salvaging of modernity through acting as a midwife for the rebirth of classical tragedy, takes the specific form of a theory of art as a representation of life in its primordial chaotic oneness and its continuous suffering wrought by the dismemberment brought upon it by Apollo, the principle of individuation. Although Nietzsche resorts to numerous masks, both "masculine" and "feminine," to stand in for various aspects of the Apollinian and the Dionysian, it is clear that he considers the original personifications of the forces of nature, life, and art to be Apollo and Dionysus, whose sexuality is ambiguous, possessing both "masculine" (excitatory/arousing) powers and "feminine" (birthing/generative) powers. In Nietzsche's account, both Apollo and Dionysus expand to encompass the fluctuating boundaries that transcend the oppositions that the scientific mind designates, such as truth versus illusion or appearance, nature versus civilization, and self-consciousness versus naiveté. It is precisely as personifications of the representationality of nature, life, art, and myth that Apollo and Dionysus rise to the level of what Henry Staten calls the "symbolic image" or "image at the limit."[29] As entities who transcend scientific dichotomies of "truth" and "lie" or "masculine" and "feminine," Apollo and Dionysus effect a slippage in these categories, revealing them to be simply another surface, and thus, hasten their eternal regress into deeper and deeper surfaces—revealing the surface-depth dichotomy to be but another Socratic construction. Precisely as mediating the primordial pain and joy of nature and life in art as the mere appearance of mere appearance, Apollo and Dionysus become signs that strive for universal signification. Coupling together the determinate image of tragedy and the universal or contentless form of music, Apollo and Dionysus become representatives of the representational character of myth itself: they become images that embody "the agony of the determinate image, its explosion and dispersal as it reaches its limit and then expires in its attempt to represent the unrepresentable universality" (17).

Furthermore, I view Nietzsche's attempts to authorize himself as the bringer of health to modernity as characterizable in two ways: (1) he styles himself, via an appeal to the authority of Wagner and Schopenhauer, as the Socrates who practices music—the physician for whom the ailing scientific world of modernity unknowingly searches—and (2) he salvages and appropriates, unto himself (as a mask for Wagner and Schopenhauer, who, in turn, serve as elevated guises for his own ambitions) and modernity, as a whole, the recurring metaphors of birthing, fertility, and generativity via his version of the Platonic myth of the reversed cosmos. It is in this manner that he is able to justify how modernity, however sickly it is, and himself, as a child of modernity, may repulse this disease of Socratism. For by showing that a progression backwards is not only possible, but even inexorably demanded by the reversal of the historical cycle, Nietzsche makes a case for the recuperation of modernity. More importantly, it is through the guidance of the pessimistic triumvirate, Schopenhauer, Wagner, and himself—men who have embraced the suffering of the Dionysian and

---

29. Henry Staten, "The Birth of Tragedy Reconstructed," *Studies in Romanticism* 29 (Spring 1990): 16.

cast this horror and nausea of existence into the beautiful illusion of the Dionysian as illusion—that such a rebirthing may occur. Yet in so far as birthing, fertility, and generation are the primary narratives that cement Nietzsche's political vision, it is the implicit mythic image of the "feminine" as mother that grants life, vividness, and force to his appeal for modernity's recuperation. Demeter, the eternal mother, ultimately emerges as more than a guise for Dionysus. Indeed, a careful excavation of Nietzsche's political aesthetic in *Birth* reveals an implicit elevation of Demeter as the entity that stands behind Dionysus, the mask for health and reproductive power. For insofar as the master trope of recuperation is not simply healing but rebirthing, it is Dionysus who serves Demeter, and not the other way around.

As proof of the implicit elevation of the principal "feminine" anthropomorphisms over the main "masculine" anthropomorphisms, I draw attention to the fact that Nature (as "maternal" in the figures of Demeter and Gaia) is a key personification/anthropomorphism that Nietzsche elevates to the mythic. Nature becomes the alienated or estranged (*entfremdete*), hostile (*feindliche*) or subjugated/enslaved (*unterjochte*) mother with whom her prodigal "son," humanity, is reconciled through Dionysian intoxication.[30] For Nietzsche, in Dionysian Greek festivals, Nature seems to display Schiller's "sentimental trait" and heaves a sigh at her dismemberment into individuals (40, 33). Reconciliation between estranged mother and son seems to occur precisely because mother and son experience the same ecstasy of dismemberment—the tearing of primordial oneness in order to produce the appearance of Apollinian individuation. In order to express this reconciliation, Nietzsche advocates a new world of symbols—a world of ecstatic bodily symbolism that is not merely a symbolism of the lips, face, and speech but more essentially a dancing that permeates the whole body, which forces each member into rhythmic, pantomimic movement (40, 33).

All these point to the invisible parasitism of the "masculine" anthropomorphisms (the main figures of Apollo and Dionysus) upon the "feminine" anthropomorphisms (such as Demeter and Gaia). It is, after all, Nature herself that is the source of both Dionysian and Apollinian. As Nietzsche declares, both the Apollinian and the Dionysian burst forth (*hervorbrechen*) from nature without the mediation of the human artist. "Man," the "noblest clay" (*der edelste Thon*) (38–39, 31), the "most costly marble" (*der kostbarste Marmor*) (38–39, 31), is kneaded and cut by nature through the chisel-strokes of Dionysian intoxication, amidst the ringing out of the Eleusinian mysteries, the province of the earth-goddess, Demeter, and her daughter, Proserpine/Persephone.

Yet Nietzsche's advocacy of the elemental character of the "feminine" is not devoid of tension. For instance, within Nietzsche's reworking of Demeter's awakening from

---

30. Nietzsche, *Birth*, trans. Kaufmann, 37; Nietzsche, *Die Geburt*, 29.

grief to joy, it is not Proserpine's return from the realm of Hades that is the crucial factor to end winter's barren tyranny. For Nietzsche, Demeter's rejoicing is the symbol of her liberation from sorrow because of the prospect of rebirthing Dionysus—a rejoicing the followers of Dionysus share in as an ecstatic and orgiastic end to individuation (74, 72). Nietzsche replaces Demeter's motherhood of Proserpine/Persephone with a newly crafted motherhood of Dionysus. It appears that the primacy of the maternal anthropomorphism must be neutralized by the replacement of a mother's rage and sorrow over the abduction of her daughter with the joy of bearing a son.

Another example of tension due to the primacy of the "feminine" anthropomorphism over the "masculine" may be seen in Nietzsche's recasting of the myths of Janus and the maenads. For Nietzsche, Janus is one of the masks of Dionysus, for the god of the Mysteries is both a mild, gentle ruler, and a cruel, barbarized demon. In Nietzsche's mythic appropriation of the dismemberment of Dionysus, it is the Titans, rather than either his maenads or nurses, who tear him limb from limb, and resurrect and worship him in the form of the smiling Zagreus. Again, in Nietzsche's mythic (re)telling, it is also Dionysus, rather than Gaia (Mother Earth) and Chaos, who generates the Olympians; Dionysus, too, is the father of humanity, rather than the Olympian divinities. Nietzsche's attempts at creating a tale of purely "masculine" source come to a head: from Dionysus's smile spring forth the Olympians; from his tears, humanity (72, 73). In Nietzsche's account, Dionysus, as Janus, is the eternal father and child, the alpha and omega of all that is, divine and mortal, and as such, usurps even Zeus who is one of his masks.

Yet what is even more striking is that Nietzsche locates one of the "feminine" anthropomorphisms outside/beyond the circle of Apollo and Dionysus. In Nietzsche's earliest account, *Birth*, the overflowing propensity of Apollinian and Dionysian forces to overcome each other has to be held in check. The dangers of not keeping this balance, for Nietzsche, are catastrophic. Searing the delicate boundary of the Apollinian dream would lead to pathology, as mere appearance would then deceive us as though it were crude reality (36, 28). Similarly, Apollo, in order to vanquish the Dionysian barbarian (as opposed to the Dionysian Greek)—characterized by that "witches' brew" (*Hexengetränk*) of sexual licentiousness, savage, natural instincts, and a horrible mixture of sensuality and cruelty—holds up the head of the Gorgon, Medusa, as an apotropaic. It is Apollo's gesture of unveiling the Gorgon's head, symbolically cast into Doric art, that cures the Dionysian, restoring to health the parthenogenetic coupling of Apollinian and Dionysian. In other words, it is Medusa, a mythic face of the "feminine" who is able to cure the Dionysian force of its excess; it is she who can restore to health a sick (i.e., excessive) Dionysus, thus enabling the healthy coupling between/within Apollo and Dionysus. Aesthetico-political redemption is configured via a figure of the "feminine" in *Birth*.

The Prophet of Good Health

Glimmers of Nietzsche's evolving political agenda emerge in *Human I*: to declare himself the prophet of good health (*grosse Gesundheit*), which entails overturning or revaluating many values. Nietzsche does not flinch in his iconoclasm: it is error, not truth, that is necessary to life,[31] for the beast in human beings demands to be lied to, necessitating the fabrication of the official lie, morality (35, 62). There are no eternal facts, no absolutes (13, 21), which are all too humanly often the confusion of effect with cause (18, 21–22; 30, 35–36). The *sancta simplicitas* of virtue secretly relishes bringing its own pile of wood to the condemned man's pyre (44, 78); and Christianity's victory over Greek philosophy indicates nothing save its coarser and more violent nature (44, 78). Thirst for pity is nothing but thirst for self-enjoyment at the expense of one's "fellow men," (38–39, 56; 69, 98) and good-naturedness, friendliness, and politeness of heart are higher virtues than pity, compassion, and self-sacrifice (38, 67). It is not unjust for a Prince to rob a plebeian of his beloved, as these men value the desired "woman" differently—one out of abundance, the other out of paucity (47, 83–84). Justice is naught but enlightened self-preservation (49, 87–88), and the social instinct is simply a remnant of our animal heritage, which evolved from the animals' instinct for pleasure—such as a female beast's delight in playing with her young, or the pleasure the two sexes derive from each other, as well as the pleasure of experiencing common sufferings, and eventually, the need to act together to ward off a threatening displeasure (52–53, 93).

In keeping with this desire to style himself as the unveiler of decadence, Nietzsche attempts to re(e)valuate the relationship between science and art in the light of his break from Wagner and Schopenhauer, the two high priests of Romanticism. "Mythology" (in the way he had used it in *Birth*) is ostensibly no longer the means through which the mere appearance of mere appearance may be glimpsed; lumped in with magic, superstition, cults, and law, mythology is now proof of humanity's propensity for drawing wrong conclusions (127–28, 227–28). No longer are science and art painfully and radically at odds with each other. It is through the "science of art" (*die Wissenschaft der Kunst*) (80, 143) that the Romantic illusion of magical and thoroughly spontaneous godlike creation may be dispelled and that the various bad habits and false conclusions, into which the intellect is lured by the (Romantic) artist, are displayed (80, 143). Nietzsche still upholds that art makes the sight of life more bearable, as he did in *Birth*, but this time, he speaks not of the beauty of illusion, but of the "veil of unclear thinking" (*den Flor des unreinen Denkens*) (82, 146) that (Romantic) art throws over things. (Romantic) art is no longer the means through which the artist gains an extra-mortal elevation; it causes him dangerously to ret-

---

31. Nietzsche, *Human, All Too Human*, 29, 40; Nietzsche, *Nietzsche Werke*, 48–49, 71.

rogress further and further into childish vehemence and irrationality, until, like Homer and Aeschylus, the inevitable fate of living death and death in melancholia claims him (84, 151).

The scientific man, instead of being the offspring of the decadent Socrates-Euripides who are accountable for the sin of murdering Attic tragedy, now becomes the further evolution of the artistic (*Weiterentwickelung des künstlerischen*) (105, 188). It now appears that the scientific and artistic, like the earlier Apollinian-Dionysian "coupling," are inextricably intertwined and necessary in order to purge modernity of its Romantic infection and to enable this sick age to evolve into a higher form.

Hints of Nietzsche's more overtly political philosophy may be detected in *Human I*. For instance, Nietzsche addresses the issue of how an individual or a race may be strengthened by hypothesizing that strong natures preserve culture, but weaker natures enable the culture to evolve. Hence, in order for an effective evolution to occur, Nietzsche advocates two steps: (1) the augmentation or intensification of the stabilizing or sustaining force through the union of minds in belief and communal feeling, and (2) the possible achievement of loftier goals through partial weakening wrought by degenerate natures. Nietzsche embeds the metaphor of innoculation at the heart of his argument. He argues that the educator's task in the formation of an individual, by analogy, is first to imbue the student with firmness and certainty, so that he may not be deflected from his intended path, and second, to inflict various injuries upon the student wherever necessary, so that something new and noble could be injected into the injured places. Similarly, statecraft's greatest aim, for Nietzsche at this point, is duration. He stresses that only after secure foundations have been established can en-nobling innoculations, the dangerous companions of duration, be invited into the *polis* (107–8, 193).

What strikingly emerges is that Nietzsche feels the need to conserve the *polis*— not the *polis* of fettered spirits, but of the free spirits. Salvation, to Nietzsche at this point, occurs through education as strengthening and innoculation—precisely through increasing "masculinization" against the "effeminate" effects of Romanticism. And Nietzsche does everything to convince his projected male and decidedly "masculine" readers that he is the proper educator, the one who has evolved from the necromantic realm of Romantic art to the life-sustaining arena of science. It is he who can redeem modernity from its progressive corruption, as evidenced in its increasing "womanization."

Nietzsche speaks with a trace of nostalgia for the "masculine" culture of Greece. In such a culture, which he sets up as an ideal, the properly "erotic" relationship, entailing an educational dimension, was between men and youths; relationships between men and women were initiated in the form of love-affairs or marriages for the purposes of child-begetting and sensual pleasure—purposes devoid of spiritual commerce. The "feminine" figures of Electra and Antigone were endured and even enjoyed—but only in art and not in real life. Greek women had no other task than to bring forth handsome, powerful bodies in whom the character of the father lived on as uninterruptedly as possible, holding at bay that ("feminine") nervous overexcitation that threatened to undermine so exalted a culture. Nietzsche claims that it was through this commerce between the sexes that Greek culture and genius was kept young and vital (121, 218).

Furthermore, for Nietzsche, it is both desirable and even possible to make "women" into "men" through education, not in the sexual sense, but supposedly, in every other sense. Through educational extortion, "women" will eventually acquire "male" strengths and virtues, but only after they have become aware of and accepted the weaknesses and vices that inhere in them—or so Nietzsche dreams. In the meantime, he exclaims with exasperation, the fundamental question is that of surviving the intermediate stage, where "woman" has still not evolved—and where "man's" natural reaction is anger at the fact that "women" have choked the arts and sciences with dilettantism, murdered philosophy through a barrage of mind-bewildering talk, rendered politics more fantastic and partisan than ever, and exacerbated the divisions in society (157, 287).

The figures of authority Nietzsche appeals to at this stage are "masculine" and patrilineal (e.g., fathers, friends, teachers, princes) (200, 369). Although there is a sense in which he still evokes images of the "feminine" as masks for several of his idealizations alongside "masculine" ones (such as the figure of good Eris), there appear to be more negative and forbidding "feminine" mythic personifications/anthropomorphisms (Solitude, Pandora) in *Human I* than in *Birth*. Of "woman" and "women," Nietzsche is most scathing of all, making them the most horrifying embodiment of the fettered spirit—the resent-full enemy of his protagonist, the free spirit.

The Physician-Invalid

Nietzsche's political agenda in *Human, All Too Human II* (hereafter *Human II*) is not very different from that which he outlines in *Human I*: the recuperation of modernity. But this time, instead of using the figure of the master educator of the free spirit, Nietzsche chooses the mask of the physician and invalid in one, who has regained health by leaving behind his own troubles, friends, duties, stupid mistakes, and painful memories, just as a physician would prescribe for his patient in order to heal him (212, 9).

Nietzsche holds that it is in the modern soul that all disease, poison, and danger is concentrated, and that it takes a man who has healed himself from its venom, a man who has drunk deeply of Wagner's "womanish" music (249, 79) and yet survived it, to become its conscience. Such a man must have evolved beyond the imperfect artist and know science (213, 10) in order to practice effectively the art of healing.

Regaining health entails the amputation of Romantic Wagnerian music that enervates, softens, "feminizes"—its "eternal feminine" drawing the "few" down rather than onwards: "*solche Musik entnervt, erweicht, verweiblicht, ihr 'Ewig-Weibliches' zieht uns—hinab*" (211, 7)! Wagner's dramatic music converts the eyes into the ears and vice versa, and causes Euterpe, the poor muse (347, 257–58), to become a monstrosity, having eyes and ears in the wrong places.

Nietzsche compares himself with Odysseus, who has many times descended into Hades, and there conversed with the shades of Epicurus and Montaigne, Goethe and Spinoza, Plato and Rousseau, and Pascal and Schopenhauer. Nietzsche draws together several allusions, both literary and Christian. One such allusion seems to be to Canto 4 of Dante's *Inferno*, in which Dante descends into Limbo, amidst the darkness that surrounds the sighs of the spirits that have lived without Baptism or Christianity, and enters into the hemisphere of light occupied by Homer, Horace, Ovid, and Lucan. Nietzsche's descent, like Dante's, is a descent into light—although in Dante's case, such light, symbolic of human reason, does not possess the heavenly perfection made possible through the presence of God.[32] The second allusion seems to be Christ as the divine sacrifice, the lamb of God who triumphantly harrows hell. Nietzsche, in contrast, sacrifices not merely sheep but his own blood in order to converse with these dread souls. It is thus in the light of Nietzsche's repeated *katabases* and *anastases*[33] (descents and returns) that the living to him often appear pale and fretful, eager for life, and these eight, inspite of their death, so full of life[34]—but "life" as such is not immediately recognizable to a sickly herd.

What is especially striking, though, is that despite his ambivalent treatment of "woman" (*Weib* and *Frau*) as well as "mother" (*Mutter*), Nietzsche's treatment of pregnancy or birthing is generally positive. It is true that there are contexts within which the figure of "mother" becomes negatively akin to Janus. For instance, Nietzsche calls joylessness the "mother of debauchery" (*die Mutter der Ausschweifung*) (230, 45) and claims that Schopenhauer was wrong with respect to why "women" possess such great pride in being pregnant: it is not in their being able to birth an intellectual prodigy, as Schopenhauer thought, but in that pregnancy serves as the

---

32. Dante Alighieri, *The Divine Comedy*, trans. Carlyle-Wicksteed (New York: Random House, 1950), 26–29.

33. For a similar emphasis on the significance of *Katabasis* and *Anastasis* in drawing parallelisms between Nietzsche and Orpheus, see John Seery, *Political Returns: Irony in Politics and Theory from Plato to the Antinuclear Movement* (Boulder: Westview Press, 1990), 2–4.

34. Nietzsche, *Human, All Too Human*, 299; Nietzsche, *Nietzsche Werke*, 169–70.

unambiguous testament of "women's" continuing desirability (309–10, 189–91). And yet, by disjoining the womb from the "mother" (257, 93) and eternal vigor from the "feminine," Nietzsche is able to salvage the power of birthing from the "womanly." For Nietzsche, this power of "birthing" or generativity becomes the ultimate *telos*, for which one must sacrifice both "eternal life" or even "life" (299, 170).

According to Nietzsche, Raphael, in his painting of the *Sistine Madonna*, splits "woman" in two: the worthy elder on the left—the vision of the future wife, a wise, loftily souled, silent, and very beautiful "woman," carrying her first-born in her arms—and the seductive "woman" on the right, who challengingly returns the onlooker's gaze with an undevout look. However, Raphael, in Nietzsche's view, brings together the young and the old in the figure of the infant messiah through painting the eye of a brave, helpful man who sees distress in the face of a child (328, 224). It is striking that in the actual painting, the woman on the left, bearing the child, is the one who actually returns the onlooker's gaze, whereas the woman on the right, the supposedly "seductive" one, keeps her eyes modestly turned down, although the pose she assumes seems to invite the viewer's eye to linger upon her face. Nietzsche appears to exercise a bit of poetic license in his interpretation of the painting, forcefully splitting the ambiguity of mother-maiden into two mutually exclusive categories. To the "masculine" child, however, he grants the paradoxical fusion of age/experience/wisdom and youth/beauty/innocence.

Similarly, Nietzsche keeps together all aspects of the "masculine," combining the wisdom of Oedipus with the scientific skill of the physician and the wanderlust of the transformed Argus. Yet he needs to split apart the power of (re)birthing—the eternal vigor of life—from the "womanly" and "motherly." As such, he begins the protracted operation of excising Demeter's womb, and transplanting it onto the composite super-"masculine" figure of Dionysus-Zeus-Apollo, the classical forefather of Nietzsche's Zarathustra, as I shall show in Chapter 3.

Artist-Scientist and "Masculine Mother"

In *The Gay Science*, Nietzsche employs two main masks to style himself as the priest of a new morality—the morality of the "gay science": (a) the mask of the artist-scientist who has seen beyond the all too human will to Truth, and (b) the "masculine mother."

Nietzsche appears to aspire to fuse together the faces of the artist and scientist in the figure of the savior of modernity. For as a scientist, he declares that the general character of the world is chaos;[35] that there are only exigencies, rather than laws in

---

35. Nietzsche, *The Joyful Wisdom*, 152; Nietzsche, *Die Fröhliche Wissenschaft*, 468.

nature (152, 468). Hence, the living being is only a rare form of dead being, as the world continually re-creates itself (152, 468) and life's most fundamental instinct is directed toward the extension of power (289, 585). Indeed, life is characterized by the babble and battle for power and primacy among warring impulses (155, 470–71). Truth, the latest to gain ascendancy through the Eleatic self-deception (154, 469–70), is the most anemic of these impulses, and requires priests as purificatory sacrifices (292, 587). The fundamental instinct to life, the most preservative of the species, is condemned as illogical and irrational by a necrophiliac culture (90, 418). Finally, error, and not truth, may be among the inescapable conditions of the life of the human being: that unfortunate creature of laughter, tears, and absurdity (64, 477–78).

In Nietzsche's account, Europe is a "female" invalid. The European, her son who is steeped in her corruption, having suckled from her diseased breasts, disguises himself in morality because he has become a sickly and crippled animal—a near abortion (293, 588).

Consequently, Nietzsche reasons that morality is simply an outgrowth of the herd instinct for survival (160, 474–75) and that consciousness evolved simply from the refinement of the need to communicate within life-threatening situations (296–97, 590–91). For Nietzsche, it is only as social animals that human beings have gained consciousness of themselves—but only as part of an endangered collective (298, 592); it is fear that motivates knowledge (300, 594).

For Nietzsche, in order to heal the widespread corruption of modernity, the "few" and free spirits must strive to become what they are: physicist-creators (263, 563). And to achieve this identity, they must purify and construct new tables of value (263, 563); and in thus creating new values, create new things (96, 422), and share in the (anti-Romantic) artist's ability to create new realities (263, 563).

The figure of the genuine artist, for Nietzsche, takes the form of the poet, as opposed to the theatrical/dramatic musician, the figure for the decadent artist, whose power ends where life begins (233, 538). Such a poet, master of his own life, generates new things through renaming and revaluating things (97, 422). Yet the scientist also possesses the Adamic power of naming with the artist, as science is the most exact humanizing of things possible—the ascent into self-knowledge precisely through remaking things in our image through naming (158, 472–73). In the figure of the redeemer of modernity, therefore, Nietzsche reasons, the scientist must meld with the artist, as evidenced by the fact that to attempt a scientific estimate of music is absurd. Artists, the concealers of naturalness (98, 423–24), are the possessors of the knowledge of appearance, not as mere appearance, as in *Birth*, but as the operating and living thing itself (189, 416–17). The ascendancy of artists is seen in that nature evolved out of art (302, 595), and not the other way around. And it is precisely via the agency of this knightly scientist-artist that a path may be hacked through the dense, entangled jungle of Socratism and Christianity toward the redemption of modernity.

The second mask Nietzsche resorts to is that of the "masculine mother." Nietzsche seeks to legitimize his claims to the naturalness and spontaneous vitality of "masculine mothers" by pointing out that in the animal world, the males are considered beautiful, but the females are the productive beings (105, 430). "Maternal love," according to Nietzsche, evolved from the animal females' gratification in being able to treat their young as property in their lust for dominion. However, pregnancy in animals has tamed maternal love and made females gentler, more expectant, more submissively inclined. Continuing on with his account of the genealogy of "masculine motherhood," Nietzsche claims that the contemplative is born from "intellectual pregnancy." Thus, he is allied to "woman" in character as a "masculine mother" (105, 430).

However, Nietzsche does make a distinction between a genuinely fruitful "masculine mother" and a foolish one. A man who is a "mother" in the grand sense is a producer. When his entire world is governed by his pregnancies and childbirths in spirit, he may reach the point where his taste and power radically diverge, such that even if births occur, they may be monstrous stillbirths—which, sadly, the "masculine mother," in his exhaustion, cannot recognize as such (331, 618–19).

Yet genuine artists, as "maternal species of men" (*die mütterliche Art Mensch*) (342, 628), are capable of a ripeness, a patience with life that is not born of exhaustion. Giving birth to works and their maturation leaves behind an "autumnal sunniness and mildness" (*herbstlichen Sonnigkeit und Milde*) (342, 628) in their originator. In such beings, the tempo of life slows down, flowing with the rich thickness of honey—not with the trembling capillary action of blood thinned and depleted of vitality.

Such beings appropriate not only the "feminine" power of birthing, but also the "feminine" power of action at a distance (99, 425). For Nietzsche, "women" exert their power precisely as masters of illusion; they effect their enchantment as heavenly, gliding creatures embodying man's better self precisely through distance, and the illusion that effects. This power is one which "woman" shares with both religion and art (108–9, 433).

For it is precisely as creatures of the future that these "masculine mothers" beckon forth to Nietzsche's "brothers" in laughter and joy from distant shores. It is precisely through their mythical distance that they revive the long dormant will to deceive (277, 575), long held anesthesized by the tyrannical will to Truth.

Similarly, it is through Nietzsche's appeal to "masculine motherhood" that he believes that the redemption of modernity may be safely carried out. For through "masculine maternity," the "feminine" (*weiblich*) that serves the useful function of beautifying and deepening life, may be used and yet sifted away from the "masculine" (*mannslich*) that safeguards and protects life (66, 398). The danger of the "feminine" lies in the fact that it initially gives in to a temporary deception and ecstacy, and eventually lapses into an incurable dissatisfaction. Thus, in order to preserve modernity, the sicklier, tenderer, and more "feminine" dissatisfaction (as evidenced in the preponderance of Romanticism) must be rooted out. And yet it is precisely through the overcoming of these embedded "feminine" poisons, that Europe, the sick "feminine" invalid owes her birthing of an intellectual sensitiveness that is the "mother of all genius" (67, 399).

To Nietzsche, the "masculine mothers" are also the "few" glimpsed in the future for whom one does philology, which always presupposes the coming of a nobler race (139, 459). To the anxious question, "Who reads the stuff I write?" (27, 366), Nietzsche answers—the heroic, not the rabble (227, 532–33); those who understand that a refined nature writes, not simply to be understood, but also not to be understood: to select its listeners, and to create distance (349, 634).

Closing Remarks

It appears that one of Nietzsche's principal and recurring tropes, even in his pre-Zarathustran phase, is that of vitality versus decadence (evolving along the lines of the dichotomy between the free versus the fettered, and the masculine versus the feminine). He believes that the "great health" (*grosse Gesundheit*) of the Greeks may yet be re-achieved, or more specifically, rebirthed. It is significant to note that Nietzsche moves from a position of midwifery to this rebirthing in *Birth*; to being the master educator of the free spirits, future beings of great vitality, in *Human I*; to being both the physician and invalid of Romantic and Christian decadence in *Human II*; and finally, to being the artist-scientist "male mother" of *The Gay Science*. For such a trend seems to indicate an increasingly intimate and bodily diagnosis of the three main cancers of modernity—its Socratism, Romanticism, and Christianity—with "woman" as their principal agent.

As midwife to the rebirthing of classic tragic drama, principally through the figures of Wagner and Schopenhauer, Nietzsche's role seems more detached and less immediate, because all he has to do is supplement or assist in this rebirthing, than when he begins to gravitate toward the role of "masculine mother": the being who must be both the vessel of beauty and the laborious and productive creature. In between these two positions, he moves from being a teacher (and kindred spirit) of free spirits, again a more lofty and detached position, to becoming an invalid who has managed to heal himself, again a stance implying a greater closeness to a problem he had earlier thought to be principally outside of himself.

Nietzsche also gradually moves away from the use of strictly mythic "feminine" figures, such as Demeter, Proserpine, Medusa, or Helen, alongside "masculine" ones, such as Silenus, Homer, Archilochus, and the satyr—as figures for or undergirding his principal mythic masks: Apollo and Dionysus, deities of ambiguous sexuality, who are personifications of the very forces of art, life, and vitality in *Birth*. Starting with *Human I*, Nietzsche's "feminine" figures tend to originate less and less from Greek tragedy/mythology, and more and more from the decadent farce of modernity. "Woman" as fettered spirit, social parasite, and deceitful mistress of manipulation gradually seeps deeper and deeper into Nietzsche's tropes.

It is true that even in *Human I* and *Human II*, there are many positive images of the "feminine." From Greek mythology, one could draw attention to Nietzsche's appropriation of Empedocles' unabashedly erotic Aphrodite as an ally against unhealthy Christian taboos concerning sexuality in *Human I*.[36] Or one could cite Nietzsche's characterization of "good Eris," fair muse of the Greeks, who enables "peaceable competition" as opposed to "war and strife," and presides over the classical competition for honor, rather than the modern race for vanity and pride (90, 160–61). Or one could point to his flattering portrait of the Graces, abundant with nobility, allowed only a brief entry into German art, the domain of Pleasantness, their less refined and provincial sister in *The Gay Science*.

Yet it is also true that in terms of general trends, more and more negative images, as well as less and less strictly mythic tropes of the "feminine" begin to populate Nietzsche's texts. Pandora becomes the treacherous pawn of Zeus who contrives to prolong humanity's suffering by trapping Hope in her gift-box in *Human I*. "Woman" as the imperfect artist and most ardent Christian believer makes her appearance in *Human II*. "Woman" as poisonous and resentful victim, and priestess of the laws of nature and society surfaces in *The Gay Science*.

There are also hints that Nietzsche possesses an uncanny insight into women's socio-political situation within nineteenth-century bourgeois Germany. His poignant portraits of the young bride's radiant smile as she gazes upon her husband as emblematic of the fleeting nature of human happiness, or of the "'noble' woman's" indoctrination into sexual ignorance and shame, only to hurl her, unprepared, into the complex experience of the proximity between animal and god on the marriage bed—reveal great insight, and perhaps, sympathy. They do not save him altogether from the charge of misogyny, but they do serve to underline the polarities that characterize Nietzsche's attitude toward the "feminine"/"woman" at this point—a polarity broad enough to encompass a spectrum of both positive and negative valuations.

---

36. Nietzsche, *Human, All Too Human*, 76; Nietzsche, *Nietzsche Werke*, 135.

One could make the argument that Nietzsche increasingly moves toward a bisexual model of the redemption of modernity, as in the composite figure of Argus-Io in *Human II*, and the figure of the "male mother" in *The Gay Science*. Yet such a stance fails to take into account that in both cases, the "feminine" becomes incorporated into or usurped by the "masculine." Io, as the ever-changing, ever-growing soul of Argus, this hundred-eyed "masculine" creature who gazes upon himself, has been swallowed up by Argus. She can no longer flee from his impaling gaze; she has become the mirror through which he may gaze upon himself as the father of the future free spirits. Similarly, "masculine mothers" appropriate unto themselves the "feminine" power of birthing, as well as the "masculine" privilege of "beauty" in the animal world—and become essentially super-"masculine" creatures who possess the "feminine" powers of creating distance and possessing the golden patience with which pregnancy imbues "mothers."

Refractory and ambivalent as Nietzsche's perception of the "feminine"/"woman" may be, it appears that Nietzsche does not ostensibly harbor doubts concerning the achievement of "great health." His political program, in *Birth*, begins with the redemption of modernity via the rebirthing of tragic culture—a rebirthing that uses both "masculine" and "feminine" mythic personifications as figures for the mechanisms through which classical nobility may be reborn via Romantic art. In *Human I*, his political vision encompasses the sifting of the free spirit away from the fettered spirit (as embodied in the figures of Romanticism, Christianity, and "woman") via the salvation from decadent Christian morality and corrupt Romantic art through science. In *Human II*, his politics takes on a more therapeutic tone, and he envisages himself as the prototype of the highest progeny of modernity—those who can recognize their decadence, and yet heal themselves; those who can learn to be grateful to the sicknesses and imperfections that plague them, only insofar as these temporary illnesses enable them to overcome themselves. Finally, in *The Gay Science*, Nietzsche continues his theme of the redemption of modernity from Romantic art through the fusion of the new composite scientist-artist and the "masculine mother."

His mythic politics, as in *Birth*, begins with ethereal personifications of various divinities, characterized by less a bodily than a spiritual bent in his differentiation of sickness from health. Yet as he progresses, most notably in *Human II*, where he begins to speak of himself as an invalid, his mythic politics seems more tangibly involved with the bodily, even if, at this point, the bodily seems aligned with the disgusting features of "nature" and "woman." For instance, regarding love for a "woman," in *The Gay Science*, Nietzsche writes that such a type of love is instigated by an instinctive hatred for nature, particularly as "woman" is prey to numerous disagreeable natural functions, and is the loathsome agent through whom the "masculine"/anti-Romantic soul is profaned by nature.[37]

Yet Nietzsche's attitude toward the "feminine" is undeniably complex in its ambivalences during his pre-Zarathustran period. For even as he speaks of the profaning hand of "woman" upon the anti-Romantic artist's soul, it is also to yet other faces of the "feminine" that he turns in order to raise up an apotropaic against the possible excesses of his attraction to science, born largely of his disillusionment with Romantic art and philosophy. Among these masks are a young girl, her mother, and Baubô.

Nietzsche narrates the anecdote of a young girl who asks her mother whether the good God is indeed present everywhere. Her mother's reply is supposedly, "I think that is indecent." Ironic humor aside, with "woman" and her supposed prudishness being the butt of a joke, Nietzsche aligns the thorough-going scientist with the figures of the Egyptian youths who penetrate their temples at night. In doing so, Nietzsche means to critique the worship of the naked goddess, Truth, and the obsession of her priests with unveiling, revealing, and laying bare. The little girl and her mother become the unconscious and farcical heroines of Nietzsche's project: the unveiling of Truth as illusion (10, 352).

Then Nietzsche coins one of his most intriguing statements, exhorting his readers to have more "reverence" for the shame-facedness with which Nature has concealed herself behind enigmas and uncertainties. Perhaps, he conjectures, truth is a woman who has reasons for not showing us her reasons? Perhaps, Baubô is truth's genuine visage—a face barely visible only to those profoundly superficial Greeks (10, 352).

Such statements have led Sarah Kofman, in particular, to argue for a Nietzsche who is actually sympathetic to the "feminine," as Baubô, within context, becomes the goddess whom the daredevils of spirit, and descendants of the Greeks, to whom Nietzsche aims his exhortations, worship. Kofman, as I have explained in my first chapter, employs detailed philological and comparative tools to make a case for the elevation of Baubô as the twin sister of Dionysus—his cosymbol of the eternal fertility of nature.

While there is some basis for such an interpretation, it is important to keep in mind the undulating landscape against which such a statement makes its appearance. The ambivalences of Nietzsche's attitude toward the "feminine" defy a linear interpretation—for they often pitch from extremely positive to extremely negative; at times they seem to transcend gender distinctions, and at times, they strongly reinforce them.

Nevertheless, what is clear, in terms of the connection between Nietzsche's political philosophy and his attitude toward the "feminine," is that Nietzsche is fairly opti-

---

37. Nietzsche, *The Joyful Wisdom*, 97–98; Nietzsche, *Die Fröhliche Wissenschaft*, 422–23.

mistic in his pre-Zarathustran phase. He believes that modernity can somehow be saved; he believes "woman" can somehow be educated to becoming more "manly"; he believes that even if one has been dangerously ill for a very long time, that absolute healing, rather than simply temporary remission, is attainable. Most of all, he believes himself cured of that crippling and emasculating disease, Romanticism. That, as I shall begin to show in the next section is one of the principal delusions he suffers from, and is a fundamental part of what powers his will-to-resentment.[38] Nietzsche, the masked Romantic, repeatedly and vehemently attempts to free himself from Romanticism, and in so doing, further attests to his decadence—his inescapable Romanticism.

38. See also Caroline Joan S. Picart, "Nietzsche as Masked Romantic," *Journal of Aesthetics and Art Criticism* 55 (Summer 1997): 273–91.

3

The Zarathustran Phase: The Phallic Mother

> The females stumbled over the long, hairy pelts that dangled from their girdles; with heads flung back they uttered loud hoarse cries and shook their tambourines high in the air; brandished naked daggers or torches vomiting trails of sparks. They shrieked, holding their breasts in both hands; coiling snakes with quivering tongues they clutched about their waists.
> —Thomas Mann, *Death in Venice*

> Surely, emphasizing rupture in this way is a kind of revenge. Incapable of bringing yourself into the world, you hated the one that gave you life, didn't you? And you reduced to nothing that power that holds aloof from your art? And made death out of native life.
> —Luce Irigaray, *Marine Lover of Friedrich Nietzsche*

Introductory Remarks

The deconstruction and reconstruction of myth is crucial to Luce Irigaray's amorous yet combative wrestling with Nietzsche in *Marine Lover of Friedrich Nietzsche*. For Irigaray, Greek myths are figurations through which one may trace the struggle between matriarchy and patriarchy—a struggle resulting in the victory of patriarchy and the concealment of the murder of the mother, a struggle whose echoes resound even today, as the maternal principle does battle to break free from the realm of night and darkness to which patriarchy has banished it.

Irigaray chooses Nietzsche as her lover-combatant as she glimpses, particularly in his myths of Zarathustra, the *Übermensch*, and the eternal return, the alluring yet pernicious death mask he dons: a mask that has become sealed on to his own visage because of his participation in the secret matricide that underlies the heritage of Western culture. For Irigaray, Nietzsche's greatest desire is to birth himself; his greatest resentment is his inability to do so. The figures of Zarathustra, the *Übermensch*, and the eternal return are simply configurations of this will to self-generation, as emblematized in the symbol of the serpent that gnaws upon its own tail—a self-circumscribed circle of joyous and necrophiliac resentment.

> Eternal is the joy that carries within it the joy of annihilation, the affirmation of destruction. In which the negative changes its sign and becomes its opposite for a new mode of being. In which man, as he reproduces himself, himself produces his becoming. Reversing the process of his generation. Wanting to create the universal of all becoming? Beyond physics. A superb distance from the birth that remains natural.[1]

Irigaray diagnoses Nietzsche's propensities for flight[2] and sun-worship[3] as symptomatic of his ambivalent desire to flee from the maternal marine element, and his resentful nostalgia for the amniotic fluid he cannot return to. His crime is his flight, as his flight is his crime[4]—into the arms of eternity, his deathly bride. To justify his being a co-conspirator in the primordial matricide, Nietzsche appeals to the courts of Apollo, the mother-killer who steals from his sister/surrogate mother, Artemis (100, 143); Athena, the idea-Woman conceived by the thought of the god-Father (94–97); and Zeus, the pseudo-mother, who condemns his twice-born son to exile from the dark nourishing soil of a mother's womb, and renders the drunken child-god skinless (123–25, 161). Yet despite the patronage of these patriarchal gods (and patriarchal constructions of "feminine" divinity), Nietzsche suffers from and eternally languishes in his dread dis-ease: his incurable womb envy.

> Zarathustra's/Nietzsche's greatest affliction is that he suffers from an envy of the womb. In his desire to achieve the impossible, namely *to give birth to himself,* Nietzsche expresses a fundamental resentment towards that which he feels ardour for and most esteems—maternal creativity. This resentment on his part towards the creative powers of woman is comparable to the resentment he detects in the will's desire to will backwards, that is to will the past and what has been.[5]

---

1. Luce Irigaray, *Marine Lover of Friedrich Nietzsche*, trans. Gillian C. Gill (New York: Columbia University Press, 1991), 27.
2. Irigaray opposes images of flight with those of plunging into the sea.
3. Irigaray opposes sun-worship with veneration of the moon, a maternal figure of the night, another mythic realm associated with the "feminine."
4. This play of words is provocative because it implies that the image of flight over the world or the expanse of the sea is a trope for the attempt to escape from or deny the "feminine."
5. Keith Ansell-Pearson, "Woman and Political Theory," in *Nietzsche, Feminism, and Political Theory*, ed. Paul Patton (New York: Routledge, 1993), 41.

Along a track parallel to Irigaray's and Ansell-Pearson's observations concerning the philosophico-political implications of Nietzsche's appropriation of the "maternal-feminine," the aims of this chapter are to show that

1. the master-myth of Nietzsche's *Thus Spoke Zarathustra* is a myth of male birthing via the Romantic rebirthing of the mythic triplets of Dionysus, Zeus, and Apollo;
2. the narrative of the hysterical phallic mother, Zarathustra, is also a political noble lie, designed simultaneously to destroy and re-create modernity via the generation of polyphonous voices that speak differently to the noble and the plebeian;
3. the masks of the "feminine" are essential to both the destruction and (re)creation of modernity that Nietzsche, through Zarathustra, hopes to bring into effect through his narration of the travails that his mythic warrior-mother undergoes during his birth-death throes.

Master-Myth: The Romantic Re-(Nascence/Surrection) of Zarathustra

Nietzsche's Zarathustra bears the proud and noble mien which Eugène Delacroix—one of the prototypes of the Romantic and the dandy—often attempted to evoke in his rhapsodic descriptions of the exotic Arabian. Certainly, Nietzsche, like Delacroix, had grown exhausted and surfeited with the decadence of nineteenth-century European culture. Both Nietzsche and Delacroix had turned to the pristine exoticism of the Oriental as a symbol of revolt against the effete, prevailing liberal and Christian culture. And indeed, Nietzsche's Zarathustra possesses Oriental characteristics, and is the prophet that calls corrupted modernity to a new age of *Übermenschen*, in whom the fierce and radiant nobility of the ancients could be reborn.

This section is an attempt to illustrate how the birthing of Zarathustra may be viewed as the result of Nietzsche's aspiration to tease apart and weave together into a new tapestry a conglomerate of myths combining the figures of Dionysus, Zeus, and Apollo, as well as the then compelling aesthetico-moral vision of the dandy. This is in keeping with Nietzsche's own attempt to construct and propagate his aesthetico-political mythology, as the prophet of the transvaluation of all values, visionary of the nightmarish eternal return, and high priest of the doctrine of *amor fati*. His appropriation of the mythic rebirths of Dionysus enables him to construct a political mythology of male birthing, thus allowing him to cast himself in the figures of mutilated father and son who is born of a male "mother." This is a heritage that claims him as a child sired by an unusual blend of Greek classicism and German Romanticism.

To begin, it is important to notice that both Zarathustra's and Dionysus's origins are obscure. Zarathustra certainly appears to be purely of mortal descent as the story begins with the abandonment of his home and lake in order to ascend the mountain at the age of thirty. Nevertheless, from the start, the source of the divine contemplativeness that enables him untiringly to enjoy his spirit and his solitude,[6] free from the malaise of boredom, depression, or loneliness for ten years, and spontaneously to commune with his animals with authority and a type of intimacy, is a matter left unexplained. He emerges as a figure humanly divine or divinely human—at cursory glance, an overtly Christlike figure. Yet as I shall show, Zarathustra is a figure whose divinely human heritage is one that is radically non-Christian—a hybrid ideal whose mythic fonts are both classical and Romantic in character.

Similarly, Dionysus is himself a god whose origins are obscure, and in whose person the human and the divine coalesce. In one myth, his mother is Semele, whom Zeus loved and promised to give whatever she requested, perhaps out of pleasure in her pregnancy. Either because Hera, Zeus's goddess-wife, persuaded Semele to ask Zeus to present himself to her in full regalia, or because Semele was simply following a rather presumptuous practice that enabled the reigning pair to impersonate Zeus and Hera, she is consumed by one of Zeus's thunderbolts when he reluctantly complies with her fatal request.[7] Zeus snatches up his unborn son from the dead maiden's womb and has him sewn into his thigh from where, in due course, Dionysus, whose name may mean "son of Zeus," just as Athena signifies "daughter of aegis-bearing Zeus," is born.[8] Dionysus thus emerges as the only Olympian god who is born of a mortal mother, and is therefore more closely associated with death than any other except Hades.[9]

The affinities linking the myths of Dionysus with the figure of Zarathustra (such as the obscurity of their origins and the ambiguous mingling of divinity and humanity in their natures) are made even richer by the fact that the Cretan Zeus and Dionysus were fused into one godhead. The "Zeus-Dionysus" of Crete was known as "Sosipolis" or "savior of the city" and appeared in the form of a child or a snake.

---

6. Friedrich Nietzsche, *Also Sprach Zarathustra: Ein Buch für Alle und Keinen*, in *Nietzsche Werke: Kritische Gesamtausgabe*, ed. Giorgio Colli and Mazzino Montinari (Berlin: de Gruyter, 1968), 5. For the English translation, for the most part, I draw from Friedrich Nietzsche, *Thus Spoke Zarathustra: A Book for All and None*, trans. Walter Kaufmann (New York: Viking Penguin, 1966), 9 (hereafter cited in the text as *Zarathustra*).

7. Keuls excavates a less amorous set of myths. She claims Zeus raped and then destroyed Semele with his thunderbolt. Cf. Keuls, *Reign of the Phallus*, 51–52.

8. John Pinsent, *Greek Mythology* (Yugoslavia: Newnes Books, 1983), 50.

9. A. Stassinopoulos and R. Beny, *The Gods of Greece* (New York: Harry N. Abrams, 1983), 107.

Zeus-Dionysus was believed to change his form as he underwent the three phases of his myth, which corresponded to the three masculine stages of zöe or life. At the first or sperm stage, the self-engendering god was a snake; at the second or embryo stage, he took the form of a minotaur or a calf-human, who was more animal than human; and at the third stage, he was both the little and the big Dionysus. As primal mother and source of zöe, his feminine counterpart was called "Rhea"; as mother and also as wife, she was named "Ariadne."[10]

It is crucial to note that this tripartite division of the mythic cycle of Zeus-Dionysus may be best characterized as genesis, betrayal, and rebirth-marriage. In the second stage, when Zeus-Dionysus is a half-calf or a premature child of the underworld, Ariadne is at the stage of pure and wild animality, which explains her infidelity, her alleged murder of her brother-son-lover, the minotaur (whose figure seems to blur into the figure of Dionysus at this point), and her escape and subsequent death. The dark events of the second phase[11] are absolutely necessary for the movement into the third or redemptive phase, in which Dionysus, the dismembered sacrificial animal, is made whole again. In the Theban version of this myth, Dionysus, having reached the stage of humanization and having grown strong from his nurses' milk, descends into the underworld to claim his sister-mother-bride, and elevates her, in full radiance,[12] to the heavens.[13]

This conglomerate of myths bears striking resonances with the initial structure of *Zarathustra*—which was itself initially conceived as tripartite.[14] In the first section of the book, Zarathustra ascends and stays in essential solitude for ten years, enjoying the company of only the sun and his animals, only to be spurred downwards again. Zarathustra's descent from the mountain is explained in terms of his spontaneous desire to expend himself as the cup, bearing the sun's golden reflection in the water it holds in its belly, which wants to become empty again.

> "Bless the cup that wants to overflow, that the water may flow from it golden and carry everywhere the reflection of your delight.
> Behold, this cup wants to become empty again, and Zarathustra wants to become man again."[15]

---

10. Carl Kerenyi, *Dionysos: Archetypal Image of Indestructible Life*, trans. R. Manheim, Bollingen Series 65, 2 (Princeton: Princeton University Press, 1976), 119.

11. This structure parallels the Christian paradigm of the dark night of the soul prior to its salvation.

12. Again, this is a pattern very similar to the Christian notion of Resurrection, or in this case, Ascension.

13. Kerenyi, *Dionysos*, 119–21.

14. Christ's Suffering, Death, and Resurrection also has a tripartite structure.

15. Nietzsche, *Zarathustra*, trans. Kaufmann, 10; Nietzsche, *Zarathustra*, ed. Colli and Montinari, 6.

However much nonaltruistically Zarathustra's descent is instigated, he falls into the role of the "Sosipolis" or the savior of the city in his sacrifice of his divine solitude in order to walk again among human beings. However, in order for him to "save," he must first destroy. This is one of many intertwining tissues making up the umbilical cord binding the figures of Dionysus and Zarathustra. In the same light, the animals with whom Zarathustra shares the greatest spiritual intimacy, the snake and the eagle, are mythically associated with the worship of Dionysus, as a sixth-century vase from Orvieto shows.

In addition, within the first section of Nietzsche's *Zarathustra*, the myth of the three metamorphoses forms the nucleus of the greater (originally tripartite) structure. The outlines of the Dionysian birth-betrayal-rebirth mythic sequence may easily be discerned in the transformation of the strong and reverent camel (which represents the pre-existing tradition), into the fierce and proud lion (which represents the rebellion against and total destruction of the existing order), and into the innocent and playing child (which represents the creation of the *Übermensch*). Similarly, the first part of the book deals with his emergence from the solitude of his mountain cave, and his genesis as anti-Christian gift-giver, which corresponds with the story of the origins of Zeus-Dionysus as "savior of the city."

The second part of Zarathustra's tale, which diffuses spontaneously into the third, contains several episodes that resonate with the dark phase of the Zeus-Dionysus cycle. The position I take is that Nietzsche's *Zarathustra* seems to appropriate or rewrite the Zeus-Dionysus mythologems for a new age. Such a rewriting is an attempt at recasting these myths to authorize Nietzsche as the new deity (savior-destroyer) of modernity. Thus, for example, in the episode of the dream of the child who bids Zarathustra to look into a mirror, Zarathustra glimpses not himself but a devil's grimace and scornful laughter (83, 101). Zarathustra himself lays bare the meaning of the dream: weeds pose as wheat (83, 101)—his teachings are being distorted and diabolically misrepresented. As a mythic precedent/parallel, Kerenyi points out that Dionysus himself is depicted as a child, with arms upraised, ecstatically gazing upon himself in a mirror, in a pyxis fashioned not before the fifth century C.E.[16] The gaiety of the scene is misleading, as behind the child lurk two armed Kouretes. One is performing a knife dance; the other, drawing his knife, is about to partake of the ceremony. The child is to be stabbed while gazing upon himself in the mirror.[17]

In Zarathustra's nightmare, the child is still a part of Zarathustra himself, symbolic of his desire to sire a new, vigorous race. Though Zarathustra is not literally stabbed by those who are supposed to serve him while he is gazing into the mirror, the

---

16. Kerenyi, *Dionysos*, 265.
17. Kerenyi, *Dionysos*, 265.

demonic vision that confronts him wounds his soul, and threatens to freeze his heart. Yet, like the infant Dionysus, whose sacrifice is but a prelude to his rebirth, Zarathustra springs up, not like a frightened man seeking air but rather as a seer and singer who is moved by the spirit (83, 102).

There are other striking areas of affinity that seem to mirror and magnify this mythologem. The soothsayer's haunting vision of a parched, dead earth and of its wailing inhabitants waking and living on in tombs (133, 168) causes Zarathustra to grieve for three days, not eating, drinking, resting, or speaking. Zarathustra then sinks into sleep, and has another nightmare. Zarathustra dreams he has become a night watchman—the guardian of tombs upon the dismal mountain castle of death. His three sole companions are the brightness of midnight, crouching loneliness, and death-rattle silence. Three ominous strokes are struck at the gate and resound as howls through the vault. As Zarathustra struggles in vain to open the creaking gate, a piercing, roaring wind tears apart the wings of the gate and casts up a black coffin before him.

The coffin bursts, blasting out an intermingling of the three ghostly sounds of roaring, whistling, and shrilling, and vomiting forth a thousand grimaces of children, angels, owls, fools, and butterflies as big as children. Zarathustra is frightened as he is thrown to the ground. He is violently awakened by his own horrified cry.

> "And amid the roaring and whistling and shrilling the coffin burst forth and spewed out a thousandfold laughter. And from a thousand grimaces of children, angels, owls, fools, and butterflies as big as children, it laughed and mocked and roared at me. Then I was terribly frightened; it threw me to the ground. And I cried in horror as I have never cried. And my own cry awakened me—and I came to my senses." (135, 170)

This is a virtual retelling of Zarathustra's earlier prophetic vision of the transmogrification[18] of his teachings, and may be interpreted as Nietzsche's rendition of the betrayal of the child-Dionysus as integrated into his own political mythology. The grimace of the child, as he is stabbed by the dancing Kouretes, is replaced by angels, owls, fools, and butterflies as big as children—fallen Adams whose monstrous distortions are amplified by the mocking, parodic laughter and ghastly noises that herald their birth. All four figures, in this context, are figures of death, as they are located in the coffin. Angels are mythic heavenly beings fashioned from the resentment against life, Christianity. Owls, Athena's pets, theoretically symbolize classical wisdom, which Nietzsche, at this point, seems to believe is unattainable or at least dubious. Fools and butterflies, representatives of possible breaks from the prevailing Platonic, democratic, and Christian traditions, seem to be likewise doomed in this vision. The threefold recurrence of the number three (three days devoid of nurturance and rest, three loathsome companions, three resounding knocks) may be a reference to and non-Christian appropriation/hyperbolization of the Christian belief in the three days of darkness, which form a prelude to the resurrection of the Messiah.

The earliest sections of the third part again play out this pattern. It begins with Zarathustra's loneliest hour, as he ascends a mountain, leaving behind his friends. The dramatic setting again bears Christian and non-Christian elements: (1) Christ's deepest hour of loneliness and despair in the garden of Gethsemane and (2) the descent of Dionysus through the waters of Lerna into Hades in order to rescue his mother-sister-bride—for which he pays the price of total effemization, and upon his return, Dionysus establishes the phallus as the cult symbol.[19] In another version of the Dionysus myth, Lycurgus attacks the nurses of Dionysus, who then flees into the sea (from whence he came) into the arms of his grandmother, Thetis.[20] The centrality of the sea to the introduction of Dionysus as a god of transfigurations is evident in the myth that narrates how Dionysus, having been seized by Etruscan pirates, transforms himself into a lion on the fore-deck of the ship and makes a she-bear materialize among the repentant, frightened sailors. The lion seizes their leader, and everyone, except the pious helmsman, is transformed into a dolphin, as Dionysus reverts back from a ferocious lion into a youth of childlike beauty.[21] Similarly, the centrality of sea imagery to the continuing political metamorphosis of Zarathustra is evident in the scene where he ascends the mountain to look down upon the black expanse of the sea, and realizes that downgoing is necessary for the birthing of the *Übermensch*, for "it is out of the deepest depth that the highest must come to its height."[22]

The vision of the eternal return and the transformation of the pale and terrified young shepherd into the laughing superman—a section that parallels the movement from the second to the third phases of the Dionysus-Zeus cycle—takes place immediately after this. On the third day of his journey with the sailors, Zarathustra speaks of the riddle-vision that he had witnessed—the cipher-vision of the loneliest. In this vision, Zarathustra climbs up a mountain, bearing on his shoulder the spirit of gravity, who appears as something in between a dwarf and a mole, both of which are nocturnal and subterranean creatures. This spirit of gravity drips leaden thoughts into Zarathustra's ear. Zarathustra encounters the gateway that binds two eternities and imperiously silences the contemptuous dwarf as he utters the doctrine of the eternal return.

---

18. By this, I refer to how Nietzsche's teachings bear "monstrous" fruit—weeds posing as wheat.
19. Kerenyi, *Dionysos*, 181.
20. Pinsent, *Greek Mythology*, 52.
21. Pinsent, *Greek Mythology*, 54.
22. Nietzsche, *Zarathustra*, trans. Kaufmann, 154; Nietzsche, *Zarathustra*, ed. Colli and Montinari, 191.

Behold . . . this moment! From this gateway, Moment, a long eternal lane leads *backwards*: behind us lies an eternity. Must not whatever *can* happen have happened, have been done, have passed by before? And if everything has been there before—what do you think, dwarf, of this moment? Must not this gateway too have been there before? And are not all things knotted so firmly that the moment draws after it *all* that is to come? Therefore—itself too? For whatever *can* walk—in this long lane out *there* too, it *must* walk once more. (158, 196)

The scene dissolves as a dog's howl turns into a piteous whine. Zarathustra finds himself upon a cliff pierced by the bleakest moonlight. Gagging in spasms, a young shepherd staggers toward Zarathustra as the dog frantically cries for help. From the shepherd's mouth dangles the tail of a heavy black serpent that had stealthily slunk into the young man's throat while he had been asleep. Horrified, Zarathustra attempts to tear off the serpent that has lodged itself into the shepherd's throat and is unable to do so. Hardening himself, the young man bites off the serpent's head and spews it far from him as he emerges radiant, laughing the golden laughter that fills Zarathustra with yearning.

The treacherous serpent, a diseased version of one of Zarathustra's favorite animals, the snake, could represent the doctrine of the eternal return that has stealthily impregnated the young shepherd. That the doctrine of the eternal return is potentially fatal is evident in both Zarathustra and the shepherd's genuine horror and nausea. That this doctrine must be rejected, by not only Zarathustra-Nietzsche and the shepherd, the representative of the coming *Übermenschen*, but also by Nietzsche's readers, is evident in Zarathustra and the shepherd's frantic efforts to dislodge the serpent. Yet, ultimately, that the birthing of the *Übermensch* is possible only through impregnation by this poisonous doctrine is evident in the shepherd's transformation into a figure of transcendent laughter only after he has bitten the snake's head off. The cyclical Zeus-Dionysian betrayal-rebirth motif undeniably recurs once again, and the vision of the eternally returning again reifies the inexorable circle of the Zeus-Dionysian cycle. But it is the young shepherd and not Zarathustra who is transformed through spewing forth the bitten serpent's head. The prophet of the doctrine of the eternal return cannot himself enter the promised land, and is left pregnant with the gnawing emptiness of longing.[23]

Animals, as presented in Nietzsche's mythic rewriting, are presented as traits or aspects of a mythic figure, such as Zarathustra's serpent representing his "wisdom"

---

23. Again, this mirrors the Christian model of prophecy in the figure of Moses, who leads the Jewish people from slavery in Egypt, and yet does not, himself, enter the promised land.

and his eagle representing his "pride." Though the original Greek myths teem with animals associated with the various mythic deities, there seems to be little extended treatment of animals, with the exception of Zarathustra's serpent and eagle, the ass, and symbolically, the city of the Motley Cow. The ass, whom the ugliest man worships in book 4, functions as the reincarnation of the "old God." Yet the ass is also an animal formerly used in the worship of Dionysus because of its indiscriminate sex drive, which is apropos of the Dionysian festival's celebration of fecundity and sexual profligacy. As a fusion of the "old" (Christian) God and the "older" (Dionysian) god, the ass seems a farcical figure for Zarathustra's attempts at birthing the overman—attempts afflicted by the ever-present temptation to reawaken the "old" God, who essentially killed off the "older" (Dionysus) by taking his place. Thus, Zarathustra's attempts to resurrect Dionysus are often thwarted by the repeated reawakenings of the Christian God. The cow, a cud-chewing animal, which repeatedly regurgitates its food, probably symbolizes the Christian and democratic traditions that Nietzsche indicts as binding modern society in an unthinking regurgitation of habit and routine.

Leaving the topic of what some of the more significant mythic animal figures may signify in *Zarathustra*, it is important to note that images of genesis and gender are crucial to understanding how Nietzsche recasts the myth of Dionysus to suit his aesthetico-political purposes. Dionysus was predominantly a god of women—he was a god who was awakened and nursed by women, a god accompanied by women, a god awaited eagerly by women who were the first to be overcome by his divine madness. Bachofen remarks:

> Throughout its development the Dionysian cult preserved the character it had when it first entered history. With its sensuality and emphasis on sexual love, it presented a marked affinity to the feminine nature, and its appeal was primarily to women; it was among women that it found its most loyal supporters, its most assiduous servants, and their enthusiasm was the foundation of its power. Dionysus is a woman's god in the fullest sense of the word, the source of all woman's sensual and transcendent hopes, the center of her whole existence. It was to women that he was first revealed in his glory, and it was women who propagated his cult and brought about its triumph.[24]

In contrast to this, it is interesting that three significant female figures Zarathustra encounters—the old woman, life (and wisdom, who reminds Zarathustra of life), and eternity—are desexualized. The first, the little old woman, seduces Zarathustra to

---

24. J. J. Bachofen, introduction to the section on "Mother Right," in *Myth, Religion, and Mother Right: Selected Writings of J. J. Bachofen*, trans. R. Manheim, Bollingen Series 84 (Princeton: Princeton University Press, 1967). Quote from Kerenyi, *Dionysos*, 130.

speak of "women" with the assurance that she is old enough so that she will immediately forget whatever he utters.[25] Its meaning is clear: she is not to be regarded as a threat insofar as she is no longer physically alluring, past the age in which the passions course through her veins with heat, and she can no longer conceive and give birth—and therefore, possesses neither the aptitude nor the willingness to make use of so dangerous a knowledge. Zarathustra then graces the old woman with his knowledge of what "men" and "women" desire in each other.

For Zarathustra, the riddle of "woman" has one solution: pregnancy. He thus contends that "man," for "woman," is simply a means for her most desired end—a child (66, 80–81).

"Man's" nature, for Zarathustra, is no riddle. His desires are simple: danger and play. Thus, he desires "woman" as the most dangerous plaything. Zarathustra contends that "man" should be educated for war, and "woman" for the recreation for the warrior; any other educational program is folly. Because the "man-warrior" does not desire all-too-sweet fruit, he has a taste for "woman" since even the sweetest "woman" is bitter. Yet surprisingly, Nietzsche places the finishing touches upon his comparative portraits of "man" and "woman" by contending that "woman" understands children better than "man" does, but that "man" is more childlike than "woman" (66, 80–81). Although it appears equally viable that as a result of "woman's" greater understanding of children, she be more like them than "man," it appears that Nietzsche wants to differentiate between "woman's" maternal power of nurturing and "man's" "masculine" power of creating anew. The child, as a new beginning, has to be brought into the strictly "masculine" realm as it is through his figure that the promise of redemption may be fulfilled. "Woman's" understanding of the child, and her capacity to nurture him, are simply a means to an end.

There is much in these statements that could tempt one to dismiss these as mere caricatures of "maleness" and "femaleness." The "man" is supposed to advance; the "woman," to retreat, or at least to appear to retreat. The "man" is supposed to be concerned with danger and play; the "woman" with bearing and rearing children. "Masculine" natures are supposed to be deep and profound; "feminine" natures are supposed to be shallow and treacherous.

Yet attempting to get beyond the observation that Nietzsche believes the "feminine" to be inferior to the "masculine,"[26] what insights may be gleaned regarding how Nietzsche's politics are shaped by his assumptions concerning "masculine" and "feminine" natures? For Zarathustra-Nietzsche, both "male" and "female" natures converge

25. Nietzsche, *Zarathustra*, trans. Kaufmann, 66; Nietzsche, *Zarathustra*, ed. Colli and Montinari, 80–81.

26. This interpretation is shared by both Ansell-Pearson and Rosen. Explicitly pitting himself against Derrida, Ansell-Pearson writes: "Nietzsche's presumptions here are sexist because he conceives of woman's 'shallowness' not, as Derrida claims, because she is a 'mystery' and an 'ambiguity,' but because she is a

upon the process of generation. The "maleness" of the warrior, expressed in play and danger, is also expressed in the "female," in a more potent form for Zarathustra because she is the most dangerous plaything.[27] The "masculine" will to power manifests itself in the desire for danger and play; the "feminine" will to power manifests itself in the desire for pregnancy. Nevertheless, "male" and "female" natures, often at odds with each other, intersect only at the level of the generation of the child, whose playfulness and vulnerability excites both recreation and a sense of danger.

Seen in this light, Zarathustra's meditations on "men" and "women" may be viewed as a retelling of the second and third phases of the three metamorphoses and an attempt at a transvaluation—the conversion of the lion (the current state of relationships between the sexes) into the child (the prototype of the superbeing, who seems implicitly to be characterized as fecund in a more spiritual than bodily sense). Yet the episode with the old woman is made even more bizarre by the fact that it is the old woman who, in effect, in my view, impregnates Zarathustra with a "little truth"—a "little truth" that he bears away with him, a treasure both dangerous and entertaining, "troublesome like a little child" (65, 80). Zarathustra's observations are merely affirmed by the old woman; she leaves, bearing nothing new. It is Zarathustra, and not the old woman, in the myth Nietzsche constructs, who must undergo the filth of giving birth.

It may be that Nietzsche's encounters with the old woman, life, and eternity also reiterate the three phases of the Zeus-Dionysus cycle: birth-betrayal-marriage. As I have just shown, Zarathustra's meditations on the nature of men and women constitute an attempt to retell the vision of the birthing of the *Übermenschen*, which he himself must undergo. Zarathustra's forays with life reveal a deep-seated ambivalence and an attraction rooted in an awareness of treachery. Zarathustra confesses to loving life deeply and most intensely when he hates life (109, 136). This is the content of the song he sings to life with her unfathomable eyes that threaten to engulf him— a song within the dancing song Zarathustra sings for the dancing girls and Cupid. It is a song that confesses how *ressentiment* lies at the very heart of the "love" with which Zarathustra relates to the "feminine."

Yet Zarathustra leaves life for eternity, to whom he sings and pledges seven times: "Never yet have I found the woman from whom I wanted children, unless it be this

---

'lack': woman needs a man to give her depth" (Ansell-Pearson, "Woman," 43). It is true that "mystery," "ambiguity," and "lack" are not necessarily mutually exclusive, but Derrida positively valorizes "mystery" and "ambiguity." Ansell-Pearson believes Derrida misreads Nietzsche's negative characterization of "woman" as "lack." Similarly, Rosen writes: "We may exculpate Nietzsche from the accusation that he advises us to beat women with whips. But he certainly intends to keep them in a subordinate position, as an ornament to men" (Stanley Rosen, *The Mask of Enlightenment: Nietzsche's Zarathustra* [Cambridge: Cambridge University Press, 1995], 120).

27. Nietzsche, *Zarathustra*, trans. Kaufmann, 66; Nietzsche, *Zarathustra*, ed. Colli and Montinari, 81.

woman whom I love: for I love you, o eternity!" (228–31, 283–87). It is with eternity, his chosen bride,[28] that Zarathustra takes upon himself, seven times, the nuptial ring of rings, the ring of recurrence (228–31, 283–87). The number seven is significant, as it also turns out to be the number—taken in terms of groups as they are encountered and captured by Zarathustra—of deformed and malodorous higher men who arise from the womb of the valley to penetrate, upon Zarathustra's invitation, the interior of Zarathustra's cave in the fourth part of the book. They may constitute seven sets (the two kings, the conscientious in spirit, the magician, the old pope, the ugliest man, the voluntary beggar, and the shadow) of aborted, monstrous progeny that Zarathustra breeds in his alliance with eternity.

The number seven, incidentally, also constitutes the number of days in the Biblical account of Genesis, for Yahweh to create a world with its various elements and teeming creatures. If I am reading this allusion accurately, then it may again be interpreted as an anti-Christian appropriation of a Christian motif: an alternative account of how the modern world, perhaps, may be re-created. However, precisely because the creatures produced through this anti-Christian genesis account are monstrous, it seems that Nietzsche himself doubted the attainability of his political vision.

Focusing more specifically on how Nietzsche's mythic politics is shaped by his attitude toward the "feminine," it is significant to remember that the classical Dionysian relationship to women was extremely complex. His follower was called a *mainas*, a "raving woman."[29] The Thyiades, the fierce warrior-women who also worshipped Dionysus, were famed for their *thyein*, "a leaping run so impetuous as to verge on flight ... [on] the high wintry mountain [of Parnassos]" (220). In Boeotia, Plutarch's place of origin, Dionysian women functioned as both nurses and slaughterers (179).

In contrast, Nietzsche appears to diminish the role of "women" in the myth of Zarathustra for he appropriates unto Zarathustra himself the process of birthing— an aspect ironically alien to Zeus-Dionysus, the god nurtured, pampered, and worshipped by women. In so doing, Nietzsche appears to heighten and exploit other aspects of the Dionysian mythic heritage such as the dual presentation of Dionysus as the hunter and the hunted—the worthy sacrificial victim necessary for the mystery of the *trieteris*: "life out of death and death out of life in an endless repetition encompassing the indestructibility of life, though it would be more correct to say that the indestructibility encompassed a repetition" (200). Similarly, Zarathustra is as the "horned kid" whose utterance of the fearful doctrine of the eternal return makes of him the lonely vessel whose destruction in the filth of birthing the superman is

---

28. It is possible to read this ironically, but that reading clashes with a recurrent theme that seems to resurface earnestly throughout *Zarathustra*: his desire for immortality, which he may gain by wedding eternity.

29. Kerenyi, *Dionysos*, 176.

necessary. Nietzsche therefore combines the two faces of Dionysus—the phallic god of fertility and the unphallic god of the mask (281–85) (the god who temporarily descends into Hades during the latter phase of the second part of the Zeus-Dionysus myth) in order to create a super-"masculine" god who desires to give birth to beings like and beyond himself. What I am aiming to show, using Kerenyi's excavations of the nature of the Dionysian rituals, is that Nietzsche strategically brings into closer conjunction two other myths: the myth of the birth of Dionysus from the thigh of Zeus and the myth of Apollo's journey to the land of the Hyperboreans. In fusing these myths, Nietzsche, through the figure of Zarathustra, creates an even more complex mythic figure—a chimera composed of Zeus, Dionysus, and Apollo. This is essential to his project of appropriating the essential mythic traits of Zeus, Dionysus, and Apollo, and grafting them on to his new deity, Zarathustra.

Kerenyi points out that in ancient Greek mythology, there are links, although admittedly frail, that connect these three gods. In the Orphic version, the affinity between Dionysus and Zeus approaches its closest conjunction. The Orphic hymn addresses the intertwining figures of the Kradiaios Dionysus, the "figwood Dionysus" and Sabazios, who is identified as the son of Kronos, and is thus equated to Zeus. In this hymn, Zeus sews Dionysus into his thigh until he can be brought to the goddess Hipta-Rhea (or the Great Mother) on the mountain of Tmolos. Kerenyi points out the significance of this myth:

> The logic of the Greek version of the myth—and this version had its impact on the Phrygian Sabazios—is marred only by the substitution of the thigh birth for the god's self-emasculation, a terrible but not meaningless act. The invention of a birth from the thigh of Zeus had its function in Greece: to cover over the god's lavish gift at the expense of his own body. The myth cruelly emphasized the necessary self-sacrifice of male vitality to the feminine sex, and hence to the human race as a whole. (275–76)

Nietzsche rejects the notion of the sacrifice of the "masculine" to the "feminine" principle in the process of creation and creates Zarathustra, the ultimate personification of the unconquered "masculine" element, who appropriates unto himself the "feminine" power of birthing. This appropriation of the image of the rebirths of Dionysus in the new composite mythic figure of Zarathustra-Dionysus-Zeus is in consonance with Nietzsche's announcement of his own rebirthing of himself as a disciple of Dionysus in the 1886 prefaces.[30]

---

30. Refer to Friedrich Nietzsche, "*Versuch einer Selbstkritik*," in *Sämtliche Werke: Die Geburt der Tragödie; Unzeitgemaße Betrachtungen 1–4; Nachgelassene Schriften 1870–1873*, ed. Giorgio Colli and Mazzino Montinari (Berlin: de Gruyter, 1988), 11–22. For the English, I relied chiefly upon Friedrich

Here, Nietzsche recasts the images of squandering and self-mutilation characteristic of the Dionysian cult as the hallmark of his own emergence from the pestilence of Wagnerian and Schopenhauerian Romanticism to new health. The Athenian version of the origins of Dionysus depict this god to be "thrice-born" but of "two mothers."[31] Analogous to the wound Zeus inflicts upon his thigh, which enables this divine male mother to experience the pangs of childbirth, so Nietzsche bears the self-inflicted wound of his attraction to tragic pessimism and redeems it by exploiting its procreative powers. Nietzsche consequently emerges as "twice-born,"[32] and of one mother; his second, self-induced birth is the sign of his mythic initiation into and political appropriation of the mysteries of Dionysus. Nietzsche's "second birth" thus ostensibly furnishes the key to his own affirmation of life, for only the experience of childbirth grants him access to the will to life rejoicing over its own inexhaustibility and indestructibility, even in the sacrifice of its highest types.[33]

Similarly, there is a set of myths that weave together the figures of Apollo and Dionysus. A watering pot by a Berlin painter, at his best during the period of the Persian Wars, depicts Apollo sitting with his lyre and bow on a large tripod. The wings that sprout from the tripod indicate his journey over the sea—which is depicted as teeming with life in the figures of the fish and the octopus—to the land of the Hyperboreans, who lived at the back of the North wind. Two dolphins plunge in mid-air, framing the flying tripod, probably signifying Dionysus, who took over Apollo's shrine in winter.[34] Apollo, the god of light and healing, returns to find Dionysus dismembered, and enables the latter to arise, whole again. It is interesting that the dolphin is one of the symbols of Apollo, as it is of Dionysus, leading Kerenyi to remark, with regard to the rites of the bacchantes: "[I]n the prophetic realm Apollo and Dionysus are scarcely distinguishable."[35]

Zarathustra is a figure in whom Apollo and Dionysus blur into each other. Zarathustra is both the one who journeys to the land of the Hyperboreans, and the one who returns to find the sickness and sundering of his teachings. Zarathustra is he who must be sacrificed, whose dismembered remains must be forged together again, for the birthing of the *Übermenschen*. Perhaps this is most concretely seen when his followers from the city of the Motley Cow bid him goodbye and present

---

Nietzsche, "Attempt at a Self-Criticism," in *The Birth of Tragedy and the Case of Wagner*, trans. Walter Kaufmann (New York: Random House, 1967), 17–27.

31. Kerenyi, *Dionysos*, 219.

32. This is another excellent example of Nietzsche's remythologization: Christ, too, was twice-born but Nietzsche casts his second birth in an anti-Christian light.

33. I wish to thank Professor Daniel Conway for his insightful comments with respect to this line of argumentation.

34. Pinsent, *Greek Mythology*, 35.

35. Kerenyi, *Dionysos*, 219.

him with a golden-handled staff on which a serpent coils around the sun. Delighted, Zarathustra's acceptance is thorough-going. He leans upon it, signifying his acceptance of the identity the staff bestows upon him symbolically, with its golden sun (emblematizing Apollo) and the serpent (emblematizing Dionysus).[36] Indeed, madness and sanity coexist in the prophetic Dionysus-Apollo as they do in Zarathustra: "there is always some madness in love, as there is always some reason in madness" (41, 45).

But with the close conjunction of the figures of Dionysus, Zeus, and Apollo that Nietzsche effects in Zarathustra, the problem of the generation of a new race reiterates rather than resolves itself. If the father is simply the son bearing himself, as the sacrificial victim is the same as the sacrificer, as the diseased is one with the healer, then how is redemption and the rise of the new age of superbeings possible?

Though he idealizes the notion of the "higher men" more than I do, Eden phrases a related aspect of this dilemma eloquently:

> The higher men are unique and stand in perpetual tension with what is common: not only what is common to other men but what is common in themselves. Their inescapable task is to create their own rules and laws; they must determine what is to be common, regular, lawlike in their natures and what it to remain untouched by the rules. This is the problem of giving style to one's character.[37]

Nietzsche himself seems aware of this absurdity, as the fourth part of the book seems naught but a farcical playing out of this dilemma. The higher men, whose deformities and stench move Zarathustra to conflicting emotions of pity, shame, anger, and affection, are parodic fragmentations of his own teachings that have gained hideous forms. The suffering, dismembered godlike Zarathustra is unable to piece himself together again, as his severing from his monstrous progeny is made complete by the reawakening of the dead god through the farcical ass festival. Pained by the inadequacies of his creations, Zarathustra must smilingly partake of the supper of convalescents.

Ultimately, the spiritual temper of Zarathustra, particularly at this point, is less classical than Romantic. The pose Zarathustra strikes is that of the dandy/Romantic, who emerges as a figure both heroic and terrorized. The dandy/Romantic refuses the resolution of the inner and the outer depicted powerfully in David's *Oath of the Horatii*, in which the pact with an external power liberates the soul from its inner torments. In taking such a stance, however, the dandy himself becomes the battle-

---

36. Nietzsche, *Zarathustra*, trans. Kaufmann, 74; Nietzsche, *Zarathustra*, ed. Colli and Montinari, 93.
37. Eden, *Political Leadership*, 118.

field of conflicting emotions. By refusing a pact with an external power, as evidenced in the dandy's refusal to fit within the staid categories of the "masculine" and the "feminine," the dandy, in effect, aspires to monadic self-legislation while living within society. Yet monadic self-legislation makes impossible the engendering of true disciples and renders absurd the aspiration to the intimacy of community. This is one of the facets of Nietzsche's hidden dandyism/Romanticism, which seems to reveal itself in Zarathustra's dream of birthing the "overman," that makes his "politics" problematic. He aspires to create a new *polis*, built upon a disillusionment with Christian and democratic principles. Yet he also realizes that the type of "community" he seeks to breed—with its anti-Christian self-legislators[38]—may not be able to cohere enough to form a community; destruction and autonomy, their common traits, may result not in the birthing but in the abortion of the new age.[39]

At this point, perhaps it is best to address how I interpret the relationship between Nietzsche and Zarathustra. This is a difficult question as it raises, to some extent, the issue of authorial intent. And there are discernible dangers in simplistically equating an author's view with a view expressed by one of his fictional creations. Yet, there are numerous occasions where Nietzsche does not seem to hesitate in identifying himself with Zarathustra, sometimes going as far as switching directly from his authorial voice to Zarathustra's, without signalling any break or disruption. For instance, in the essay entitled "Attempt at a Self-Criticism," his retrospective review of the *Birth* after he had written *Zarathustra*, he writes:

> No! You ought to learn the art of *this-worldly* comfort first; you ought to learn to laugh, my young friends, if you are hell-bent on remaining pessimists. . . . Or, to say it in the language of that Dionysian monster who bears the name of Zarathustra:
> "Raise up your hearts, my brothers, high, higher! And don't forget your legs! Raise up your legs, too, good dancers; and still better: stand on your heads!
> "This crown of the laughter, the rose-wreath crown: I crown myself with this crown; I myself pronounced holy my laughter. I did not find anyone else today strong enough for that.[40]

---

38. To some extent, this could be read as a parody of Kant's emphasis on self-legislation as the basis of ethics. However, Kant does not have Nietzsche's appeal to the amorality of nature and power that provides much of the justification for Nietzsche's rebellion against legislation by the state or a religious institution.

39. To attempt to render dialectical the portrait of the dandy as masquerading what he wants/desires to be is actually to simplify the ambiguity of his stature. He would then be a figure who is/desires to be what he appears to be—which is not a very helpful model for attempting to understand the ambivalences and ambiguities of Nietzsche's writings.

40. Nietzsche, "Self-Criticism," 26–27; Nietzsche, "*Selbstkritik*," 22.

Furthermore, in *Ecce Homo*, Nietzsche crowns his *Zarathustra* as "the greatest present that has ever been made to [mankind] so far."[41] He bases this claim upon a further claim—that it is a book of tremendous height and depth, through which "no prophet is speaking, none of those gruesome hybrids of sickness and will to power whom people call founders of religions" (219, 257). Like Nietzsche, Zarathustra is not an alleged "improver of mankind" but a mouth that speaks in halcyon tones, whom only the most select can hear underneath the thunderous hammer whacks, which the plebeian take as a rallying cry for (self-)destruction (219–20, 258). The high degree of identification or affinity between Zarathustra and Nietzsche leads me to the hypothesize that, in many respects, Zarathustra functions as Nietzsche's mythic mouthpiece.

Lou Andreas-Salomé comes to the same conclusion in her portrait of Nietzsche:

> Zarathustra, then, is also the child, as well as the god of Nietzsche, the act or created art-form of an individual, linking this individual with the whole lineage of man and with the *essence of man*. He is "the created as well as the creator," the "stronger person of the future," and the one who towers over the suffering, human Nietzsche-manifestation—he is the "over-Nietzsche."[42]

Zarathustra, as Nietzsche's projected mythic alter ego, serves as a complex self-portrait of Nietzsche. Although, at certain points, it is advisable to differentiate between Zarathustra and Nietzsche due to the hermeneutic problem of ascribing authorial intent, whenever it is relevant to draw out how tightly these two entities appear to be bonded, I shall do so, in an effort to glimpse beyond the mask that Nietzsche appears to view as his own face. Naturally, I shall also strive to keep these two entities as distinct as possible during my discussion, whenever it is most relevant to do so.

Two objections to this hypothesis may come up at this point: (1) that Nietzsche, as an author, speaks through all of his characters, and not simply one, and (2) that the virtual equation of Nietzsche and Zarathustra simplifies Nietzsche's (esoteric) rhetoric. The first is certainly a valid point, and it is true that every author deflects her voice through the characters s/he creates; and indeed, in Nietzsche, one has the sense that the darker sides of Nietzsche speak through even the most odious creatures he creates, such as the ugliest man. However, in my view, it appears that Nietzsche often sets up such characters as foils against which the nobility and anti-Christian

---

41. Friedrich Nietzsche, *Ecce Homo*, in *On the Genealogy of Morals and Ecce Homo*, trans. Walter Kaufmann (New York: Random House, 1989), 219; Friedrich Nietzsche, *Ecce Homo*, in *Nietzsche Werke: Kritische Gesamtausgabe*, vol. 3 (Berlin: de Gruyter, 1969), 257.

42. Salomé, *Nietzsche*, 139.

morality that Nietzsche wishes to propagate may gleam even more brightly in Zarathustra. Hence, although the bearlike hermit, whom Zarathustra meets during his initial descent, is a double of Zarathustra (as evidenced by his communion with nature), this hermit is a decadent double: a cracked mirror that emphasizes Zarathustra's greater nobility and wisdom, demonstrated by Zarathustra's knowledge of the death of god, of which the hermit knows nothing. The centrality of Zarathustra's perspective is what binds the narrative together; and since Nietzsche does not textually seem to establish a gap between his views and Zarathustra's, either in *Zarathustra* or elsewhere, I think this approach is a fruitful way of arriving at an intelligent hypothesis concerning Nietzsche's probable political and philosophical aims.

To the issue of possible oversimplification, I counter that Nietzsche's rhetoric does not lose its complexity by hypothesizing Zarathustra as his mythic mouthpiece. Zarathustra is a complex figure, who undergoes adventures that cry out for interpretation. He is a figure who is both enlightened yet mortal, prone to the weakness of pity—traits Nietzsche certainly ascribed to himself as an "untimely man," whose last act prior to his descent into madness was embracing a horse that was being brutally beaten by its owner. The complexity of Nietzsche's rhetoric does not diminish, even if we were to take Zarathustra as a proverbial lens that concentrates the rays of Nietzsche's insights. It is Zarathustra who most perfectly speaks and performs Nietzsche's esoteric and exoteric languages; hence, no esotericism seems to be lost in viewing him as functioning as a mythic mouthpiece for Nietzsche. This is not to provide a facile reply to the hermeneutic issue of ascribing authorial intent, but a constructive attempt—similar to playing a game of chess which builds from an observation of clustering patterns and probable future moves—for arriving at an intelligent formulation of the broad contours operative in Nietzsche's political philosophy. Naturally, I am not claiming that Nietzsche's intentions are transparently expressed by Zarathustra; on the contrary, Zarathustra's actions and utterances are far from unambiguous. Nor am I claiming that I am capable of entering Nietzsche's mind by scrutinizing Zarathustra's rhetoric. What I am attempting to do is to see where the hypothesis of interpreting Zarathustra as Nietzsche's constructed mythic alter ego can lead me, in terms of understanding how Nietzsche probably views his politics in relation to the issues of the "feminine"/"woman"—and to locate, more or less, how Nietzsche's persistent Romanticism interacts with or sculpts his attraction to classical culture.

Zarathustra and Nietzsche, like the dandy/Romantic, seek the uniqueness of their own beings, and set themselves stubbornly against work, utility, nature, woman, progress, and democracy. Like the dandy/Romantic, they allow themselves to experience the ravishing power of emotions; and like the dandy, they both nevertheless aspire to retain their self-control under all circumstances, "to resist the onslaughts of the world, and to die stoically, like the hunted wolf in Vigny's fable, which suffered and died without deigning to utter a word."[43]

Thus, the mask of the classical Dionysus, the god of theater and horror, for whom the elements of pity and terror are essential to catharsis, becomes transformed into the civilized mask of the dandy, with his white gloves, polished ankle boots, jewelry, and lace. It is the mask of someone who knows the folly of all he attempts to do, and holds within himself the gall of this bitter realization with a contemptuous smile—thus adhering to the dandy's/Romantic's own mythic ideals of combining the extremes of willpower and passion, and of blending classical impassivity with a sharp, personal awareness. It is a mask "forged by scorn and held in place by pride . . . [which enables the dandy] to feel that his living flesh . . . [has] become one with the superimposed artificial mask" (133). The delivery of one of Zarathustra's final speeches bears the imprint of this scornful and heroic assumption of suffering impassivity.

In this final section, Zarathustra momentarily lapses into a cry for pity for the higher man. He then stiffens, his face turning into bronze, as he hardens himself with the thought that he is not concerned with happiness but with his work.

> "Pity! Pity for the higher man!" he cried out, and his face changed to bronze. Well, *that* had its time! My suffering and my pity for my suffering—what does it matter? Am I concerned with *happiness*? I am concerned with my *work*.[44]

In keeping with this attempt to describe the Romantic temperament, Jean Lorrain describes a masked ball at which the guests, seeking further amusement, take off their masks. They tear off the mask of one reluctant guest—only to find out that he does not wear a mask. The shocking conclusion lays bare one of the fundamental mythic tenets the dandy carefully espouses—the horrific and glorious anticipation of his own death.

> The dandy allowed himself to undergo the daily ritual of dressing with meticulous correctness, running the risk of being taken for a mere fop. . . . every day, he was dressing like a man who is preparing, with minute attention to the slightest detail, for his own execution.[45]

Beneath the bravado of Zarathustra's tumultuous and enraptured shouts, one glimpses the secret longing for the night-kingdom of death immortalized in Novalis's *Hymns to the Night*. Zarathustra, who takes upon himself the weight of the doctrine of *amor fati* and the vision of the eternal return, cries out for the brightness of mid-

---

43. Michel Le Bris, *Romantics and Romanticism* (New York: Rizzoli International Publications, 1981), 132.
44. Nietzsche, *Zarathustra*, trans. Kaufmann, 327; Nietzsche, *Zarathustra*, ed. Colli and Montinari, 404.
45. Le Bris, *Romantics*, 133.

night, and shuns the boorishness of day—the quintessential heroic pose of the dandy/Romantic.

> "Leave me! Leave me! I am too pure for you. Do not touch me! . . . My skin is too pure for your hands. Leave me, you stupid, boorish, dumb day! Is not the midnight brighter?"[46]

This is the hidden cry of someone who accepts with heroic impassivity the burden, filth, and destruction of giving birth to the *Übermensch*. The phallic mother seeks the secretly blessed fragrance and smell of eternity—"of the drunken happiness of dying at midnight, that sings: the world is deep, deeper than the day had been aware" (321, 396). These are the cry and the yearnings of a man who seeks his own glorious, sensual, and heroic death. These are the utterances of a phallic mother who seeks immortality in the throes of attempting to birth the *Übermensch*—while he remains cognizant that these labor pains are death throes. This is a man who would have well understood the conjunction of the erotic sensualism and deathly pallor of Delacroix's *Massacre at Chios* and *The Death of Sardanapalus*. This is a man who drinks deeply of the heady and deadly draught of Romanticism, and drunkenly awaits the embrace of death beneath a visage of vitality and health.[47]

Glossolalia (Speaking in Tongues): Politico-Mythic Authorization

Frances Oppel captures, in clean strokes, a powerful sketch of Irigaray's diagnosis of Nietzsche's womb envy and resentment.

> Irigaray attributes two desires to Nietzsche: one to be a mother, and the other to return to the womb. These are two very different projects expressive of opposite wishes and thus of major ambivalence toward birth itself.[48]

Keith Ansell-Pearson comes to a similar conclusion. He draws attention to Nietzsche's ambiguous glorification of not only "woman," but also the female reproductive organs—which Nietzsche uses as a figure for the eternal fecundity and creativity of life.[49] Ansell-Pearson sets these next to Nietzsche's "evasion of his—and

---

46. Nietzsche, *Zarathustra*, trans. Kaufmann, 321; Nietzsche, *Zarathustra*, ed. Colli and Montinari, 396.
47. See also Caroline Joan S. Picart, "Nietzsche as Masked Romantic," *Journal of Aesthetics and Art Criticism* 55 (Summer 1997): 273–91.
48. Frances Oppel, "Irigaray with Nietzsche," in *Nietzsche, Feminism, and Political Theory*, ed. Paul Patton (New York: Routledge, 1993), 94.
49. Ansell-Pearson, "Woman," 39.

our—human, all too human origins, [which] results in a hatred of the mediocre, the handicapped, the feminine, and the natural" (42).

And indeed, the refractory character of Nietzsche's attitude toward the "feminine," particularly in the guise of "mother," is crucial to understanding how Nietzsche styles himself as the redeemer of modernity. As I have established in the preceding section, Zarathustra, functioning as Nietzsche's mythic alter ego, appropriates unto himself the complex mask of Dionysus-Zeus-Apollo in order to fashion for himself the figure of Zarathustra as phallic mother. Such a mythic being possesses the unbounded "feminine" power of fecundity and birthing along with the "masculine" virtues of the warrior. The virtues of pregnancy and playing thus become fused in this *über*-figure who seeks to create or birth beings like himself.

Nietzsche's consummate artistry is evident in his crafting of this mythic being, if art is to be understood as an illusion that enhances life, or strengthens the will to power. Yet art, for Nietzsche, is intrinsically political, in so far as it is a stimulus to life, and is ostensibly aimed at the destruction and recreation of the polis from the modern vision-pestilence of chaos and its philosophical minion, nihilism. Modernity's dis-ease, for Nietzsche, is its resentment against time, its desperate search for meaning within a universe in which the death of god has been proclaimed, its barrenness and infertility, signaling the nightmarish coming of the last men.

Like a voice crying out of the wilderness, Zarathustra aims to lead the already noble "few" from Egypt to Jerusalem, substituting the poetic-prophetic ecstacies of Dionysus-Zeus-Apollo for the tablets of Moses. Yet in order to effect the grand exodus, Nietzsche must accomplish two tasks: (1) winnow the "rare" from the "common," and (2) destroy the decadent order of modernity.

Nietzsche seeks to accomplish both goals through the deployment of what Stanley Rosen calls Nietzsche's "double rhetoric."[50] By this, Rosen essentially means two things: (1) the pulsing fluctuation between the rhetorical registers of pessimism and optimism (247), and (2) the transformation/debasement of the esoteric into the exoteric (248).

Both Nietzsche and Zarathustra cast their golden fishing rods to catch disciples—men who will be willing to suffer the heavy burden of an age ripe with longing for the coming of the *Übermenschen*. He knows that his catch will be of variable quality—some noble; others, ignoble. To solve the problem of separating the plebeian from the rare, Nietzsche appears/feigns to exotericize the esoteric. That is, Nietzsche seems to recast the language of the "few" into the language of the "many." In other words, he makes it easy for those with the ears of the jackass to believe that they are his true heirs, thus hastening their own self-instigated destruction. Yet to the ears of

---

50. Rosen, *Mask of Enlightenment*, 247.

the Hyperborean, Nietzsche speaks differently—he sings, as convalescents do, of the possible coming of a child who may give birth to a star. As Rosen points out:

> Nietzsche's dilemma is that he can destroy only in the hope that out of the ashes of the present will arise an infant who is also a creator of a new table of values. Nietzsche knew, as his letters show, that his invocation to creativity would be radically misunderstood or at least radically misapplied by those who believed themselves to be at once supermen and his disciples. (xiv)

A crucial part of Nietzsche's deployment of his double rhetoric—of creation and destruction, optimism and pessimism, and esotericism and exotericism—is his figure of Zarathustra as the phallic mother. To the plebeian, Zarathustra becomes the noble lie through whom they may be lured back to life—only to hasten their deaths. Zarathustra, as male virgin mother who seeks warrior-heirs, becomes the general who sends his deformed and malodorous troops to die in battle, a fitting sacrifice to the higher cause of the *Übermensch*. Zarathustra, as self-generating wheel, whispers the noble lie of the will to power to the jackass-eared, lulling them into the life-invigorating forgetfulness of the horrifying vision of the eternal return. Zarathustra, sun-communer and eagle-snake biting his own tail, causes the modern adders to bite their own tails, and die from their own poisons.

To the noble, Zarathustra as phallic mother assumes a different visage. For although Zarathustra is indeed pregnant with the vision of the *Übermensch*, his golden son lies entwined within the arms of his dark twin—the vision of the eternal return. Zarathustra is indeed pregnant, but his is a hysterical pregnancy: one characterized by shrill cries and erratic mood swings—a pregnancy that knows no relief from birth pangs and is haunted by the vision of the filth of after-birthing. Zarathustra can only generate the near-abortions of the higher men—hideous siblings to the *Übermensch*, who revel in either clever, nihilistic magic tricks or a cowlike tranquility. Zarathustra may enable the shepherd to bite off the deadly serpent's head—but it is not he who is transformed into the *Übermensch*; nor is it he who laughs the golden laughter that emanates from this elevated being.

It is to such Hyperboreans that Zarathustra, functioning as Nietzsche's mythic mouthpiece, reveals glimpses of the suffering servant of the *Übermensch*. To their clear eyes, the phallic mother offers fleeting glimpses of the skin rash that infests him—the Romanticism that threatens to infect, and maybe abort, his most precious progeny: the shining vision of himself purged of his three cancers—modernity, Christianity, and Romanticism.

Nietzsche's political project therefore dooms him to an inescapable *ressentiment*, spawned partially by the necessity of revenge against the herd, as well as by the persistence of that "feminine" and Romantic heritage that courses through his blood. Nietzsche realizes that in the face of the inexorability and endless repetition of the eternal return, human happiness lies in the will to create—a will all too humanly doomed to frustration and the temptation to revenge. All creation thus becomes naught but "enthusiastic lying" (189). The noble lie of creating a life-sustaining mythology becomes the supreme art—the art of the masked convalescent, who may reveal his pockmarked face only to those who possess Hyperborean eyes.

It is true that the "feminine" makes its appearance in ways different from the mask of "maternity" in *Zarathustra*. For instance, "woman" is described as a tyrant and slave incapable of "friendship," and knowing only "love"—which is supposed to be inferior to "friendship." "Woman" has not yet overcome the "cat," "bird," or at best, "cow" stage. Nietzsche has made the cat's pussy-footing an infamous symbol of malicious sneakiness; the bird, which is not as majestic and proud as the eagle, is a degenerate and emasculated version of the king of the skies; the cow, a cud-chewer, is a symbol of both the complacent, continual regurgitation and savoring of tradition, as well as a source of milk and nourishment, however poisoned.

> Therefore woman is not yet capable of friendship: she knows only love. Woman is not yet capable of friendship: women are still cats and birds. Or at best, cows.[51]

In addition, Nietzsche styles wisdom as a brave, mocking, violent "woman" who loves only warriors (41, 45); and later he makes the remark that it takes someone who is "man" enough to release the "woman" in "woman."

> There is little of man here; therefore their women strive to be mannish. For only he who is man enough will release the woman in woman. (169, 209–10)

Furthermore, modern "man's" ribs are impoverished because the Christian god stole one from his side to make a "little female."

> "Probably some god secretly took something from me while I slept. Verily, enough to make himself a *little female*. Strange is the poverty of my ribs." Thus have some men of today already spoken. (italics mine; 120–21, 151)[52]

---

51. Nietzsche, *Zarathustra*, trans. Kaufmann, 57; Nietzsche, *Zarathustra*, ed. Colli and Montinari, 69.

52. "*Und er sprach: 'es hat wohl da ein Gott, als ich schlief, mir heimlich Etwas entwendet? Wahrlich, genug, sich ein* Weibchen *daraus zu bilden! Wundersam ist die Armuth meiner Rippen!' also sprach schon mancher Gegenwartige*" (emphasis mine).

Chen may be used as an endearment; but it may also be used in a derogatory fashion. Nietzsche uses the words *klein* and *wenig*, and the suffix *chen* to signify "littleness," meager-ness, mean-ness, or deficiency. He implies, in keeping with his earlier characterizations of her, that "woman" is the supreme parasite, whose apparent richness is simply stolen from "man" by a "womanish" Christian god—a god of pity and hidden malice. Indeed, throughout *Zarathustra*, Nietzsche warns of modernity's continual shrinkage and miniaturization; the moderns are continually getting "smaller and smaller" (171, 212), making geniuses of "inverse cripples." These "inverse cripples" are enormous eyes, ears, mouths, or bellies attached to thin bodily stalks with tiny, envious faces: subhuman beings with too much of one thing and too little of everything else.

> "An ear! An ear as big as a man!" I looked still more closely—and indeed, underneath the ear something was moving, something pitifully small and wretched and slender. And, no doubt of it, the tremendous ear was attached to a small, thin stalk—but this stalk was a human being! If one used a magnifying glass one could even recognize a tiny envious face; also, that a bloated little soul was dangling from a stalk. (138, 174)

Yet the "littlest" of the "little" in this Lilliputian nightmare seems to be "woman."[53]

Thus, Nietzsche associates the "womanish" with the servile, the sham-wise, the world-weary, the priestly—and warns of the aspirations of the base to rule over the noble, dark aspirations that are soon to be impaled under the harsh and glaring light of the great noon, when the masks of goodness and mercy shall be revealed as such.[54] Nietzsche, the apocalyptic anti-Christian prophet, dreams of the great noon when the "few"/"masculine"/"great" may be separated from the "many"/"feminine"/"little."[55]

> The sham-wise, however—all the priests, the world-weary, and all those whose souls are womanish and servile—oh, what wicked tricks has their trickery always played on selfishness. . . .
> But for all these the day is now at hand, the change, the sword of judgement, *the great noon*: much shall be revealed there![56]

---

53. Nietzsche revalues "littleness" though he talks about his "smallest ears" compared with the "long ears" of the plebeian.

54. Nietzsche, *Zarathustra*, trans. Kaufmann, 191; Nietzsche, *Zarathustra*, ed. Colli and Montinari, 235.

55. This parallelism is faulty in some ways in that maternal power is something to be appropriated whereas the "many"/"little" have nothing to give. What again emerges is Nietzsche's ambiguous characterization of the "feminine" as simultaneously powerful and disempowered.

56. Nietzsche, *Zarathustra*, trans. Kaufmann, 191; Nietzsche, *Zarathustra*, ed. Colli and Montinari, 235–36.

The "feminine" also makes its appearance in *Zarathustra* in the "goodness" of "little girls," the superstitiousness of "old women," the ignorance of a "woman." By implying a contrast between the "goodness" of "little girls" and the "goodness" of the warrior (47, 55), Nietzsche emphasizes the "masculinity" and superiority of his new table of values over the old. By depicting "old women" as the keepers of the myth of the huge, fiery rock before the gate to the underworld, Nietzsche implies that these "old women" are vigorous worshippers of the decadent fire-hound. Zarathustra vanquishes the "old women's" fire-hound through his narration of the countermyth of a different fire-hound who inherits his laughter from the golden heart of the earth. This noble fire-hound does not spew forth ashes, smoke, and hot slime as the decadent fire-hound does; golden laughter flutters from him like colorful clouds (132, 166). Zarathustra's noble fire-hound is another figure for the *Übermensch*. It is significant that Zarathustra's myth-telling is enough to drive the decadent fire-hound, a mythic creature fearfully and vehemently worshipped by the "old women," back into his cave, his tail between his legs like a frightened dog, his head bowed. This mythic battle is couched in the form of a mythic narrative Zarathustra-Nietzsche passes on to his disciples, not only to explain his mysterious disappearance, but also to strengthen them.

Moving on to another portrait of the "feminine," Zarathustra speaks with irony of the "woman" who prevents her child from coming to him, particularly as the child wanted to come to him. She warns of Zarathustra's eyes, which could do harm to children by scorching them. It is important to listen to the Christian undercurrents and their anti-Christian subversion in this scene. Christ, the divine son conceived by the virgin, also loved children, and often welcomed them in his loneliness. Zarathustra, the phallic anti-Christian "mother," is thwarted from the company of a child by an inferior "mother"—who coughs in argument against the strong winds of Zarathustra's happiness (168, 208).

In many ways, these are all too familiar masks Nietzsche fashions of the ever-malleable "feminine": the tyrant-slave, the breeders of malice and superstition, the unenlightened, the "small." Yet in their baseness and whoredom, these "feminine" masks are the very means Nietzsche via Zarathustra employs in order to separate the "rare" from the "common," based on where the eros of his potential disciples is directed: upwards (in a manner that promotes life) or downwards (in a sickly and self-indulgent manner). Thus, Zarathustra advocates falling into the hands of a murderer rather than falling prey to the dreams of a "woman in heat." In so doing, Nietzsche, through Zarathustra, effectively castigates the only type of "ascent" that debased "men" have gloried in—lying with a "woman" (54, 65).

The prospect of lying with the "woman-whore" becomes the Apocalyptic test through which the eagles and serpents may be separated from the birds, poisonous adders, cats, and cows. Joining the ranks of the "rare" requires disdainfully repulsing decadent sensuality—that bitch that charmingly begs for a piece of spirit when she is denied a piece of meat, that bitch that leers enviously out of every pious Christian's eyes (54–55, 65–66). Becoming part of Nietzsche's army requires being able to learn the "right art of giving," which necessitates not giving to those obliging, lascivious, and forgetful creatures—"women" (270–71, 331–32).

Zarathustra also styles himself as Oedipus who has himself tied to a column in order to avoid peril. Yet Zarathustra's siren is a tarantula—a "female" demoness who demands Christian justice and punishment. And Zarathustra's revenge against the tarantula's bite is his refusal to dance the tarantella. His disciples must follow his example, and resist the poison of the deadly spider; in order to join his army, they must not dance her dance but his.

> Alas, then the tarantula, my old enemy, bit me. . . .
> Indeed, it has avenged itself. And alas, now it will make my soul, too, whirl with revenge. And to keep me from whirling, my friends, tie me tight to this column. Rather would I be a stylite even, than a whirl of revenge. (102, 127)

Zarathustra speaks positively of the "feminine" only when she comes in the guise of unbounded fertility or maternal fecundity as a trait men could adopt. Hence, he speaks with reverence for the wild, changeable, and eternally fruitful depths of life. Of his equally wild wisdom, Zarathustra speaks tenderly, calling her a lioness who has given birth to her beloved upon a lonely mountaintop, and who runs foolishly through a desert to seek a suitable bedding place for her youngest one. Her youngest one, the product of both wild wisdom and foolishness, is but another figure for Nietzsche's visions of the eternal return, and the coming of the *Übermensch*.

Thus, within Nietzsche's politico-mythic constellation, the "feminine," and neither "woman" nor woman, is necessary for both the destruction of the old order and the birthing of the new one—as whore, tarantula, and pregnant lioness.[57] The "feminine" is a principle of chaos—of destruction and creation—swallowing and spewing forth universes.

Concluding Remarks

Nietzsche's pre-Zarathustran texts are remarkable for the plurality of micro-narratives that teem and abound in an undulating sea of forces, each attempting to wash away the debris and pollution of modernity, Romanticism, and Christianity. Although numerous mythic personages, both "masculine" and "feminine"—such as Dionysus and

---

57. It is again of striking import, in terms of Nietzsche's attempts at remythologization, that lions were used by the Romans to kill and devour Christians.

Apollo, or Baubô and Medusa—populate his earlier works, most notably in *Birth* and *The Gay Science*,[58] these retain their essential nature as personified mythologems—fragments that make no sustained attempt to cohere together to form a larger narrative.

As I have shown, *Zarathustra*, on the other hand, is characterized by a more coherent master-myth. It is the grounding myth of a phallic "mother" who takes unto himself the heritage of Dionysus-Zeus-Apollo to create an *über*-figure who possesses both the bravery of the warrior and the fecundity of the pregnant "woman." Thus, son, father, and brother blur into each other, becoming a self-generating wheel. Zarathustra fervently urges his disciples to be mothers who suffer from birth pangs in order to become newly born children: "To be the child who is newly born, the creator must also want to be the mother who gives birth and the pangs of the birth-giver."[59]

Zarathustra is rife with images of pregnancy and motherhood. Zarathustra proclaims love of one's child and work as the only love that extends from the depths. Yet this love of "child" and work is not in keeping with the Christian notion of altruism. Love of one's "child" and work, for Zarathustra, is self-love, and the only genuine sign of "pregnancy."

> For from the depths one loves only one's child and work; and where there is great love of oneself it is the sign of pregnancy: thus I found it to be. (161, 200)

Pregnancy is one of the new virtues of Zarathustra's new beatitudes. Blessed are those who are heavy with lightning bolts that laugh and flash the eternal Yes, and whose dark bosoms drape the mountains like clouds waiting to kindle the light of the future, he proclaims, during one of his rapturous moments (228, 283). Zarathustra's greatest desire is to be ready and ripe—with clouds heavy with lightning and swelling milk udders—at the time of the great noon. This is the noon at which the shadowy masks of Christianity and Romanticism will be exposed to the harsh glare of light (214, 265).

It is true that there are indications that Nietzsche discriminates between a noble and an ignoble birth. For instance, Zarathustra cites the ill-matched as the most poisonous and vengeful, and appeals to his brothers that they may use the "garden of marriage" not simply to reproduce, but reproduce beyond themselves (211, 260).

In yet another section, Nietzsche, through Zarathustra, differentiates a genuine marriage by its reverence from a sham marriage that is characterized by mere contentment. However, whereas he remains vague as to the nature of a "marriage" involving reverential heterosexual partners, he paints a stark image of its opposite: how a hero in search of truths ironically conquered (or was conquered by) a little dressed up lie. In addition, the reverential marriage Zarathustra eventually most ardently advo-

---

58. *Fröhliche Wissenschaft* can also be translated as "Joyful Wisdom."
59. Nietzsche, *Zarathustra*, trans. Kaufmann, 87; Nietzsche, *Zarathustra*, ed. Colli and Montinari, 107.

cates seems expunged of any "feminine" participation. The hallmark of such a "marriage" is that his "brothers" are motivated purely by an intense longing for the *Übermensch*—analogous to the way an arrow, quivering in a bent bow, points at its mark.

> Thirst for the creator, an arrow and longing for the overman: tell me, my brother, is this your will to marriage? Holy I call such a will and such a marriage. (71, 88)

The phallicity of Zarathustra's motherhood becomes increasingly clear as his pronouncements regarding the patrilineal character of regeneration-redemption repeatedly recur. He enjoins his brother-disciples to conceive not of the Christian god, but of the *Übermensch*. As their best creation, the *Übermensch* becomes the means through which they may become like the self-generating serpent. Through the fathers and forefathers of the *Übermensch* (which Zarathustra's disciples would presumably sire), Zarathustra's "brothers" could re-create themselves in the image of their *über*-vision. Though they, like the prophet Zarathustra, Nietzsche's mythic alter ego, cannot enter the promised land, they may do so through their highly evolved spiritual progeny, and by that lineage, gain immortality (85–86, 105).

Finally, Zarathustra encourages his malodorous higher men to walk in the footprints of their fathers' virtue, as they may climb no higher than their fathers' will allows them (291, 359). These are subtle but unmistakable signs of how patrilineal descent is the crucial factor in determining who is to be saved from the holocaust of the self-destruction of modernity, and who is not.

Yet despite the fact that Nietzsche does outwardly advocate a clear delineation of sickness and health, and nobility and decadence, he does speak differently to different audiences, as the hunchback, listening to Zarathustra speaking with his disciples, observes (141–42, 178).

To the weak in age or virtue, Zarathustra, as Nietzsche's mouthpiece, employs a twofold rhetoric. On the one hand, he attempts to convince his possible followers that they are his genuine heirs and attempts to recruit them for his army of warrior-mothers, who prepare the way for the coming of the *Übermensch* in suffering and joy. One the other hand, he advocates that they allow themselves to be overthrown, in order that they may be reborn more vital and virtuous.

> [L]et yourselves be overthrown—so that you may return to life, and virtue may return to you. (132, 165)

The two methods of persuasion spontaneously fuse into each other, producing a powerful appeal for expenditure for the sake of a higher cause—the redemption of decadent modernity through the birthing of the *Übermenschen*.

Yet to his nobler audiences, Zarathustra speaks differently—as a poet, who knows and acknowledges that poets lie. To these Hyperboreans, he reveals that he is the physician attempting to heal himself. To their clear eyes, he unveils the swollen bite of the tarantula. And to their ears, he whispers the doctrine of the eternal Yes in the face of the eternal return, as echoed upon the lips of the ugliest man—the killer and awakener of the old god. By framing the utterance of *amor fati* twice—first, through Zarathustra's battle with the dwarf who encumbers his climb up a mountain, and second, through the ugliest man's praise of Zarathustra's healing influence—Nietzsche renders the message of the eternal Yes ambiguous, resounding differently in jackass and Hyperborean ears. To the jackass-eared, it is an exhortation to the untrammeled expression of the will to power; to the hyperborean-eared, it is a confession of residual unhealthiness. To the "long-eared," it is the assurance of the coming of the redeemers of modernity, the *Übermensch*. To the "short-eared," it is the posing of a tremulous anxiety over the outcome of doctrines that could be very easily deformed, resulting in the possible annihilation of modernity.

> "My friends, all of you," said the ugliest man, "What do you think? For the sake of this day, I am for the first time satisfied that I have lived my whole life." . . .
> "Was *that* life?" I want to say to death. "Well then! Once more!" (317–18, 392–93)

The ugliest man's utterance marks the culmination and end of the ass festival—a celebration of which only convalescents have need. As Zarathustra's son, the ugliest man is the mouth through which Zarathustra, as Nietzsche's literary creation who embodies the type of heroism Nietzsche advocated, reveals his hidden resentment, in keeping with his pronouncement that the son is the unveiled secret of the father (100, 125). What occurs at this point seems to be a complex ventriloquistic maneuver: Nietzsche puts Zarathustra's words into the mouth of the ugliest man, the most monstrous "higher man"—antithesis of the "Overman." In so doing, Nietzsche ironizes Zarathustra's dream of birthing the *Übermensch*, by making his doctrine of *amor fati* distorted through its utterance by the ugliest man. Through the inverted cripples—those monstrous higher men—Nietzsche himself has birthed through the teachings of Zarathustra, who may be seen to function as his mythic alter ego, Nietzsche confesses his dis-ease: his lust for and envy of the maternal womb. Through their decadent dances and songs, Nietzsche unveils the resentment that ails him unto death—his inability to birth beyond himself, his inability to birth himself in the figure of the *Übermensch*.

4

The Post-Zarathustran Phase: Emasculate Conception

> *Zarathustra* is the work of a regenerate, of someone who already had one foot in the tomb and then finds himself cured of a long illness. Thus he does not owe the passion of the "Yes" par excellence to his mother but to his father. . . . In the chapter consecrated to *Zarathustra* he asserts that in order to understand this ideal he needs a single but essential thing: *triumphant health*.
>
> —Sarah Kofman, *"A Fantastical Genealogy"*

> German-ness for Nietzsche is tied up with indigestion, constipation, corruption, and complete insensitivity to culture. It is all that he experiences as abject, all that reminds him of the "baseness" of his own maternal heritage.
>
> —Jean Graybeal, *"Ecce Homo"*

Introductory Remarks

Sarah Kofman's "A Fantastical Genealogy: Nietzsche's Family Romance" makes use of a recently released section of *Ecce Homo*'s "Why I am So Wise" in the latest Colli and Montinari edition to show how Nietzsche's venomous rejection of his mother and sister points toward a hidden, incestuous desire for them (35–52). For Kofman, what is most indicative of Nietzsche's incestuous love for his sister and mother (using a Freudian symptomatology) are two things: first, the vehement extent to which he attempts to dismiss them as *canaille* (rabble, plebeian) and as constituting a *Höllenmaschine* (hell-machines), and second, glimmers of an admission that he has never met any woman, except for his sister, with whom he thought himself completely compatible.

> Nietzsche sees himself, basically, as the victim of a plot hatched by the two women [his mother and sister] against him. . . . In their "venomous" aspect

they are fearsome and dangerous; as "vermin" they arouse repugnance and horror above all.

This "horror" is so "unspeakable" (*unsagliches Grauen*) that it can only be the flip side of a more or less forbidden love, for which it functions as a counter-investment. (43)

Yet Nietzsche's primordial ambivalences toward his mother and sister gain even more striking prominence against the backdrop of his unambiguous elevation of his father to the spheres of the celestial and divine. Nietzsche's extreme adoration of his father is possible only in so far as he kills off his father in order to inherit from him the superhuman Yes to life (37–38). It is only by emphasizing his father's early demise that Nietzsche is able to paint a portrait of himself as the continuance of this all-too-brief spark of nobility, and to trace his spontaneous ability to commune with the lofty and noble to a purely paternal lineage.

Kofman's central thesis is that Nietzsche constructs for himself "an entirely different kinship, the fiction of a fantasmatic genealogy, a true family romance in the quasi-Freudian sense of the term, since it is always a question, for Nietzsche as for the child making up a romance, of creating a more 'noble' and illustrious family than the one from which he derives physiologically" (36). Thus Nietzsche kills off his father to become his true heir. As Kofman puts it: "The original Zarathustra could transform himself into the new one—into Nietzsche's Zarathustra, the child of love, the child of sin, who weighs on his conscience because, far from paying his debt to his father through him, he denies the father at the very moment when he seems to be filled with gratitude toward him" (38). He seduces/reduces his mother and sister to vermin, and apotropaically raises the head of Dionysus against their poison. He then creates for himself a new family with Cosima and Richard Wagner as his surrogate parents, with Napoleon, Caesar, and Alexander as his ancestors.

What Kofman ultimately shows is that Nietzsche, in *Ecce Homo*, attempts a remythologization of his genealogy—a political aim that congeals already in his earlier text, *Zarathustra*. As I have shown in Chapter 3, in my reading of *Zarathustra*, Nietzsche styles himself as the Romantic heir to the Dionysus-Zeus-Apollo mythologems and as phallic mother-saviour of modernity in order to birth the vision of the coming of the *Übermensch* alongside its dark siblings—the eternal return and the monstrous higher men. In this chapter, the questions I aim to answer are the following: (1) In what ways does Nietzsche's remythologizing[1] of the problem of modernity, and how he sees his role in relation to this problem, differ with respect to his earlier attempts at creating a noble genealogy for himself? (2) How do figures of the "femi-

---

1. By "remythologizing," I mean the modification or revision/re-creation of mythic accounts.

nine"/"woman" arise in relation to this remythologizing? (3) What political philosophies and accounts of modernity arise from my reading of Nietzsche's re-genealogizing of himself and the future of modernity?

What I aim to show is that Nietzsche's later attempts at remythologizing move along four axes:

1. an increasingly pessimistic view concerning the possibility of modernity's recuperation from its sickness;
2. an increasingly overt trend toward misogyny, with a flattening out of Nietzsche's earlier ambivalences toward the "feminine" to become a vituperative spitting out of any "female" inheritance as well as an unrelenting condemnation of the rise of the "borification of woman"—"feminism";
3. an increasing attempt to make his remythologization (i.e., a revision of past mythic accounts) appear as a demythologization (i.e., an apparent negation of any sort of appeal to mythic foundations)—in other words, an increasing tendency to blur the boundaries between the esoteric and the exoteric, in line with the probable project of intensifying modernity's death throes;
4. a movement from a political agenda of catalyzing modernity's self-destruction to focusing purely on Nietzsche's own self-preservation.

Post-Zarathustran Remythologization

Unlike Nietzsche's pre-Zarathustran texts, where a rich panoply of mythic figures abound, Nietzsche's post-Zarathustran texts employ decreasing numbers of overtly (Greek) mythic figures. This is in line with Nietzsche's attempt to appear to demythologize his remythologizing of himself, thus dangerously blurring the line separating the esoteric (the language/code of the "noble"/"few") from the exoteric (the language/code of the "plebeian"/"many") in the hope of escalating modernity's fatal descent into decadence. It is through this exoterization of the esoteric that Nietzsche hopes to claim for himself the title of hammer of modernity, dynamite of the twilight of the idols. For it is precisely by blurring these boundaries, i.e., making the exoteric incitement to and enhancement of (self–)destruction easy for the plebeian and crass to hear, that Nietzsche hopes to effect modernity's deeper descent into corruption. Along a parallel track to this increasing exoterization is a heightened misogyny directed more specifically at "woman" rather than the "feminine," and a masked gravitation toward an advocacy of the utter destruction of modernity, culminating in Nietzsche's attempt to preserve himself.

Beyond Sphinx and Circe: Master versus Slave Moralities

In *Beyond Good and Evil,* Nietzsche makes use of a few mythic figures to set up what he now views as the problem of modernity. For Nietzsche, this problem is that "truth," supposing she were a "woman," has so far proven to be aloof to the advances of philosophers and has emerged, unwon, from the clumsy and inexpert courtship of these "lovers of truth." The will to truth that drives philosophers and scientists to foolhardy adventures is as a Sphinx that refuses to answer questions. The problem of the value of truth results in a dizzying tag game of questions and answers. Based upon my reading of the text, it appears that it is the will to truth, rather than Truth as such, that Nietzsche seems to put at issue here insofar as the will to truth cannot justify itself as a moral imperative. In his account, the will to truth tempts to "many a venture,[2] that famous truthfulness of which all philosophers so far have spoken of with respect—what questions has *this will to truth* not laid before us" [italics mine].[3] This Sphinx, the will to truth, remains wrapped in the cryptic language of riddles; in order to speak her language, one must learn to ask questions such as, "Why not a will to untruth and uncertainty, or even ignorance?" (9,9). In other words, why not replace a will unto sickness with a will unto health?

Philosophers, babbling like children or old women (98, 108), sacrifice themselves for this Virgin-Sphinx, and the result, for Nietzsche, is the loss of a philosophical sense of humor, and the unfolding of a satyr play—assuming that philosophy, as a tragedy, is finally moving into its long-drawn yet inevitable ending (37, 39).

The degradation of the age is evident, for example, in the skeptic's worship of the Sphinx and Circe. By consoling himself with the reasoning that since uncertainty, that Sphinx-Circe, is not devoid of charm, and that Circe, too, is a philosopher, the skeptic reveals that he is plagued by that most spiritual expression of nervous exhaustion and sickliness. The goddesses to whom he pays homage infuse his blood with a poison that makes him sick of his will to life. This disease spreads unevenly and in many forms. Its most lethal hold is upon those niches where "culture" has established its bastion the longest and "barbarism" has been most effectively held at bay. "Objectivity" and "being scientific" are but dressed up camouflages for this paralysis and self-hatred of the will to life (130, 142–43). Christianity is another such disguise, with its elevation of the "effeminate" virtues of charity and pity. Indeed, in a man devoted to the Nietzschean task of "knowledge" rather than "truth," pity is ridicu-

---

2. This is a possible allusion to Oedipus and the sirens.
3. Friedrich Nietzsche, *Beyond Good and Evil: Prelude to a Philosophy of the Future,* trans. Walter Kaufmann (New York: Vintage Book, 1989), 9. Friedrich Nietzsche, *Jenseits von Gut und Böse: Einer Philosophie der Zukunft,* in *Nietzsche Werke: Kritische Gesamtausgabe,* ed. Giorgio Colli and Mazzino Montinari (Berlin: de Gruyter, 1968), 9.

lous, hanging like delicate hands from the hulking frame of a man-eating Cyclops (92, 102). Nietzsche attempts a "psychology" of his age by examining the deities it worships. That it venerates goddesses—and goddesses who are "poisonous" rather than healthy, who "effeminize" rather than "masculinize"—seems to him the ultimate testimony to modernity's desperate state.

Despite the deepening pessimism in Nietzsche's tone, there are senses in which at this point, the destructive pole of his politics interacts with a more creative pole. Given the decadence of the age, Nietzsche advocates the rise of an Oedipus figure—one who possesses within himself the profound enjoyment of masks alongside the will to a severe discipline and cruelty in his spirit. Such an Oedipus, for Nietzsche, will be capable of "translating man back into nature" (161, 175). Hardened in the discipline of science, he, like Oedipus, sees beyond the numerous vain and enthusiastic interpretations spawned by decadents, and, like Odysseus, is deaf to the pipings of old metaphysical bird catchers, who seek to seduce him with their praise of his lofty origins. Again, Nietzsche strategically elides the figures of Oedipus and Odysseus to form a supermale entity, the antidote to the poisonous Sphinx-Circe pair.

It is interesting that Nietzsche does not address how Odysseus, until Hermes comes to rescue him, happily stays Circe's prisoner; nor does Nietzsche address how Oedipus, although he is able to answer the Sphinx's riddle and break her spell over the city, takes a step further into the involuntary embrace of his destruction. This is another example of how Nietzsche rewrites Greek mythology to create super-"masculine" entities devoid of their weaknesses in the original myths.

> [W]ith intrepid Oedipus eyes and sealed Odysseus ears, deaf to the siren songs of old metaphysical bird catchers who have been piping at him too long, "You are more, you are higher, you are of a different origin! (161, 175)

That this composite Oedipus-Odysseus is both blind and deaf seems, at one level, an ironic portrayal. Yet Oedipus, precisely when he is torn away from his Jocasta, his mother-wife, through her suicide, and has torn out his own eyes, sees more clearly than when he had his physical sight. Odysseus, with his ears sealed, is protected from the poison of the siren's song. Again, the recurrent pattern seems to be on remythologizing the figures of Oedipus and Odysseus in a manner that glorifies "masculine" traits in isolation from "feminine" traits.

Such an Oedipus-Odysseus blurs into the figure of the worshipper of Dionysus—this god who masters, rather than adores, his Ariadne. She, emblematic of the all too human, becomes the clay upon which Dionysus may mold a stronger (*stärker*), more evil (*böser*), more profound (*tiefer*), and more beautiful (*schöner*) race (236, 249). Nietzsche overtly aspires to be this Oedipus-Dionysus worshipper, but in order to make such a claim, he must authorize the validity of his heritage by appropriating unto himself the grand position of father of the philosophers of the future. This is one of the clearest indications of his gravitation toward an increasingly misogynistic politics as opposed to an ambivalent one, characteristic of his pre-Zarathustran and Zarathustran phases.

Nietzsche styles himself as the father of the philosophers of the future. For Nietzsche, these philosophers set themselves against the softhearted and "effeminate" tastes of democracy (134–35, 146). Such philosophers not only smile scornfully but also experience a genuine nausea over everything that is "enthusiastic," "idealistic," "feminine," and "hermaphroditic"—offspring of that all too widespread decadence that infects everything modern (134–35, 147).

They, according to Nietzsche, must resist the prevalent herd morality (*Heerdenthier-Moral*) (115, 126), a tranquilization through the illusion of green pastures. As (at)tempters and experimenters (*Versucher*) (52, 55), his followers should be as eternal children-sages, to whom the concepts of "truth," "God," and "sin" are but as a child's pain appear to an old man; world-affirming souls who embrace the eternal return and shout insatiably, "*da capo!*" again and again (68, 73).

Hardness and severity are the chief traits of these philosophers of the future, as they must be unyielding in their reestablishment of master morality over the decadent mushrooming of slave morality. As commanders and legislators, they must hammer out values for the future, resisting the tendency to become a mere repository of past values—knowing, creating, and legislating the primordial will to power (136, 149).

They must also be super-"masculine" types, distinctly different from their effeminate counterparts, such as the "levelers" (*Nivellirer*) (54, 57), those pseudo-free spirits who strive for herdish security and comfort; the *homines religiosi*, the highest type among the "burnt children" (*verbrannten Kinder*) (71, 76) who enjoy life only by maliciously falsifying its image; and the objective men/ideal scholars whose only forte is the "feminine" task of mirroring, of spreading themselves out tenderly for fear that light footsteps and the quick passage of spiritlike beings may escape them (126–27, 139).

These philosophers of the future belong to the race of geniuses, who either beget or give birth, unlike the modern scholar or average man, who is like an "old maid" (*alten Jungfern*) (125, 137)—infertile, ignoble, ignorant of the two most important functions of man: begetting and birthing.[4] Another "effeminate" type of man, for Nietzsche, is the sociologist who is prey to the deadly hatred of suffering, and the "almost feminine inability to remain spectators" (116, 127) to someone's suffering—i.e., he does not possess the "masculine" hardness not to react.

---

4. Again, Nietzsche returns to the project whose outlines we see in *Zarathustra*—the creation of a super-"masculine mother" who possesses the "masculine" virtues of the warrior and the fertility of the mother.

In addition, Nietzsche takes great pains to show that the "masculine" pity (*Mitleid*) of these philosophers of the future is different from the "unmanly"/"feminine" (231, 246) pity (*Mitleid*) of the teeming Christian masses. Christian "pity" (*Mitleid*) is built upon the sick dream of abolishing suffering; the "pity" (*Mitleid*) of the philosopher of the future desires to raise modernity's level of suffering, so as to abolish all that is weak, fragile, and effeminate that a modern, democratic, and Christian culture preserves.[5]

> Well-being as you understand it—that is no goal, that seems to us an *end*, a state that soon makes man ridiculous and contemptible that makes his destruction desirable. (153, 167)

For Nietzsche, the appearance of feminized men[6] as well as masculinized[7] women[8] is symptomatic of the generalized corruption of the era. In Nietzsche's view, a crucial factor in this deepening decadence is the hybridization caused by modernity's embrace of democratic and Christian principles. The German soul, with its riddles and contradictions, is the epitome of this hybridization; its "profundity" is simply a result of dyspepsia, of a labored and sluggish digestion—because of its omnivorous diet as well as its unaristocratic genealogy (179, 194). Modernity's hybrids are weak human beings, whose only desire appears to be the cessation of the war that they are (111, 122)—hence, their desperate search for various forms of narcotization.

Yet the pervasiveness of disease, for Nietzsche, is an ambiguous environment. For on one hand, it does cultivate an environment hostile to the "higher types"/"philosophers of the future" and confers a greater survival advantage to the rabble or base herd animals. Yet on the other hand, these same cruel mechanisms may yield higher and higher types, whose physiological makeup becomes increasingly similar, thus generating a nomadic type—a type possessing the vigorous art and power of adaptation. The conditions that encourage the leveling of man into the useful herd animal are likely to produce exceptionally dangerous and attractive types. The environment that

---

5. Nietzsche uses the same term, *Mitleid*, to speak of both the "masculine" and "feminine" types of pity. For example, exclaiming about the "unmanly" type of pity that is praised in Christian and "womanish" circles, Nietzsche writes: "*Die Unmannlichkeit dessen, was in solchen 'Mitleid' getauft wird, springt, wie ich meine, immer zuerst in die Augen*" (Nietzsche, *Jenseits von Gut unde Böse*, 246).

6. Examples of "feminized men" include the leveler, the religious man, the objective man, and the scholar/average man.

7. Hence, at this point in Nietzsche's politics, women are condemned whether they are "masculine" or "feminine."

8. An example of a "masculinized woman" is Madame de Stael, who wrote *De l'Allemagne* (Paris, 1810), and described Germans as gentle, good-hearted, weak willed, and poetic. Nietzsche, *Beyond Good and Evil*, 133; Nietzsche, *Jenseits Gut und Böse*, 146.

nurtures cows is a prime ground for the cultivation of tyrants as well. Tyranny, for Nietzsche, is meant principally in the spiritual (and "masculine") sense. Such a tyrant can emerge if a strong human being is subjected to training cleansed of Christian, democratic, and "feminine" prejudices, and if he possesses the tremendous multifariousness of practice, art, and mask.

> The very same conditions that will on the average lead to the leveling and mediocritization of man—to a useful, industrious, handy, multi-purpose herd-animal—are likely in the highest degree to give birth to exceptional human beings of the most dangerous and attractive quality. (176, 191)

Nietzsche, at this point, seems to admit that given the modern condition of hybridization, there is no purely "noble" being free from the taint of plebeianism or vulgarity. Yet he resurrects his dream of the *Übermensch* via the conjecture that if a being, born with powerful and contradictory drives, were also to gain the subtle art of waging war against himself, then higher types may be produced. The philosopher of the future may be born if and only if a being resists the herd's imperative to happiness as tranquilization. Such a being, tortured by the conflicting demands of his hybridized state due to the loss of the narcotizing influence of herd mentality, may transcend the pangs of his hybridization, and thus enable the emergence of a purer, less infected race, as seen in the examples of Caesar, Alcibiades, and Leonardo da Vinci (102, 112).

Yet the ultimate task of the father of the philosophers of the future, despite his hybridized state, is to inscribe unambiguous demarcation lines separating "master morality" (the moral code of the philosophers of the future) from "slave morality" (the moral code of the herd-animal, the Christian, the "feminine"). The strictness of the demarcation is crucial because given modernity's allowance of hybridization, "master morality" (*Herren-Moral*) and "slave morality" (*Sklaven-Moral*) may coexist, not only within a society or culture, but even in an individual, leading to his contradictory impulses. The resultant attempts at mediation or interpenetration render "master morality" in danger of suffering from various degrees of impurity. In order to salvage whatever remnants of purity there are to melt down for the philosophers of the future, one must be as exacting as possible in judging the value of these alloys of varying contamination.

For Nietzsche, "master morality," prior to its defeat by "slave morality," legislated the "good" as opposed to the "bad" based on exalted, noble states of the soul as distinguished from the contemptible, ignoble states of the soul. In addition, such a "noble" set of moral categories flowed principally from an assessment of the type of human being, and only secondarily, the act itself. Hence, within the boundaries of "master morality," the genuinely "noble" helps another not from Christian pity (*Mitleid*), but from an urge born of an excess of power (*Überfluss von Macht*) (205, 219–20). Finally, "noble"/"master" morality values both friendship and the art of being/having enemies; it is a morality that values the capacity for and duty of long gratitude and long revenge—a "manly" morality in which the warlike and playful virtues are celebrated (204–6, 219–21).

In contrast, "slave morality" is essentially a morality of utility, and bases its judgements less on an assessment of the type of soul a human being has, than upon the effects of her actions [Note: I use "her" because for Nietzsche, slave morality is "feminized," and at this point, I am still tracing out Nietzsche's position.] "Slave morality" seeks to reverse and usurp the categories of "master morality." Replacing the category of "bad" with "evil," slaves adhere to the belief that it is those who inspire fear who are "evil," whereas, for the master, it is those who inspire fear who are "good" and those who cannot inspire fear who are "contemptible"/"bad." "Slave morality" replaces the master-virtues of friendship and war with love as passion, and substitutes enthusiastic reverence and devotion for aristocratic thinking and evaluating (207–8, 221–22).

For Nietzsche, the repository of all that is plebeian—i.e., the being whose blood is greatly steeped in the slave's craftiness—is "woman." With the rise of the democratic order, spawned by the intermarriage between masters and slaves, "woman" is the vessel within which the residue of the slave's vanity is most concentrated. It is she, bearer of that most deadly atavism, vanity, of which the philosopher of the future must be most wary. "It is 'the slave' in the blood of the vain person, a residue of the slave's craftiness—and how much 'slave' is still residual in woman, for example!" (209, 224). This same trend toward a decreasing use of mythic allusions and a sharp rise in violence and misogyny is evident in *Twilight of the Idols*.

Twilight of the Descending Lines of Life: Hammering Cornarism

There are even fewer mythic figures populating Nietzsche's *Twilight of the Idols* than *Beyond Good and Evil*. The only mythic figures developed to some extent are Apollo and Dionysus. Nietzsche returns to a discussion of these two figures in relation to the topic of what makes art what it is, particularly within the context of the twilight of the idols. For Nietzsche, frenzy (*Rausch*)—i.e., being swelled, taut, overloaded with strength—is indispensable to art. Art, as an expression of the will to power, involves the power of transformation: of violation so as to make things mirror the creator's power. The essential aspect of frenzy (from feasts, contests, cruelty, destruction, meteorological influences, narcotics, the will) is that it gives the artist a feeling of increased strength and fullness.[9]

Nietzsche revises his thesis slightly from *Birth* by stating that both Apollo and Dionysus experience frenzy, as opposed to the earlier book where frenzy seems an attribute exclusive to Dionysus. Apollinian frenzy, in this new version, entails an excitement of the eye that gains the power of vision.[10] Dionysian frenzy excites and enhances the whole system, replacing every form of mimicry and acting, such as representation, imitation, transfiguration, and transformation, with metamorphosis, thus enabling Dionysus entry into any skin, any affect (68, 111).

Again, an examination of the principal mythic figures that Nietzsche uses provides us with a general idea of how the various elements fit into Nietzsche's developing attempts at a reconfiguration of the problem of modernity. Within the context of an era so steeped in decadence, where art is misunderstood as either *l'art pour l'art* ("art for art's sake") or the anti-artistry of Christianity, Nietzsche feels it essential to emphasize the notion of art as an act of transformation and enrichment through over-fullness or excess. Nietzsche rejects the Christian as well as the Darwinian perspectives because they view the world from impoverished lenses, and transform everything into thin and consumptive versions of their robust selves. Darwin, for Nietzsche, was wrong in that he viewed life as a struggle for survival/existence rather than as a struggle for power.[11] Nietzsche reasons that starvation and impoverishment are unusual circumstances, and occur only when life is diseased. Otherwise, richness, profusion, and absurd squandering are what generally characterize life (71, 114).

The implication of Nietzsche's critique, even if it is flawed from a Darwinian standpoint, is that it is precisely only within such a mortally sick era that Darwinian and Christian ideas could not only take root, but also bear their deformed and poisonous fruit. The stage is set for Nietzsche's philosophizing with a hammer—or of separating the healthy from the sick.

One of Nietzsche's principal configurations, the tropes of health and sickness, surfaces with great vividness in *Twilight of the Idols*. One of the principal tests he uses to sift away the robust from the diseased is to assess whether the individual is a repre-

---

9. Friedrich Nietzsche, *Twilight of the Idols*, trans. Anthony Ludovici (New York: Gordon Press, 1974), 66; Friedrich Nietzsche, *Götzen-Dämmerung*, in *Nietzsche Werke: Kritische Gesamtausgabe*, ed. Giorgio Colli and Mazzino Montinari (Berlin: de Gruyter, 1969), 110.

10. It is possible that Nietzsche, here, is again revising his mythology. Both Oedipus's eyes and Odysseus's ears have to be saved for this developing super-"masculine" entity.

11. Naturally, a Darwinian could defend his paradigm against Nietzsche's attack by stating that the framework of a struggle for existence does entail the notion of squandering. The natural selection of the fittest is a ruthless affair, entailing the perishing of all save those who happen to have the characteristics that best enable/equip them to adapt and survive. Part of the problem is that Nietzsche interprets Darwin's framework to mean the desperate survival of the individual, whereas Darwin is more concerned with the survival of the species, despite its prodigal expenditure of individuals.

sentative of an "ascending" or "descending line of life" (85, 125). As an ascending line of life, an individual is exceptional, and every care must be taken to ensure not only his preservation, but also his well-being, as he carries within himself the whole history of humanity, and life itself ascends through him. An individual of the descending line of life, for Nietzsche, is of little value, and his parasitism upon the ascending line of life should be kept to a minimum, as he brings nothing but decay, degeneration, and sickness wherever he goes (85, 126).

Among the descending lines of life, Nietzsche counts Socrates, Christianity, and "woman." Among the ascending lines of life, he enumerates the figures of Apollo and Dionysus, which I have just discussed, and the "law of Manu," which I will reserve for discussion later in the chapter, where a detailed analysis of what it means to "ascend" in keeping with this religious-political Indian caste system is crucial.

Nietzsche indicts Socrates on several charges as representing a descending line of life: (1) that Socrates, through his final words (which revolved around the topic of offering a cock to Asclepius), revealed that he had long thought life was simply a protracted period of sickness, and that the cock was an offering of thanks to the god for having finally relieved the sufferer from this dread disease (9, 61); (2) that the ugliness of Socrates, particularly within strictly Greek norms, was sufficient proof of Socrates' declining development, or of his inescapable plebeian origins (10–11, 62–63) (Nietzsche points out that this very same indictment was leveled against Socrates by the physiognomist who read every conceivable crime in the face of Socrates, and that Socrates himself calmly verified the validity of that reading); (3) that Socrates' decadence is attested to not only by the wantonness and anarchy of his instincts, but also by the hypertrophy of his logical faculty and his characteristic sickly sarcasm—a strange condition that spawned the anti-Greek equation of reason with virtue and happiness (11, 63).

Yet if Socrates was, particularly within Greek society, a monstrous buffoon, plebeian and ignoble through and through, Nietzsche asks, how did he get himself taken seriously? How did Socrates successfully negotiate the vanquishing of nobility via the elevation of dialectics—the tool of those who are incapable of simply commanding (noble/ascending), and need to give reasons in order to be obeyed (plebeian/descending)?

Nietzsche answers these questions by showing that Socrates was a source of both fascination and repulsion to the ancient Greeks. Repulsion, on the grounds of his ugliness,[12] his commonness, and his sickness. Fascination, on the grounds that he

12. Socrates was also probably viewed as a political threat of sorts by the authorities then but Nietzsche does not mention this, as he is more concerned with extending, as far as is possible, his metaphor of "sickness" (using the classical belief in the correspondence of states within the physical and spiritual) to explain how it is that someone like Socrates could both fascinate and repulse ancient Athens, and thus, come to possess the influence and power he exerted, even in his decadence and eventual death.

created a new erotic *agon* (dialectics, particularly with young men), and that he appeared to be in complete control over his extreme instincts. Socrates saw through the noble facade of his declining age, and realized that an all-pervasive decadence was seeping through ancient Athens. At a time when the instincts had grown extreme and tyrannical, and their competition to rule each other was at its highest pitch, the crafty Socrates, according to Nietzsche, realized that a countertyrant was necessary. Socrates effectively crowned that countertyrant: reason. The essential choice, given this context of pollution and decay, seemed to be between perishing in the anarchy of the instincts or becoming absurdly rational. Socrates realized this, and knew that his era longed for his (apparent) cure (13–15, 65–66).

For Nietzsche, Socrates became influential because of his awe-inspiring ugliness; to an age that knew itself to be dying and that was desperately in search for a cure, he appeared as a physician and saviour. He, as the extreme case of apparently self-contained decadence, seemed to hold the answer as to how one could control the diseased anarchy of the instincts and survive. Yet Socrates, according to Nietzsche, knew that there was only one genuine physician and one real cure to the illness that plagued him and his fellow Athenians. That physician/saviour/cure could only be death (16, 67)—hence, Socrates' grateful thoughts on offering a cock to Asclepius during the twilight moments of his life. Yet his cure was also his most effective revenge against his era, successfully sowing the seeds of Christian morality: fear, guilt, and the equation of happiness, virtue, and reason (16, 67).

Despite the death of Socrates, Nietzsche claims that Socrates' descending lineage lives on in Christianity. Christian ideals, with their fables of an "other" and "better" world, continue Socrates' revenge against life through their presumptuous and pessimistic judgement concerning this-worldly life. Nietzsche, still functioning as a psychologist, claims that judgements of value concerning life have value only as symptoms of the health of the culture that makes such pronouncements—because the value of life cannot be estimated (10, 62). Only the dead—or those with a foot beyond life (which Nietzsche later claims to be true of himself in *Ecce Homo*)—can possibly make any sort of pronouncement regarding life.

Christianity, with its modernized Platonic tyranny over the instincts, suffers from the same degenerate hatred against life. Its practice and cure against the anarchy of its instincts is castratism; its "highest" forms are either the eunuch-saint (30, 79), or the moralist bigot and prig who paints his own portrait upon the wall and exclaims, "Ecce homo!" (31, 81). Christianity's recourse to radical means—to the attempted extirpation of a craving—reveals its degeneracy, its inability to impose moderation upon itself. Its deadly hostility to sensuality is reflective of its need for asceticism as the spiritualization of this hatred of life. "Only degenerates find radical methods indispensable: weakness of will, or more strictly speaking, the inability not to react to a stimulus, is in itself simply another form of degeneracy" (27, 77).

Aligned with Christian morality and religion is a psychology of error based upon a confusion of cause and effect. Philosophers (as well as Christians) tend to confuse "first" with "last" concepts (19, 70)—hence, they consecrate the "original sin of reason, the immortal unreason" (34, 83): virtue is the cause of happiness. For Nietzsche, a healthy/ascending line of life would read it the other way—that happiness is the cause of virtue. Similarly, philosophers/Christians state that indulgence in license and luxury results in physiological decay; for Nietzsche, this decadent view mistakes the real cause for the effect. He thus holds that a healthy/ascending morality would see that physiological degeneration precedes license and luxury. It is only when an era is undergoing its death throes that it is most extravagant; or to put it slightly differently, an exhausted nature needs greater and greater stimulation in order to maintain its semblance of life.

> The Church and morality say: "A race, a people perish through vice and luxury." My reinstated reason says: when a people are going to the dogs, when they are degenerating physiologically, vice and luxury . . . are bound to result. (34, 83)

Nietzsche calls this decadent confusion of cause with effect "cornarism" after the (in)famous Cornaro who wrote a book recommending a meager diet as the cause of his long and happy life. In reality, according to the dietitian-psychologist Nietzsche, Cornaro mistook effect for cause. Cornaro's diet was the effect of his slow metabolism, rather than the necessary cause of his long life. To have attempted to eat more than he did, given his metabolism, would have been suicidal (33, 82).

Similar to the modern's/Christian's "cornarism" is his erection of the structures of "will" (*Wille*), "consciousness" (*Bewusstseins*), "spirit" (*Geistes*) and "ego" (*des "Subjekts"*) (36, 84) in the name of finding the cause of an action/event. This illusion/error, instead of confusing cause for effect, simply attributes causation to a false cause. The modern wishes to believe that in willing, one causes. Yet the "will," to Nietzsche, does not explain anything; it simply accompanies events. Sometimes, it is even absent from the flow of these events. Consciousness, motive, spirit, ego are but fables, fictions, plays on words, articles of faith, projections, all-too-human creations (37, 85).

The third error/illusion the modern philosopher/Christian suffers from is the error of imaginary causes. In brief, this means that one mistakes the representations that were produced by a certain state to be the causes of that state. These representations—initially produced because of the desire to explain away the unfamiliar, and therefore, to hold at bay the fear spawned by contact with the unfamiliar—eventually harden to habitual categories. Hence, a banker explains things in terms of his business; a Christian, in terms of sin; a girl, in terms of love. For Nietzsche, the whole realm of morality and religion lies precisely under this error of imaginary causes. They constitute "explanations" of disagreeable feelings—because of evil spirits, acts of sin, or as punishment or payment for something one should have refrained from doing. They also function as "explanations" of agreeable feelings—trust in God, a "good conscience," or faith, hope, charity, and all the Christian virtues. All of these "causes," for Nietzsche, are simply imagined and constitute a subset of the first error or fallacy. One is in a state of hope precisely because of the basic physiological feeling of being strong and rich; one trusts in God precisely because such feelings of fullness and strength bestow one with a sense of rest, and not the other way around (40–41, 88–89).

The fourth illusion that Nietzsche diagnoses as a symptom of the decadence of this modern/Christian/Platonic descending line of life is the error of "free will" (*freien Willen*) (41, 89). For Nietzsche, the doctrine of the free will was invented specifically because the priests wanted to create the right to punish (for God, of course). By inventing free will, and its necessary Christian companion, responsibility, punishment became a right to be exercised by the priests. "Men" were considered "free" so they could be held responsible for their actions, and pronounced "guilty" by the priests, who were often at the head of ancient tribes. Thus "free will" was but another snare used to capture and tame man, producing "improved" and sickly beasts.

Yet the lowest point of descent for this Platonic-Christian line of life is its intersection with "woman"/"female." The "true world" becomes a fable as it gets increasingly "subtle, insidious, incomprehensible—it becomes female, it becomes Christian [*sie wird feiner, verfänglicher, unfasslicher,—sie wird Weib, sie wird christlich*]" (24, 74). Punning from the Edenic story in Genesis, Nietzsche states that "woman" is a creation of "man" from the rib of his ideal—his God (2, 55). Making the connections between "woman" and "sin" even stronger, Nietzsche claims that the "perfect woman" (*volkommene Weib*) (3–4, 56) perpetrates "literature" the way she does a small crime: in passing, yet making certain that it is noticed by someone. "Literature," like a petty crime, becomes an ornament of vanity through the machinations of Nietzsche's "perfect" and Christian "woman."

Nietzsche's tirade against "woman" is vociferous and vicious in *Twilight of the Idols*. It is as if "woman" is a particularly insidious idol who deserves an exceptional number of whacks with his hammer. Hence, he writes that "woman" is mistakenly considered "profound"/"deep" (*tief*) because "man" seldom manages to fathom her depths. On the contrary, Nietzsche claims, she possesses no depth at all and she is not even deserving of the description "shallow" (*flach*) (5, 57). There seems to be no hint of even a ceasefire in the Nietzschean battle of the sexes, for Nietzsche writes that if "woman" has "manly virtues" (*männliche Tugenden*) (5, 57), then "one" (i.e., "man") feels like running away; if, on the other hand, she is devoid of any such "manly" virtues, then she herself runs away.[13]

Furthermore, Sainte-Beuve, a writer in whom Nietzsche finds nothing of value, is deep down a "female," endowed with a "female"'s lust for revenge (*Weibs-Rachsucht*), and a "female"'s sensuality (*Weibs-Sinnlichkeit*) (61, 106). *De Imitatione Christi*, one of the books Nietzsche claims not to be able to hold in hand without undergoing a violent physiological reaction, reeks of the perfume of the "Eternal-Feminine" (*Ewig-Weiblichen*) and thus is a book palatable only to Frenchmen (because of their effeminate tastes, as evidenced in the preponderance of "the woman" and the amatory in French dialectics) (78–79, 120) or to Wagnerians (who are mostly women) (62, 107). Finally, George Sand—for Nietzsche, that female descendant of decadent Rousseau—has the charm of a "female"'s coquetry with "male" attributes, with the manners of naughty boys—a "self-satisfied cow" (64, 108) with something German (in the bad sense) in her blood.

Save for one salutary reference to a "feminine" figure, Circe—Nietzsche quips that a genuine artist needs only *panem et Circen* (bread and Circe, as art/sorceress) instead of *panem et circenses* (bread and circuses)—Nietzsche's writings concerning "woman" or the "feminine" are vitriolic. It is she, it seems, who lies at the bottom of the innermost circle of this descending line of life. As such, it is she whom he must attack without compromise, using his most poisonous weapons. Very little, if any, is seen of his earlier rapid shifts, from the extremely positive to the extremely negative, in his ruminations on *Weib* or *weiblich*.

How the Convalescent Was Always Healthy

Nietzsche's attempts at an apparent demythologization of his writings through a remythologization of his own genealogy reaches its clearest and yet most refractory formulation in *Ecce Homo*. The title, *Ecce Homo*, itself spawns numerous interpretations as it is used by Nietzsche to describe Napoleon's surprised and admiring reaction to his encounter with a real German man (in stark contrast to Madame de Stael's descriptions of them) in *Beyond Good and Evil*; yet Nietzsche also uses the same expression, "*Ecce Homo*," as the exclamatory flourish of the smug and self-satisfied moralist bigot and prig who paints his own portrait on the wall for all to see in *Twilight of the Idols*.

---

13. This again illustrates the quintessential double bind for women in Nietzsche's post-Zarathustran depiction of them.

Walter Kaufmann clearly interprets Nietzsche's use of "*Ecce Homo*" to signify a naked statement of self-identification. Hence, in his introductory exegesis of why Nietzsche chose to use this title, he writes: "*Here* is a man! Here is a new, a different image of humanity: not a saint or holy man any more than a traditional sage, but a *modern* version."[14] In addition, Kaufmann interprets "*Ich bin der und der*"[15] as "I am such and such a person," an apparent preparation for a unidimensional way of reading the last line of the first section of the preface: "Above all, do not mistake me for someone else."[16]

Yet "*Ich bin der und der*" may be interpreted contrapositively as "I am he and he," implying either a fragmentation or dissimulation, or both in the speaker—a method of writing that echoes the satyric author who has made the mask his signature. Similarly, "*Ecce Homo*" is uttered by Pilate: the same man, who, in Nietzsche's eyes, is the only hero of the New Testament for having asked, "What is truth?"[17] These seem to be clues that something appears to be amiss with a linear way of interpreting Nietzsche, especially when he claims to have taken off his masks.

The counterposition of these two methods of interpretation illustrate how the esoteric and exoteric modes of discourse blend together into a complex polyphony, or at times, even a cacophonous babble in Nietzsche's last completed book prior to the onset of his madness.

In addition to its strikingly condensed, enigmatic, and aphoristic style, *Ecce Homo*, even more than Nietzsche's earlier books, resists being packaged into sections. No sustained discussion of (Greek) mythic deities, save for a few references to Dionysus, occurs here. Nietzsche's main myth here, how a convalescent eventually regains health, is intimately tied up with his principal political tactic: that of creating a "fantastic" (in the Freudian and Kofmanian senses) family genealogy to prove that from the very start, he was, at bottom, healthy and that is why he is able to regain his health completely, despite his long and painful convalescence.

To begin, Nietzsche claims that his "good fortune" lies in his "fatality"—i.e., expressed in the form of a riddle, his "wisdom" lies in his dual descent from his father, through whom he is dead, and from his mother, through whom he continues to live and grow old. While it appears that there is some salutary value in Nietzsche's

---

14. Walter Kaufmann, introduction to *Ecce Homo*, 204.
15. Nietzsche, *Ecce Homo*, in *Nietzsche Werke*, 255.
16. Nietzsche, *Ecce Homo*, 217, 204.
17. It is possible to interpret this reference to Pilate as signaling Nietzsche's taking over the place of the crucified Christ. In the same way Pilate utters the fatal words, "What is truth?" as he allows Christ's torture to commence, Nietzsche must be led to his descent in order to ascend in the form of the *Übermensch*. The issue then becomes one of reconciling how Nietzsche could conceive of himself as radically anti-Christian and yet ironically reify the same pattern of sacrifice and resurrection that Nietzsche claims is spurred by the resentment from which he attempts to separate himself.

attributing his continuing survival to his mother, it is important to notice that Nietzsche superlatively valorizes his paternal heritage over his maternal one, which he speaks of with great hostility and repugnance. His father occupies the "highest rung" on the ladder of life; his mother, the "lowest." He dares to call himself a "beginning" by virtue of his paternal lineage; and he admits to his decadence by tracing his maternal lineage.

> I am, to express it in the form of a riddle, already dead as my father, while as my mother I am still living and becoming old. This dual descent,[18] as it were, both from the highest and the lowest rung of the ladder of life, at the same time a *decadent* and a *beginning* . . .[19]

Furthermore, in the Colli-Montinari 1969 edition (as opposed to the standard version), which makes use of material Nietzsche sent to his publisher only a few days before his collapse into madness,[20] it is significant that Nietzsche takes great pains to attribute the superhuman capacity for saying Yes to life to his father, and that he attempts to weave a narrative of his noble and pure polish descent (*Ich bin ein polnischer Edelmann pur sang*)[21] from his paternal side. His being a "pole" is rhetorically important to him, for he wishes to establish that he is not of the realm of the "very German" (which he attributes to his mother and sister). Yet of his mother and sister, he says simply that they embody the incalculable meanness/commonness of instincts; they are *canaille* (rabble/riffraff) and constitute a *Höllenmaschine* (hell-machine). It is a great blasphemy to his (and his father's) divine nature that his mother and sister are related to them. And the most profound and horrifying objection to the eternal return, at this point, is neither the eternal recurrence of either the smallest man or the last men, but the eternal recurrence of his mother and sister (266).

Instead of following this route to the Freudian discovery of a secret incestuous desire for his mother and sister that Nietzsche appears to suffer from, as Kofman does, I want to trace how this elevation of the paternal to the divine and ethereal, and this reduction of mother (and sister) to the most debased of the plebeian, contours

---

18. "Descent" involves a play on meaning here. It could mean "inheritance," which is a comparatively neutral term. But if it means going "down," as opposed to "ascent," it may be read as a reluctant admission that Nietzsche sees himself as a decadent trying to heal himself.

19. Nietzsche, *Ecce Homo*, 223; Nietzsche, *Ecce Homo*, in *Nietzsche Werke*, 262.

20. For a concise comparison of how the "standard" and this long-suppressed document (i.e., Colli-Montinari edition) differ, refer to Jean Graybeal, "*Ecce Homo*: Abjection and 'The Feminine,'" in *Language*, 77–93.

21. Nietzsche, *Ecce Homo*, in *Nietzsche Werke*, 266. I am relying principally upon the Colli-Montinari edition for this section as Kaufmann's translation is based upon a different version of *Ecce Homo*.

Nietzsche's political philosophy—particularly in terms of one of his master tropes, the opposition between sickness and health.

It is via this twofold heritage, of being dead and alive, that Nietzsche claims for himself the title of teacher par excellence of the revaluation of values. He, knowing what perspectives from above and from below look like, is the best authority on how a frog perspective may be transformed into a hyperborean/*Übermensch*ian view. Because he has an acutely developed sense of smell for the signs of ascent and decline, he is in the best position to describe how a long suffering convalescent can again emerge into health. He can legitimately claim that because he knows how, only he can effectively reverse perspectives, and begin a revaluation of values.[22]

Having thus fortified his credentials as physician-patient par excellence, Nietzsche then goes on to describe how he, an admitted decadent, has somehow completely healed himself. His answer is simple—and not altogether different from a version of the law of Manu, biographically applied. The secret of recovery is that of being healthy, at bottom. Only those who have been noble (i.e., "strong" or "vital," hence, able to resist illness or decadence) from the very start may be healed from the poisoned stings of modern, Christian, "feminine," and Romantic *ressentiment*. Those who have been born sick or are typically diseased can never gain health—they are simply incurable and inhuman disasters (223, 264).

His recovery, by his account, is practically magical, almost like a conversion experience. One day, suddenly, all of his capacities leaped forth in their scintillating perfection, and he found himself grateful for all that his life had ever been, with no desire that anything be changed. He found himself, he claims, as he had always been—(apparently) with never having had a desire for honors, women, and money (255, 293).

In keeping with this thoroughgoing thankfulness for his life—his unqualified Yes to what his life had been—Nietzsche expresses his gratefulness for the nutrition, place, climate, and recreation that have nurtured and molded his nobility (255, 293). He proclaims his freedom from any sort of pathological trait—so free in fact, that he claims that even when he suffered from severe illness, he never became pathological (*krankhaft*) (257, 294). His formula for human greatness, for being noble enough eternally to embrace life, or for remaining essentially healthy amidst an age of decadence, is *amor fati* (love of fate).

> My formula for greatness in a human being is *amor fati*: that one wants nothing to be different, not forward, not backward, not in all eternity. Not merely bear what is necessary, still less conceal it—all idealism is mendaciousness in the face of what is necessary—but *love* it. (258, 295)

---

22. Nietzsche, *Ecce Homo*, 223; Nietzsche, *Ecce Homo*, in *Nietzsche Werke*, 264.

In keeping with this general desire to prove how he suffers from no pathologies, Nietzsche revises his relationship with Richard Wagner. Unlike his earlier diatribes, Nietzsche here honors Wagner with the title "great benefactor of my life" (*nenne ich Wagner den grossen Wohlthäter meines Lebens*)[23] and admits that they have profoundly suffered from each other—even more than "men" of this century are capable of suffering from each other, he claims. He does not disabuse Wagner of his earlier epithets of "poison," "hashish," and "romantic," but he does claim that Wagner, even as a toxin, was the cure par excellence for everything "German" (249, 287) (in the same way his mother and sister are "something very German"). Wagner's unforgivable sin is that he, who could glimpse the heights, condescended to the Germans—he became *reichsdeutsch* (249, 287), the highest form of rabble, lover of that decadent and corrupting hag, Germany.

Similarly, he lavishes praise upon Cosima Wagner, under the banner of the profundity of French (i.e., non-German) culture. To Cosima, he showers the title, "the first voice in matters of taste that I have ever heard," (243, 283) and then moves on to detail a host of other exalted/instructive members of French culture, such as Pascal, Montaigne, Moliere, Corneille, and Racine (which again reverses many of his vitriolic remarks regarding French culture and French authors in his earlier books).

Nietzsche is anxious to make such claims to fortify further his pronouncements concerning his freedom from sickness, which he identifies as a type of *ressentiment*. The danger of being afflicted with this dread disease is that it burns up one's resources, and exacerbates its painful symptoms, producing a rapid consumption of nervous energy, and a pathological increase of harmful excretions, such as that of the gall bladder into the stomach (230, 270), the physiologist-psychologist, Nietzsche, claims. Recasting the law of Manu into yet another form, Nietzsche states that *ressentiment* is particularly harmful to base natures, yet it constitutes their most natural inclination; like fireflies to fire, they gravitate spontaneously toward it and are consumed by it (230–31, 270–71).

Nietzsche attempts to give yet another account of how a sick person may cure himself. However, that cure, which he calls "Russian fatalism" (*russischen Fatalismus*) emerges as simply another term for *amor fati*: that ability to accept oneself as if one were fated, not wishing oneself (or anything) different (231, 271).

Yet lest this "Russian fatalism" be mistaken for Christian piety, Nietzsche vigorously returns to his theme of reawakening the "manly" virtues of war, and of valuing one's enemies as well as being capable of being a worthy enemy. He differentiates aggressive pathos from vengefulness and rancor. Aggressive pathos is an attribute of the "strong"; vengefulness and rancor is a mark of the "weak," especially "woman."

---

23. Nietzsche, *Ecce Homo*, 250; Nietzsche, *Ecce Homo*, in *Nietzsche Werke*, 288.

The aggressive pathos belongs just as necessarily to strength as vengefulness and rancor belong to weakness. Woman, for example, is vengeful: that is due to her weakness, as much as is her susceptibility to the distress of others. (232, 272)

Nietzsche's misogyny comes full circle: his hatred of the maternal can be redeemed as a nonpathology only through his elevation of Cosima to the heavenly sphere of mythic mother, replacing his own biological mother. Once he has accomplished that, he can again channel his energies toward the destruction of the "effeminate" (dis)order and ultimately, as I shall show in the next section, preserve himself from this destruction.

Political Agenda: From Destruction to Self-Preservation

Nietzsche's political agenda, in his post-Zarathustran writings, rapidly progresses from advocating a thorough demolition of modernity to a preoccupation simply with saving himself. To accomplish his (d)evolving political aims, Nietzsche appropriates various roles for himself. Among the masks he dons are the new psychologist (*Beyond Good and Evil*), the physician of modernity (*Twilight of the Idols*), and the self-preserving sick noble (*Ecce Homo*).

The New Psychologist: Ushering In the Extramoral Period

In order to bolster further his claim in *Beyond Good and Evil* of being the father of the philosophers of the future, dismantlers of modern morality, Nietzsche resorts to the tools of the "new psychologist" (*neue Psycholog*).[24] To do this, Nietzsche attempts an account of the genesis of modern morality from its premoral origins, and looking forward to its extramoral futurity. He claims that his project is the symptomatology of intention—the means through which a genealogy of the rise of morality may be excavated, as well as the mechanism through which an extramoral period may be ushered in. For Nietzsche, the premoral period was an intention-free period; within it, an action was judged according to its retroactive success or failure. During the moral period, a stage modernity is still mired in, "intention" became the key to the value of an action: it became the all-exhaustive origin and history of an action. Contrastively,

---

24. Nietzsche, *Beyond Good and Evil*, 21; Nietzsche, *Jenseits von Gut und Böse*, 21.

Nietzsche aims to usher in an extramoral period—a period characterized by the suspicion of "intention" or the "conscious" and gravitates more toward interpreting the imperceptible signs of the "unintentional" as more genuinely revelatory. Within such a schema, "intention" is but a symptom and sign—a "skin" that reveals and conceals—that must be interpreted alongside a panoply of other symptoms and signs. Isolated and elevated to the only important category in judging an action, "intention" is meaningless (44, 47).

For Nietzsche, fear is the mother of morals. "Love of neighbor" is a conventional, arbitrary illusion that springs from fear of one's neighbor. Certain strong and dangerous drives, which were formerly crucial to advancing into new territory, become more and more dangerous as society becomes increasingly entrenched. The (d)evolution of herd morality slowly arises as drives that threaten the security of the community are branded as immoral or abandoned to slander (113–14, 124–25).

Moralities are artifices that exude the nook odor of old nostrums and the wisdom of "old women" (*Altweiber-Weisheit*) (109, 120). Moral judgements and valuations constitute the revenge of the spiritually inferior—the slaves—against their spiritual superiors—the masters. Morality is malice spiritualized, wielded as a weapon by those who have not been favored by nature, who reward themselves with the honey of revenge. "Moral judgements and condemnations constitute the favorite revenge of the spiritually limited against those less limited . . . malice spiritualized" (147, 160). For Nietzsche, the best example of this most vicious and spiritual revenge is the Christian Church's proclamation of the sainthood of the "female" (64, 69). By this, he means that the triumph of Christian values is the slave revolt of the spiritually inferior, the rabble, the common. For instance, Madame de Guyon's *unio mystica et physica*, for Nietzsche, reeks of womanly tenderness and lust; it is often a disguise for both the hysteria of the "old maid" and the pubescent immaturity of a "young girl" or "youth" (64, 69).

In order to reveal this slave/"feminine" revolt for what it is, and perhaps hasten its demise, Nietzsche takes upon himself the task of stating "a few truths about 'woman as such'"—with the ironic proviso that his pronouncements be understood as *his* truths. "After this abundant civility that I have just evidenced in relation to myself I shall perhaps be permitted more readily to state a few truths about 'woman as such'— assuming that it is now known from the outset how very much these are after all only—*my* truths" (162, 176).

Undoubtedly, Nietzsche's nuancing of his pronouncements regarding "women" as simply *his* truths is important to keep in mind. It is reflective of how, at this point, he still retains a certain intellectual distance from the increasingly powerful grip of misogyny upon him and his developing political philosophy. Yet this ironic distance does not exculpate Nietzsche from his venting his bile against "woman"'s supposedly catlike and therefore, unpeaceful nature, despite "man"'s illusions on her seeming peacefulness (87, 96); neither does it negate the fact that Nietzsche thinks "women" with scholarly ambitions are sexually dysfunctional (89, 98), and that "woman"'s genius in finery is due to her secondary role in relation to "man" (89, 98). For Nietzsche, in matters of love and revenge, "woman"'s nature is more barbarous than "man"'s (88, 97); in anything else but these matters, "woman"'s gaming performance is simply mediocre (115, 93). It is at this point that Nietzsche's blurring/collapsing of the spheres of the "feminine" (which he had earlier treated in a more ambivalent fashion) with the "female" (which he tends to speak of derogatorily) leads to an all-out attack on "women" and the "feminine"—the scapegoats upon whom the sterility of modernity and Nietzsche's own impotence must be dumped.

Continuing in the same vein, politico-culturally, that "woman" desires to become self-reliant, in Nietzsche's view, is one of the worst developments of the "general uglification of Europe" (*der allgemeinen Verhässlichung Europa's*) (162, 176). Unlike earlier signs of the generalized decadence of modernity, which Nietzsche takes pains to identify as merely symptoms, rather than causes, Nietzsche leaves it ambiguous as to whether or not "woman"'s desire for enlightenment about herself and what she wants from "man" are simply manifestations of this generalized condition of decadence or are actually symptoms that can also be causes: a symptom that serves to intensify this crippling dis-ease.

In his element, Nietzsche warms up to his political project of harnessing the "feminine"/ "woman" (the earlier distinction between these two essentially collapses at this point). Not only does "woman" have so much reason for shame—with her inescapable pedantry, superficiality, schoolmarmishness, petty presumption, and licentiousness. More importantly, "she" is about to lose her principal virtue or great art, the lie, as she also loses her "natural" fear of "man." Nietzsche claims that it is only this art and instinct—to mere appearance and beauty—that "man" reveres in "woman." Nietzsche goes as far as proclaiming that in reality, "woman" does not even want "truth" as it is repugnant and alien to her very nature (163, 177).

Using the authoritative formula, "we men" (*Wir Männer*), Nietzsche appeals to "woman" that she not go on compromising herself through her quest of enlightenment. In one of the few passages where he joins forces with the Church, Nietzsche claims to echo "man's thoughtfulness and consideration for woman" (*Manns-Fürsorge und Schonung des Weibes*) (164, 178) in the aphorism: *mulier taceat in ecclesia* ("woman" should be silent in Church). He quotes Napoleon's *mulier teceat in politicis!* ("woman" should be silent when it comes to politics) to the all too eloquent Madame de Stael in preparation for his own *mulier taceat de mulier* ("woman" should be silent about "woman") (164, 178).

As "psychologist" of "modernity," "morality," "truth," and particularly of "woman," Nietzsche diagnoses the fundamental problem of "man" and "woman" to lie in their abysmal and primordial antagonism (166, 181); thus, he claims that to aspire toward an equality of rights between these deadly enemies is a sign of shallowness. The increasing trend toward "feminism"—which involves teaching slaves that they may be equal to their masters—is both a sign and cause of modernity's increasing decadence, with its blurring of the "noble" order of rank. For Nietzsche, modernity has lost sight of two important Greek insights: first, the necessity for slaves in order to support a "higher" civilization (169, 183); and second, the originally Oriental wisdom regarding the treatment of "woman"—that she should be treated severely and misogynistically. Particularly concerning the gradual development of a Greco-Asian antiwoman attitude, Nietzsche praises the "necessary" (*nothwendig*), "logical" (*logisch*), and "humane" (*menschlich-wünschbar*) character of pondering upon this insight concerning how "woman" has been historically treated by "virile" and thriving societies (166, 181).

As "psychologist" of "woman" and "modernity," Nietzsche apocalyptically paints a dismal picture of the crumbling retrogression of woman alongside the deepening sickness of modernity. He proclaims the coming of a new age, not without resonances with two of his earlier nightmarish Zarathustran visions, the coming of the monstrously subhuman "last men" or the increasing dimunition of the moderns. This time, he proclaims the slow dawning of the "borification of woman" (*die Verlangweiligung des Weibes*)—the modern murder of this unicorn, this "horned animal" (*das Thier mit Hörnern*), which has both attracted and inspired fear in European "man."

Nietzsche's overtly forming pessimism regarding "woman" forms a striking parallel to his deepening pessimism regarding the purity of the categories of "few"/"rare" and the "many"/"common" within the "hybridized" modern polis. There are, admittedly, still glimmers of optimism that slightly offset his predominantly negative image of "woman" (such as his ironic and playful praise of Madame de Lambert's prudent motherly advice to her son that he should not allow himself anything but follies) (165, 179) as well as his pessimism regarding modernity (such as his recuperation of the dream of the *Übermensch* via the vision of a self-mastering hybrid inflicted with a contradictory nature). Yet Nietzsche's pronouncements, regarding the future of modernity, as well as "woman," are markedly less ambivalent, more bleak, more dis-eased compared with those in his earlier works. This increasing pessimism, regarding modernity and the "feminine"/"female" reaches its starkest formulation in *Twilight of the Idols.*

The New Physician: Exploding Modernity

The opposition between the "ascending" and the "descending" lines of life that Nietzsche brings up in *Twilight of the Idols,* in many senses, is reminiscent of other dichotomies Nietzsche has already brought up earlier, such as the healthy-sick, few-many, rare-common, herd-animal-*Übermensch* polarities. Yet what is noticeably new is the ruthless and radical procedure he now espouses regarding the preferential treatment of the "ascending" over the "descending" lines of life. Nietzsche puts on the mask of the physician of modernity in order to prescribe (and authorize) one of his most dangerous medicinal (and medi-cynical) experiments. He contends that it is the physician's new responsibility, and in the interests of the ascending life, to crush the descending lines of life—to combat them in the areas of the right to procreate, the right to be born, the right to live. Political power must be wielded to exterminate all the weakness, poison, and decadence that modernity, with its soft and "womanly" ideals, has preserved.[25] All vermin, cows, and parasites must be ruthlessly killed for the sake of the ascending line of life.[26]

In line with this more overtly ruthless tactic of separating the healthy from the sick, Nietzsche valorizes the "law of Manu." This law, built from within the rigid caste system of India, was geared toward breeding four particular races at the same time—the priestly type, the warrior type, the type geared toward agriculture and trade, and a race of servants, the Sudras. Yet these four races or types were bred only against their opposite, the unbred man, the Chandala. In order to protect these four bred races from that outside their boundaries, the Chandala had to be made sick and weak. Hence, the only nourishment s/he was allowed were garlic and onions, as holy scripture forbade giving them grain, or fruit with grain, or even water or fire. This same law/religious mandate held that the water they need should not be taken from rivers, wells, or ponds but from passages leading to swamps and holes made for the footsteps of animals. Yet even this filthy and murky water was not to be used to wash their laundry or to bathe, as it was considered already an act of "grace" (*Gnaden*) that they were even allowed to have water to quench their thirst. Finally, no Sudra woman, even if she belonged to the lowest caste, could assist a Chandala woman in childbirth; even Chandala women were not supposed to assist each other during this moment of great vulnerability (45–48, 94–95).

Nietzsche does not flinch in detailing the many horrors of this effective method of policing the "unbred" man—the spate of murderous epidemics and horrifying venereal disease that led to the formulation to yet another religio-political norm: "the law of the knife" (*das Gesetz des Messers*) (47, 95). Thereafter, male Chandala children were circumcised; similarly, the internal labia were excised from female Chandala children. Manu's pronouncements regarding the Chandala justify this inhuman

---

25. Nietzsche, at this point, sounds strikingly like Hitler, or if one were using a strictly historical timeline, vice versa.
26. Nietzsche, *Twilight of the Idols*, 88; Nietzsche, *Götzen-Dämmerung*, 128.

treatment, condemning them as the heinous fruit of adultery, incest, and crime—hence, the legitimacy of prohibiting them from enjoying the same rights as the "virtuous," the people of "race." Even the right to write with the right hand, as well as to write from left to right, were claimed exclusively for those "bred," as opposed to the "unbred" (47, 95).

Deliberately setting up the law of Manu as the counterpoint to the New Testament, which he dismisses as foul-smelling, Nietzsche lavishes praise upon Manu's treatment of the Chandala, through which glimpses of "Aryan humanity, quite pure, quite primordial" (47, 95) may be seen. As opposed to the democratic and Christian propagation of hybridization, the law of Manu harshly displays that the notion of "pure blood" is the opposite of an innocuous concept (47, 95).

Yet Nietzsche claims that the Chandala hatred against the "humaneness" of the law of Manu has become more subtle, transforming itself into a religion and even genius. Christianity, for Nietzsche, is this successful Chandala revolt—the counterrevolution against breeding, against race, against privilege: the perfect anti-Aryan religion. The religion of "love" based upon the undying hatred that consumes the downtrodden, the wretched, the poor, the base, the plebeian. "Christianity is the transvaluation of all Aryan values, the triumph of Chandala values . . . the immortal revenge of the Chandala as the religion of love" (48, 95–96). For Nietzsche, freedom from the sickness of an age that produces weaker and softer "men"—"men" more tender and more easily hurt (90-91, 130)—necessitates the return to valuing indifference as a strength and to cultivating the necessary "pathos of distance" to keep the healthy from being infected by the sick (90, 131).

Furthermore, in Nietzsche's view, modern institutions are no longer of any good because as the instincts of the moderns have become base or "feminine"/ "womanly," so have their institutions become steeped in decadence. What is necessary is a rejuvenation of the "manly" instincts, which delight in war and victory, and tyrannize other, more "womanly" instincts, such as that of pleasure. The warrior, whom the moderns need to resurrect, according to the physician-educator Nietzsche, spits upon the "well-being" dreamed of by the "effeminate" crowd of shopkeepers, Christians, cows, "females," Englishmen, and other democrats (95, 133–34). Such effeminate creatures have forgotten that the basis of a "higher" culture is that of having a Chandala race—a class of slaves. It is thus one of the follies of modernity that it is eradicating its means to a higher culture; it is educating its women (99, 137).

Nietzsche, at this point, seems to employ a twofold rhetoric in order to achieve his political aim: the salvation of the endangered ascending lines of life from the teeming descending lines of life. First, he speaks of the great need for "educators" (*Erzieher*)—teachers who possess the elevated skills of seeing, thinking, and writing, as opposed to the "brutal training" (*brutale Abrichtung*) that transforms young men into usable (*nutzbar*) and abusable (*ausnutzbar*) government servants (55, 101). Such educators (and Nietzsche implicitly claims that he is of that type) are different from the "higher wet nurses" (*höhere Ammen*) (55, 101) modern Germany inflicts upon its youth insofar as these educators themselves have noble origins, and as such, can teach these noble skills to equally noble youth, who have not yet been corrupted to the core by the decadence around them. These three skills—of seeing (of accustoming the eye to calmness and postponing judgement until each individual case has been grasped from all sides) (55, 102), of thinking (as a technique, a will to mastery, a dance) (57, 103), and of writing (dancing with one's feet as well as with concepts) (58, 104)—are essential to cultivating and preserving a "noble" culture. Some glimmer of hope for the partial salvation of modernity seems to lie in Nietzsche's optimism that both "noble" educators and students may yet be found in the sewer called modernity. Yet it is equally important to note that even in this apparent ray of light, Manu's inexorable law holds. Only those who are naturally "strong" and "noble" may have this education. "All great and beautiful things cannot be a common possession: *pulchrum est paucorum hominum*" (56, 101).[27]

Second, he employs a darker and more destructive battle cry. He claims that politicians and preachers of virtue have treated "morality" as a bed of Procrustes, upon which the hapless victim may be stretched or hacked up in order to make him/her fit perfectly into their aims. Hence, such politicians and preachers have dreamed nostalgically, like crabs, of "walking backwards"—of returning to the garden of Eden. Nietzsche's uncompromising condemnation is evident in the tone he adopts against such a doctrine, which is reminiscent of his vision of a return to the golden age in *Birth*. No even partially noble being is free to be a crab, he argues. The most such a noble being can do within such a sick era is to go forward, deeper and deeper into the heart of decadence, or dam it up in order to effect a more vehement and sudden explosion. It is this self-destructive project that he calls modern "progress."

> But not everyone can be a crab. It cannot be helped: we must go forward,—that is to say step by step further and further into decadence.... We can hinder this development and by doing so dam up and accumulate degeneration itself and render it more convulsive, more *volcanic*: we cannot do more. (101, 138)

There is an increasingly Apocalyptic character in Nietzsche's proclamations regarding the fate or future of modernity. Genuinely great men or geniuses, for Nietzsche, stand in relation to the age in which they live in the same way that the strong do in relation to the weak. They constitute the finale to an age. Geniuses or great men are

---

27. The English translation precedes the Latin aphorism above.

born only when for a very long time, a tremendous force has been dammed up, and tensely coiled, awaits expenditure. Thus, such men are necessarily squanderers—explosives capable of wreaking tremendous upheavals. Yet the danger with the emergence of such geniuses (and he implicitly appropriates for himself that title) is that after their expenditure, there is nothing save an exhausted wasteland. A period of barrenness and sterility follows in the wake of the roaring overflow of their banks: "The danger which great men and great ages represent, is simply extraordinary; every kind of exhaustion and of sterility follows in their wake" (103, 139–40).

In such geniuses, the instinct of self-preservation is weakened; self-expenditure is their all-consuming passion. Yet they are often misunderstood by their time, and they bear the pallid and fatal Chandala mark upon their foreheads, not because others brand them with this, but because they feel themselves so utterly alienated from the values of their age (105–6, 141).

Nietzsche's ambivalences toward being misunderstood point to themselves in *Twilight of the Idols*. This is particularly evident in Nietzsche's remarks concerning his style (which he aligns with the "ascending" styles of Thucydides and Macchiavelli) (114, 150) as opposed to the decadent/"descending" style of Plato, whose hybridized, boring, moralistic, and pre-existently Christian style of writing reveals its plebeian roots (114, 149). The style he claims for himself (in line with the other "ascendants") both facilitates comprehension yet provokes contradiction (22, 72). In section 24 of "Skirmishes in a War with the Age," Nietzsche states that the tragic artist must communicate his confrontation with the fearful and questionable if he is truly an artist or genius of communication; and yet in section 26, only two sections later, he claims that those who communicate themselves no longer sufficiently esteem themselves, as language seems to have been invented only for the average, medium, and communicable (81, 122).

In addition, the deliberately refractory character of Nietzsche's style speaks for itself in other sections. For instance, in section 1 of "Things I Owe to the Ancients," Nietzsche attributes his "noble" way of writing to its Roman roots, involving a minimum in the extent and number of signs, and yet a maximum in energy produced or the effect of these signs. Anything other than this discriminately chosen mosaic of words is mere garrulity and therefore plebeian for Nietzsche (113, 149). His self-proclaimed ambition as a writer is to state in ten sentences what everyone else says in a book, in addition to what everyone else does not say in a book (111, 147).

Yet the obvious problem that rises from this more compressed, more refractory, radically ambivalent style of writing is that the messages meant for the ears of the ass, and those meant for the ears of the hyperborean, meld into a more confusing cacophony, particularly for the plebeian ass. Nietzsche seems deliberately to cultivate this style in order to intensify his political aims that one can tease out as early as

Zarathustra, as I have shown in Chapter 3. One of these aims lies in making his less than noble followers believe themselves to be his true followers, enlist them in the project of squandering themselves for the vision of the coming of the *Übermenschen*, and thus, catalyzing the general explosion of modernity. Nietzsche's rhetoric concerning the need to breed a race of nobles, now built upon the ancient example of the law of Manu, is frighteningly more ruthless than his earlier discourses. His political aim of crushing all the poisonous, the Christian, the "female" is thoroughgoing.

His other aim lies in revealing the great dangers that lurk in the wake of his risk-filled and "noble" task—a message that only those with the ears of the hyperborean can hear. Hence, he warns of the destruction wreaked by the expenditure of the genius or "ascending line of life." He foretells an age of barrenness and exhaustion, not entirely dissimilar to his description of the coming of the last men in *Zarathustra*. Most importantly, he admits that a philosopher may be silent out of the nobility of soul; or contradict himself out of "love;" or may lie out of politeness precisely when he possesses a certain (dangerous) knowledge (106, 142).

Nietzsche, at this point, seems convinced that his message to the ass-eared will be the more widely heard, spurring the intensification of his injunctions toward violence, toward an increased corruption of the age, toward either a head-on collision with, or damming up of the explosive forces of, modernity. Again, glimmers of how the "feminine" figures in relation to his predominantly more destructive and pessimistic philosophy are revelatory. Nietzsche ends section 19 of "Skirmishes in a War with the Age" with a dialogue between Dionysus and Ariadne. In this conversation, Ariadne asks her divine philosopher-lover why he pulls her by her ears. He counters that he finds a kind of humor in her ears, and wonders why they are not longer.

> "O Dionysus, thou divine one, why dost thou pull mine ears?" Ariadne asks on one occasion of her philosophic lover, during one of those famous conversations on the island of Naxos. "I find a sort of humour in thine ears, Ariadne: why are they not a little longer?" (75, 117–18)

Longer ears refer back to the ears of the ass. Ariadne becomes the embodiment of the crass and plebeian audience that Dionysus-Nietzsche targets. The humor and laughter of this later Nietzsche bears less a resemblance to the golden laughter he dreamed of in *Birth* than a type of laughter that resonates with and resounds his hammer blows.

Even the more positive strands of his later political philosophy, involving the breeding of noble types, are woven from a preeminently misogynistic model. In addition to the example of the Indian law of Manu, Nietzsche refers back to ancient Greece, where the men, according to Cicero, were superior to women even in beauty

(143, 107). Such an "ideal" society, which actively persuades the body and breeds the soul along noble lines, builds its notions of beauty and genius upon the exclusion and suppression of its "other"—"woman." As we have also seen in *Beyond Good and Evil*, as Nietzsche's pessimism concerning the possible salvation of modernity deepens, his images of "woman" (*Weib*) and the "feminine" (*weiblich*) grow increasingly misogynist.

The Self-Preserving Sick Noble

Nietzsche continues the political distinction between the "long-eared" (plebeian) and "short-eared" (noble) in *Ecce Homo*. It is at this point that the intersection between his attitude toward the "feminine" as well as the "female" and his mythic politics comes into view. He claims to have the "smallest ears"[28] (*die kleinsten Ohren*)[29]—an obvious counterpoint to Ariadne's/the ass's ears. It is by virtue of having these smallest ears that he claims that he is of immense interest to "women." In addition, as part of his self-appropriated Dionysian dowry, he claims to be the "first psychologist of the eternally feminine" (*der erste Psycholog des Ewig-Weiblichen*) (266, 303). As such, he supposedly possesses the keenest insight into the essential nature of "women"— who all, according to his all too legitimate position, love him, save for those "abortive"/"emacipated" ones. Nietzsche's pronouncements regarding the nature of "woman" and how she fits into the polis are, by now, hardly surprising.

For Nietzsche, "woman" is more evil and more clever than "man" and yet "good nature" in a "woman" is a degeneration (insofar as she lives by Christian virtues) (267, 304). One "cures" or "redeems" a "woman" only by giving her a child (267, 304). The fight for equal rights is a symptom of a generalized decadence, as every physician knows, Nietzsche claims (267, 304). All "feminism"—in women and men—shuts the door to audacious insights (264, 301). Emancipated "women"—those unnatural monsters ill-favoured by nature—actually hope to wreak revenge upon their sex by lowering the rank of "women" in society (266, 304). A "woman," insofar as she is truly a woman, resists "rights" in hand and foot as the state of nature, after all, grants her the first rank. Yet the only way she can effectively exercise this "natural" supremacy in the polis is precisely not to give up her "femininity"—her un-"manliness."[30]

---

28. This could be a reference to Nietzsche's revaluation of Odysseus and his blocked ears. The question then becomes whether Nietzsche meant "small ears" to possess an acute sensitivity not available to the "long eared," or whether being "small eared" meant being deaf to the siren's song of the rabble, especially "woman's" voice. Naturally, both characterizations are not necessarily mutually exclusive.

29. Nietzsche, *Ecce Homo*, 263; Nietzsche, *Ecce Homo*, in *Nietzsche Werke*, 300.

30. As I have pointed out in my introductory chapter, feminists who condemn Nietzsche as anti-

Thus, Nietzsche reauthorizes himself as the preeminently healthy convalescent who healed himself by shoring up his credentials with also being the "first psychologist of the eternally feminine." It is by virtue of this self-endowed authorization that he claims that he is able to make even more legitimate pronouncements regarding who is healthy and who is sickly, who is strong and who is weak, who may yet be healed and who must be relegated to the shards of modernity. It is "woman"—with her rancor, vengefulness, and Christianity—who is the irredeemably decadent enemy and victim upon whom the sins of modernity must be heaped, and who must be kept, harnessed, on the outskirts of the polis of the healthy who must preserve themselves.

In addition, there is one other way Nietzsche implicitly authorizes himself as the convalescent-healer of a decadent age (a title that is reminiscent of the charges he levels against Socrates in *Twilight of the Idols*). Through his expositions on nutrition/diet and the various physiological effects of substances such as alcohol or water upon one's stomach (238–39, 278); as well as on place and climate, such as his pronouncements on how dry air, clear skies, and rapid metabolism are necessary for health (240–41, 279–81); or on recreation, in which he strongly recommends reading that allows the (masculine) reader journeys away from his own seriousness (24, 282)—Nietzsche implicitly elevates his bodily and spiritual requirements to be the norm for being a convalescent who can heal himself. It is via a focus upon his physico-spiritual travails—his near-blindness,[31] his constant gastric trouble, his ever-looming nervous attacks and migraines—that he is able to make a claim that such bodily aches are but symptomatic of a state of vitality. It is only by highlighting the frailties of his body as effects of, and not causes of, health that he can make the claim that the true cause of health is innate vitality—according to his own terms, as his own "proof" of how nobility or baseness of soul is intimately intertwined with and yet prior to physical ailment or physical overcoming. His body becomes the living testimony to his having been a convalescent, and yet, at bottom, his having been preeminently healthy all throughout his illness.

Nietzsche seeks to dissociate himself from his decadent Socratic counterpart by laying claim to four things: (1) that he, unlike Socrates, is a *Doppelgänger*, with at least a second, maybe even a third face—and hints at it, unlike the crafty Socrates who implicitly claims to have but one mask; (2) that he, unlike Socrates, does not suffer from the temptation toward moralizing or aspiring to become an "improver" (217, 256) of humankind; (3) that he, unlike Socrates, does not pretend that all may be taught, through the democratic and plebeian principle of dialectics and the insti-

---

feminist draw from his post-Zarathustran texts, and they are accurate in doing so. What is lacking in their accounts, though, is how Nietzsche, after a considerable degree of ambivalence, eventually arrives at this misogynistic and politically ruthless position.

31. Again, this is a possible reference back to Oedipus, with whose figure he often aligns himself.

tution of the Christian conscience, to heal themselves; and (4) that he, unlike the devotee-gathering (Christian) Socrates, demands that his disciples "deny" him in order for him to return to them (220, 259).

Yet, perhaps the most striking observation regarding Nietzsche's political philosophy, at this point, is its rudimentary character. He no longer talks about how the modern *polis*,[32] as a whole, may be re-enlivened (as in his pre-Zarathustran phase); or how only the *polis* of those who have learned his art of interpretation may be saved (as in his Zarathustran phase); or how one can hasten or intensify the self-destruction of modernity (as in his earlier post-Zarathustran phase). Instead, he seems preoccupied with the topic of explaining how he became what he is. As a being dead and noble in his father, and alive yet decadent in his mother, Nietzsche seems to return, yet again, to that Zarathustran dream of siring/birthing himself. As Greybeal observes:

> On a literal level, the riddle "as my father I am already dead, while as my mother I still live and grow old" might seem simply to point to the actual biographical facts at the time of his writing. Nietzsche's father had died when Nietzsche was four years old; his mother would live until 1897, nine years beyond the composition of *Ecce Homo*. Yet it is *as* his father and mother that he claims to be both dead and alive; in what sense does he see himself *as* his own parents?[33]

In the sense that Nietzsche saw himself as one "posthumously born": "*Ich selber bin noch nicht an der Zeit, Einige werden posthum geboren.*"[34] In the sense that he deliberately cultivated a "multifarious" writing style to re-sire/birth himself as the true disciple of Dionysus—the self-engendering god, the god twice-born from his father's thigh, the son as the father resurrected. Yet Nietzsche seems aware that his (re)conception of himself as teacher of the doctrine of *amor fati* is an emasculated conception.

---

32. It is true that Nietzsche does not overtly use the term *polis*. But there are many instances where, in his nostalgia for the culture and political organization of the ancient Greeks, it seems he constantly sought to return to some model of the ancient *polis*. Hence, he thought it possible to save modernity in his pre-Zarathustran phase through the resurrection of classical Greek politico-aesthetics, or, in his Zarathustran phase, to effect the coming of the *Übermenschen* via his training of the few who could learn his "art of interpretation," and hopefully, become his "disciples" (which still implies some form of political organization, however loosely defined). It is true though that a contradiction, at least in Nietzsche's political enterprise, is especially evident here. For if Nietzsche's "disciples" must reject him in order to become truly like him, and if their principal traits are independence, individualism, rebelliousness, and overflowing power, how are they ever going to form a "new" type of *polis*, or more loosely, society beyond modernity? Nietzsche himself seems aware of this contradiction, as I have shown in my analysis of book 4 of *Zarathustra* in Chapter 3.
33. Graybeal, *Language*, 78.
34. Nietzsche, *Ecce Homo*, 296; Nietzsche, *Ecce Homo*, in *Nietzsche Werke*, 296.

142   Resentment and the "Feminine"

For now, his political goal is neither the revitalization of modernity, nor the innoculation of the noble "few" against the plebeian "many," nor the amputation of modernity as a whole. His political goal now seems to be simply self-preservation: explaining how he became what he is and how he can keep himself healthy. For by explaining how he is essentially and inexorably healthy, he can claim that he is absolutely free of *ressentiment*—and can authorize himself as the sole ascending line of life in an era of decadence, who can, hopefully, rebirth himself in his future sons gifted with the smallest ears. The genealogy of Nietzsche's persistent dis-ease of *ressentiment*, particularly against "woman"/the"feminine," has been one of the main strands of this chapter.

Concluding Remarks

One of the most striking characteristics of Nietzsche's post-Zarathustran writings is the trend toward decreasing references/allusions to (Greek) mythic figures. By the time Nietzsche composes *Ecce Homo*, only brief references to Dionysus remain. On the one hand, this seems in line with Nietzsche's overtly expressed aspirations toward mastering a condensed, highly provocative style of writing—which he calls "Roman"[35] —employing minimal signs, while maximizing effect. Yet on the other hand, such an observation concerning Nietzsche's developing style(s) does not explain why Nietzsche gravitates toward this way of writing, or how the evolution of his style corresponds with the (d)evolution of his political philosophy, particularly with respect to the notions of the "feminine" or "woman."

One of the principal points of this chapter has been to show that by adopting this aphoristic, refractory, and increasingly openly biographical mode of writing, Nietzsche has sought to condense his esoteric and exoteric messages to such an extent in his post-Zarathustran writings, that by the time he writes *Ecce Homo* (which, on the surface, appears to be Nietzsche's benevolent act of taking off his masks), the exoteric message of self-destruction (of the plebeian "other") dominates the esoteric message of self-preservation (of the noble "same"/self, or at least, Nietzsche himself). The apparently utter exoterization of his doctrines accomplishes two aims: (1) to make his ass-eared followers believe they are his true heirs, thus catalyzing their (and modernity's) self-expenditure; and (2) to make his hyperborean followers aware of the dangers that follow in the wake of the sounding of a hammer that smashes idols, as

---

35. Using Strauss's and Rosen's language, this means he writes exoterically—using a style that seems more literal, less symbolic, and less allegorical—but also more esoterically, even more discriminating in its sifting of the "many"/plebeian from the "few"/noble.

well as to alert them to the need to remain "healthy." By appearing to unveil himself, with but the subtlest hints that at least a two-fold rhetoric is again at work, Nietzsche aims to ensure that only those with the smallest and most sensitive of ears may hear his whispered warning.

Nietzsche's move toward seeming to demythologize[36] his writings is also aligned with his less visible move to remythologize[37] his politics as well as his authority as a political thinker. Hence, in *Beyond Good and Evil*, he styles himself as the father of the philosophers of the future—those beyond the "feminine" and Christian categories of "good" and "evil" characteristic of modernity; in *Twilight of the Idols*, he takes the stance of being the only ascending line of life in an era of supreme decadence; in *Ecce Homo*, he claims to be the only convalescent who has completely healed himself.

It is true that strictly and grammatically speaking, Nietzsche uses figures and tropes rather than mythic deities or figures here. But he essentially uses these figures/tropes to fill in for the mythic deities he seems to banish. Yet as father of the philosophers of the future, he still carries the mantle of Zeus, the supreme Father of them all. As the only "ascending line of life" in modernity, he still bears a kinship with the combined figures of Apollo and Dionysus, through whom genuine art and life may rebirth themselves. As a convalescent who has completely healed himself (because he was always preeminently healthy, anyway), he still bears distinct affinities with Dionysus, who possesses the preeminent health to be pieced together again, despite his dismemberment. In other words, the claim I am making is that Nietzsche precisely *appears* to downplay the role of mythology exoterically, only to result in an even more subtle esoteric mythology disguised as a nonmythology.

The tools Nietzsche uses in order to establish his authority as a political thinker also vary as he moves across these three post-Zarathustran texts. In *Beyond Good and Evil*, it is via his capacity as "new psychologist" that he is able to diagnose morality as malice spiritualized, and to trace Europe's deepening corruption to its adoption of democratic and Christian principles. This increasing democratization and Christianization results in the allowance of hybridization—i.e, the mixing of "higher" and "lower" types in societies and even individuals, producing softer, weaker "men." In *Twilight of the Idols*, it is via Nietzsche's heritage as a continuance of the ascending line of the law of Manu that he is able to diagnose the four great cancers that plague modernity—the error of "Cornarism" (confusion of cause and effect), the error of false causes, the error of imaginary causes, and the error of "free will." In *Ecce Homo*, it is by virtue of his twofold heritage, dead as his noble and non-German father, and alive as his decadent and German mother, that Nietzsche claims that a revaluation of values is possible only with him.

36. By "demythologize," I mean outwardly to avoid a mythic frame.
37. By "remythologize," I mean to replace one mythology for another, seemingly anti-mythic one.

His political aims change subtly as well. In *Beyond Good and Evil*, he is concerned with producing a "higher" type, who, by achieving control over the anarchy of his debased instincts, would ensure the rebirth of master morality. In *Twilight of the Idols*, his focus splits into two: (1) re-enlivening the law of Manu, to breed a noble type and crushing all the plebeian, weak, and resentful types that democracy and Christianity preserve; and (2) hastening or damming up modernity's inevitable self-destruction. In *Ecce Homo*, he takes on the project of rebirthing and preserving himself as the sole modern heir to Dionysus and noble health.

One of his recurrently paired figures, the dualistic tropes of health versus sickness recurs and mutates in keeping with his political aims. In *Beyond Good and Evil*, he seems to say that an unproblematic distinction between the two is not possible. Given the degree of decay that characterizes modernity, there is no purely "noble" being. The best that one can hope for is a hybrid who possesses/is possessed by anarchic and powerful drives, and yet manages to control them—in isolation from the herd imperative to happiness. In *Twilight of the Idols*, however, he gravitates toward a more black and white delineation between the noble/healthy and the base/sick, drawing up a sharp contrast between ascending and descending lines of life—and prescribing a more ruthless method of breeding "nobles" and exterminating the "plebeian." In *Ecce Homo*, he seems to oscillate between his two earlier positions because on the one hand, he admits that he, the most noble modern, is also a decadent; yet on the other hand, he claims to have completely healed from his convalescence because he was inherently healthy from the very start.

Despite these mutations, Nietzsche's post-Zarathustran political philosophy, via the prism of his seemingly master trope of sickness versus health, sounds and resounds the following themes:

1. Europe's increased democratization and Christianization has led to the creation of hybrids, who are at war with themselves because of the various admixtures of the "noble" and the "base" in them;
2. Such a corrupt age favors the proliferation of the "sick" over the "healthy";
3. The "European problem" lies in finding a way of cultivating a new caste to rule Europe;
4. Given that the teeming vermin outnumber the "healthy," the new physician must crush and destroy these parasites for the well-being and preservation of the "ascending";
5. The only "ascending" line of life produced by modernity, Nietzsche himself, must preserve himself in the aftermath of the inevitable self-destruction of modernity by rebirthing himself in his future followers with the "smallest ears";

6. There is no guarantee that after he, the genius/explosive/hammer of modernity, has expended himself, that a new age of "nobility" may arise from the resultant age of barrenness and sterility that follows in the wake of such squandering.

Finally, how Nietzsche's politico-medical philosophy intersects with his notions of "woman" or the "feminine" are also crucial to understanding the (d)evolution of his thought. In *Beyond Good and Evil*, there are still traces of an ambivalence toward the "feminine"/"woman." In the figure of truth as a woman yet unwon by clumsy philosophers, the "feminine" seems positive. In the figure of the will-to-truth as a Sphinx,[38] the "feminine" is ambiguous. In the figure of the Sphinx-Circe that the skeptic worships, the "feminine" is negative. Yet the overall trend seems to be an increasingly negative valuation of "woman" and the "feminine" in Nietzsche's political world. Hence, "real men" are distinguished from "effeminate men" because they are not infected by the "womanly" trait of being unable not to react, they do not distort the world into corrupt and "little" perspectives, and are capable of more than mirroring and spreading oneself out before a "light-footed spirit." Similarly, the occurrence of hybrids, not simply across the "noble"-"plebeian" divide, but also across the "masculine"-"feminine" polarity (thus generating "feminized men" and "masculinized women") is undeniable proof and a contributing cause to the escalating corruption of modernity. "Woman"'s aspirations toward self-reliance is an indication of the successful revenge of those "abortive" ones against their own sex, and is a symptom of the general "uglification" of Europe. What is necessary in order to alleviate this general effeminization of the era is to revert back to the wisdom of the Orientals (and their heirs, the Greeks) in their increasingly sadistic treatment of "women."

Nietzsche's negative treatment of the "feminine"/"woman" grows even more unambiguous in his later writings. In *Twilight of the Idols*, the spreading of the four lethal errors is associated with how the "true world" becomes a fable by becoming increasingly "female." Christianity, the religion and genius of Chandala hatred, is the supremely base institution of an era in which the instincts have gone bad; its elevation of the "feminine" values of pity and mercy is a testament to the success of the Chandala/slave/"feminine" revolt. What is necessary, on the one hand, is the reconstruction of institutions along "manly" and "noble" virtues of seeing, thinking, and writing, and on the other hand, crushing and destroying all that reeks of the plebeian,

---

38. There seems to be a fundamental ambiguity in Nietzsche's *Beyond Good and Evil* as to whether the figure of the Sphinx refers to Truth itself, or to the inexplicable will to truth. I have taken the second reading in my interpretation as it seems to be the more accurate, if one were to try to remain as closely as possible to the original text. Naturally, it is possible that both readings are implied by the text. Cf. Nietzsche, *Beyond Good and Evil*, 9; Nietzsche, *Jenseits von Gut und Böse*, 9.

the rancorous, the "female"—thus reconstituting a new noble hierarchy along the lines of a pathos of distance that separates the healthy from the sick.

Nietzsche's misogyny is also quite evident in *Ecce Homo*. Here, he traces his inherent nobility to his dead father and his having been a convalescent to his mother (and sister). While he speaks of his father as a celestial being from whom he inherits the eternal Yes to life (*amor fati*), he denigrates his mother and sister as *canaille* and *Höllenmaschine*, and calls them the most profound and terrible objection to the vision of the eternal recurrence. What is valuable about his maternal and German heritage is that it allows him to know the view from below. The ability to overcome it, or to reverse perspectives, is purely a paternal (and therefore, divine or transcending) heritage. It is true that Nietzsche speaks positively of one woman in *Ecce Homo*—Cosima Wagner. But he is able to do so under the rubric of classifying her with other French (i.e., non-German) elevated beings, the rest of whom are male. Nevertheless, Nietzsche does claim that he is "the first psychologist of the eternally feminine." In keeping with this title, which he claims is part of his Dionysian dowry, he says that not only does he have access to "woman"'s evil and clever nature, but also that all "women" cannot help but love him (save for those "abortive"/"emancipated" ones), fascinated as they are by his "small ears." The reference to "small ears," a testimony to his "noble" or hyperborean nature, implies that "women" suffer from (to steal from, reverse, and deform Freud) "small ear envy"—as they themselves suffer from their congenital "long ears." The only way one can make "woman"'s ears shorter, for Nietzsche, is to give her a child. Yet it seems that Nietzsche's persistent dream has not been of giving "woman" a child, but of himself becoming "feminine," thus being able to give himself a child,[39] just as the composite Zeus-Dionysus-Apollo figure created through Zarathustra shows in Chapter 3.

---

39. *Das Kind* is neutral, but Nietzsche associates the traits of playing and unencumbered creativity, in *Zarathustra*, with "masculinity."

5

Looking Back, Looking Forward

> Exploring his "Heraldic Universe," he declares, "I am a man . . . I am an artist . . . I am God!" Hardly original; the romantics, Nietzsche pre-eminently, had killed God and simultaneously had confirmed history by enthroning a new deity rooted in their inner consciousness.
> —Richard Pine, *The Dandy and the Herald*

> Unless one lives and loves in the trenches it is difficult to remember that the war against dehumanization is ceaseless.
> —Audre Lorde, *"Age, Race, Class, and Sex: Women Redefining Difference"*

A Genealogy of Nietzsche's Will-to-*Ressentiment*: Summary and Conclusions

In Chapter 1, I have described, and located (within the broad arena of Nietzsche studies, political philosophy, and feminism) the main concerns of this book. In brief, I have drawn attention to the undulating planes of gender, myth, and politics in Nietzsche's (d)evolving visions of the "feminine"/"woman" and modernity as symptomatic of the will-to-resentment that drives Nietzsche's philosophy. By "feminine," I have generally meant anthropomorphisms drawn from Greek deities (such as Gaia or Demeter, for instance), functioning as symbols for Nature, the source of both the Apollinian and Dionysian forces, as well as the unbounded vitality of life. By "woman," I have generally meant actual historical women whom Nietzsche mythologizes as vermin, parasites, or as the most concentrated repositories of disease in modernity. Nevertheless, the boundary lines separating both interact in a very complex manner, especially in Nietzsche's post-Zarathustran phase, where Nietzsche, in *Ecce Homo*, for example, has Cosima take Demeter-Gaia's mythic status as "mother of health," and relegates Franziska and Elizabeth to the dark realm of "hell-machine."

In the introductory chapter, I have sketched the outlines of a program for cutting open the tumor that feeds upon the mater-ial of Nietzsche's political philosophy: the deeper noble lie of the dichotomy dividing sickness from health beneath the more superficial noble lie of political salvation/resurrection via the "art of interpretation." In addition, I have described, in general terms, the political, gendered, mythic, and embodied approach I employ—attempting a genealogy of my own methodological genealogy via reference to the theoretical frameworks provided by Strauss, Dannhauser, Blondel, Kristeva, and Irigaray, among others. Finally, I have provided a brief review of the general history of philosophical discussions on Nietzsche in relation to the "feminine," and, when it was relevant to do so, summarized, compared, contrasted, and plotted out the relevant arguments of several crucial texts by thinkers such as Derrida, Kofman, Irigaray, among others, which have sought to address the question of how Nietzsche figures the relations of the "feminine"/ "woman." In doing so, I have attempted to create a space for my own project within the larger schema of how Nietzsche may be reconfigured in relation to political philosophy, aesthetics, and gender studies.

In Chapter 2, "Exca/Elevating the 'Feminine,'" I began with an examination of *Birth* (1872), *Human, All Too Human* (1878), and *The Gay Science*[1] (1882), as texts representative of Nietzsche's pre-Zarathustran phase. This chapter's title, "Exca/Elevating the 'Feminine,'" alludes to two things: (1) my own appropriation of Nietzsche's "subterranean" critical method; and (2) the content of Nietzsche's politico-aesthetic at this early stage, which elevates mythic figures of the "feminine" alongside "masculine" ones.

I began with these texts because in them, Nietzsche's use of myth in relation to the feminine and the salvation of the *polis* is clearly still benign and even empowering. Nietzsche's use of myth, at this stage, is analogous to that which Stanley Rosen ascribes to Plato with the myth of the reversed cosmos in *The Statesman*. For Rosen, the purpose of the myth of the reversed cosmos is to illustrate the ambiguous nature of the relation between physics and politics but not to resolve this ambiguity, since this very ambiguity resists resolution.[2]

What I have shown is that the figures of Dionysus and Apollo in *Birth*, for instance, mediate the tension between politics and aesthetics, illusion and reality, and the "masculine" and "feminine"—embodying, but not fully disclosing, the ambigu-

---

1. *Die Fröhliche Wissenschaft* has also been translated as *The Joyful Wisdom* by Thomas Common.
2. Stanley Rosen, "Plato's Myth of the Reversed Cosmos," in *The Quarrel Between Philosophy and Poetry* (New York: Routledge, 1993), 67.

ous and dialectical relationship binding these poles. Myth, as employed within this phase of Nietzsche's philosophy, is a manner of imaging or symbolically depicting and (re)conceiving the nature of life and culture, in that space in between the universal and the particular. What results in Nietzsche's pre-Zarathustran phase is a political aesthetic. By this, I mean a harmonious interpenetration between Nietzsche's political project of sa(l)ving modernity and his aesthetic interests in the power of illusion or appearance as breaking the Christian dichotomy between "truth" and "lie" where "truth" is equated with "good" and "lie" is judged as "evil."

It is important to take note of two things in line with what has been this project's developmental or genealogical approach: (1) that Nietzsche, at this stage, is optimistic enough to believe that modernity may still be saved from its corruption and decadence; and (2) that Nietzsche, at this point, does not attempt to repress the "feminine" (as opposed to "woman," a negative mythic figure, which Nietzsche begins constructing as early as *Human, All Too Human*). As he moves across his masks of midwife (*Birth*), master educator of the free spirits (*Human I*), physician-invalid (*Human II*), and artist-scientist/"male mother" (*The Gay Science*), Nietzsche repeatedly returns to his self-declared mission: the restoration of "great health" (*Grossegesundheit*) to modernity, and with that, the winnowing of the healthy from the sick. "Woman," even at this early stage, seems the counterpoint to the "feminine"; she is the most dangerous among the sick—the most potent repository of the poisons of Christianity and Romanticism. Yet there is also a sense in which Nietzsche reveals flashes of insight (and perhaps even sympathy) for the plight of "woman" trapped in nineteenth-century German bourgeois society. For instance, in *Human, All Too Human*, he uses the radiant smile of a young bride gazing upon her husband as the poignant symbol for the fragile and illusory nature of human happiness, and he is critical of the taboos surrounding the education of women regarding sex. He even goes as far as formulating the "Law of the Sexes," in *The Gay Science*, stating that "woman" cannot help being what she is because her nature is to be willing to become what her "man" wills. Naturally, these observations do not necessarily exonerate Nietzsche from the charge of misogyny, nor has the task of ridding Nietzsche of his tarnished image ever been one of my concerns. What I have been concerned with is showing that in Nietzsche's pre-Zarathustran phase, "feminine" imagery is tacked on to political optimism; the generative powers of modernity are linked to the relatively nonmisogynistic treatment of "feminine," and in some rare flashes, of "woman-as-victim."

In his pre-Zarathustran phase, the subject of my genealogy of Nietzsche's gendered politics in Chapter 2, Nietzsche's myth of the redemption of modernity, as figured in the resurrection of the figures of Apollo and Dionysus as images of life, aims to function as an antidote to modernity's impotence. It aims to mediate between the ambiguity binding the borders of illusion and reality by positing an aesthetico-political solution to modernity's unhealthiness, without tearing apart and resolving this ambiguity.

How does Nietzsche's political vision relate to his view of the "feminine"? In my reading, Nietzsche's early political optimism also sculpts his encounters with the "feminine." Following Sarah Kofman, I have drawn out the consequences of Nietzsche's lines from *The Gay Science*: "Perhaps truth is a woman who has reasons for not letting us see her reasons? Perhaps her name is—to speak Greek—Baubô?"[3] As I have shown in my analysis, Nietzsche elevates the many faces of the "feminine" to mythic equivalents of their "masculine" counterparts, as masks for one of his principal political doctrines: the recovery of "great health" as aligned with the eternal recurrence of life. Apollo and Dionysus, the archetypal mythic figures through whose (apparent) coupling this "great health" may be restored, employ various masks, both "feminine" and "masculine": Helen and the satyr, Antigone and Cassandra, Homer and Archilochus. Similarly, Nietzsche uses the figure of Medusa as the apotropaic to the excessive/sick Dionysus; it is a mythic "feminine" who is able to restore to health the unhealthy Dionysus, enabling the apparent embrace between the Apollinian and Dionysian forces: an embrace that does not negate the gendered duality of "masculinity" and "femininity" within these gods themselves. Finally, Nietzsche also implicitly elevates the "feminine" anthropomorphism of Gaia-Demeter to the power behind Apollo and Dionysus, for it is from her that both of them spring. Even if Nietzsche's hidden elevation of the "feminine maternal," at this point, can be excavated, it is equally evident that there is some tension in this act. Nietzsche, in remythologizing Demeter's role as Mother-Nature, recasts her in the role of a mother joyfully anticipating the birth of her son, Dionysus, rather than a mother wrapped in grief over the rape and disappearance of her daughter.

This same tension exists in Nietzsche's conjoining of the figures of Io, the "feminine" figure watched over, and Argus, the hundred-eyed watcher, as the image for the new "soul" for the new heroic age in *The Gay Science*. For in making Io the key to Argus's attainment of profound self-knowledge, Nietzsche elevates the "feminine" alongside the "masculine" as figures for the redemption/healing of modernity. Yet by allowing Io to be forever impaled by Argus's gaze, by enabling Io to be swallowed by or fused into the figure of Argus, Nietzsche domesticates the "feminine."

Notwithstanding these tensions, it is evident in the pre-Zarathustran phase that Nietzsche's attitude toward the "feminine"/"woman" (as compared with his Zarathustran and post-Zarathustran phases) is relatively more benign. Alongside his belief/conviction that modernity can be saved is his reluctant admission that the "feminine" coexists, intertwined with the "masculine" in the irrepressible self-(re)production of life, power, and the *polis*.

3. Nietzsche, *The Gay Science*, 38.

The logic that I have used to structure Chapter 3, "The Phallic Mother," flows from the way in which the roles of myth and gender in Nietzsche's evolving politics change in *Zarathustra* (1883–1885). Here, myth no longer functions as a mediator of ambivalences and as an antidote to modernity's illness, but as a noble lie designed to save not the entire *polis*, but only those who have learned his "art of interpretation." The noble lie redeems only those who can behold his esoteric teachings as such; the rest are unsalvageable and damned. Thus, in this chapter, I have derived my notion of the function of myth in relation to Nietzsche's political philosophy from Strauss and Dannhauser, with their emphasis on the centrality of a "noble lie" functioning to enable human beings to embrace life in its absurdity. In my reading of it, *Zarathustra* is Nietzsche's attempt at teasing apart, and weaving together, into a new mosaic a conglomerate of myths binding the figures of Dionysus, Zeus, and Apollo (as well as the then-aesthetico-moral vision of the dandy) in Nietzsche's own attempt to construct and propagate his own aesthetico-political mythology as prophet of the transvaluation of values, visionary of the nightmarish eternal return, high priest of the doctrine of *amor fati*. Nietzsche's appropriation of the mythic rebirths of Dionysus through the figure of Zarathustra enables him to cast himself in the figures of the mutilated father and son who is born of a "masculine mother." Nietzsche's political optimism seems gradually to give way to a pessimism that attempts to harness the "feminine" power of fertility to a "phallic mother."[4]

The fact that this rebirthing of Nietzsche-Zarathustra-Dionysus is "noble" may be seen in that the final goal of Nietzsche's constructed myth—of himself as a "masculine mother" giving birth to the *Übermenschen* (beings who are heirs to the vitality of the Greeks rather than the corruption of the moderns)—a life-sustaining myth. It appears, at one level, to foretell the birthing of a new age devoid of all the infirmities of modernity. That this myth is a lie is seen in that at another level, this redemptive vision is an absurdity, as the fourth part of Zarathustra seems to show. In my reading of *Zarathustra*, the higher men, whose deformities and stench move Zarathustra to conflicting emotions of pity, shame, anger, and affection, are parodic fragmentations of his own teachings that have gained hideous forms. The suffering and dismembered godlike Zarathustra is unable to piece himself together again, as his severing from his

---

4. Judith Butler makes a similar point regarding the insideness-outsideness of the "feminine" in a phallogocentric economy, in relation to her analysis of Irigaray's attack on the form/matter, soul/body, meaning/matter dichotomies. She writes: "Irigaray's intervention in the history of the form/matter distinction underscores 'matter' as the site at which the feminine is excluded from philosophical binaries. . . . The economy that claims to include the feminine as the subordinate term in a binary opposition of masculine/feminine excludes the feminine, [and] produced the feminine as that which must be excluded for the economy to operate." Cf. Judith Butler, "Bodies that Matter," in *Engaging with Irigaray: Feminist Philosophy and European Thought*, ed. Carolyn Burke, Naomi Schor, and Margaret Whitford (New York: Columbia University Press, 1994), 149.

monstrous progeny is made complete by the reawakening of the dead god through the farcical ass festival. Pained by the inadequacies of his creations, Zarathustra must nevertheless smilingly partake of the supper of convalescents—the quintessential ironic image undercutting this myth's apparently redemptive function.

Another way of framing my analysis (drawing partially from Rosen's Straussian influenced reading of Nietzsche as employing a twofold rhetoric with messages for the esoteric/"few" alongside those for the exoteric/"many") is to say that Nietzsche uses a double rhetoric through his use of the figure of the "masculine mother." For the plebeian/"many," Zarathustra's utterances become the noble lie through which they may be lured back to life—only to hasten their deaths, and the destruction of this decadent age. To the noble/"few," Zarathustra reveals his pregnancy to be hysterical and sterile—one that can generate only the near-abortions of the higher men, one that cannot guarantee the coming of the *Übermenschen*.

In relation to the issue of "woman," Nietzsche's political ambivalences in interaction with the "feminine" attain a new pitch in *Zarathustra*. For although he appears to empower the (desexualized) "feminine" figures of the old woman, Life, Wisdom, and Eternity, he appropriates for Zarathustra the "feminine" power of birthing. In addition, the conversation with the old woman regarding women is rhetorically ambiguous. It is heavily laden with qualifications, as a conversation between Zarathustra and a woman who no longer has the capacity for childbearing, and whose final pronouncement is announced with the phrase, "Thus spoke the little old woman." This phrase possibly renders her a mask for Zarathustra, particularly as that pronouncement is immediately followed and authorized with the closing phrase, "Thus Spoke Zarathustra." Nevertheless, what consistently emerges, despite Nietzsche's numerous ambivalences toward the "feminine" is that he considers the "feminine"[5] as necessary for both the destruction of the old order and the birthing of the new one—as whore, tarantula, pregnant lioness; a principle of chaos, swallowing and spewing forth universes.

From there, I moved into Chapter 4, "Emasculate Conception," where the dynamic binding myth and gender in Nietzsche's evolving political philosophy in his post-Zarathustran phase grows even more complex and polemical. The title of this chapter, "Emasculate Conception," in keeping with my general reading of Nietzsche as a "phallic mother," aimed to point out how Nietzsche's attempts at birthing the *Übermensch* are essentially exercises in abortive stillbirths or the spawning of monstrosities insofar as they are rooted in resentment. Again, since I am tracking how Nietzsche's politics and attitude toward the "feminine" sculpt each other, I pay particular attention to how Nietzsche chooses to use or banish images of the "feminine"

---

5. I contrast the "feminine" with "woman."

in relation to his apocalyptic vision of the end of modernity. On the one hand, he appears outwardly to advocate humanity's need for a noble lie in order to stave off the nihilistic threat. Indeed, in keeping with this reading, Keith Ansell-Pearson's analysis of the *Nachlass* notes arrives at the conclusion that Nietzsche is led to the overman because he is in need of a vision of a type of humanity which is able to endure and affirm the abysmal thought of the eternal return.[6]

Ansell-Pearson shows that both the doctrines of the birthing of the *Übermensch* and the will to power, particularly in *Beyond Good and Evil* (1886) for instance, indicate Nietzsche's attempts at crafting a life-sustaining mythology against the vision of the eternal recurrence; the myth of the *Übermensch* is the noble lie crafted to endure the threat of the eternal return, whose entrance marks nihilism's knocking at the door. Yet, as his descent into madness grows more and more discernible, Nietzsche attempts to live without such a noble lie, identifying the painful symptoms of his own body with the dismemberment of Dionysus—envisaging himself as corporeal vessel of the noble lie, the horned kid who must be sacrificed for the resurgence of life and vitality, the hammer that must explode modernity and its idols.

In other words, in my analysis, Nietzsche moves from envisaging Nature as a maternal body that births the Apollinian and Dionysian forces of life during his pre-Zarathustran phase, to mythologizing Zarathustra's body as the penultimate super-"masculine" body that has appropriated the "feminine" power of birthing to itself, and finally, to his own body as a reincarnation of the Dionysian body that must be dismembered in order to effect, perhaps, the resurgence of life after the amputation of the cancer of modernity.

In his pre-Zarathustran phase, Nietzsche figures the "feminine" body as an "other" that could function as an equivalent mythic mask, alongside his "masculine" figures, for his doctrine of the irrepressible vitality of life and therefore, the possible salvation/recuperation of modernity. In his Zarathustran phase, the "feminine" body becomes dismembered in Nietzsche's attempt to create a super-"masculine" body that appropriates to itself the "feminine" womb and its power of birthing through its (in)fusion of the figures of Dionysus, Zeus, and Apollo into one mythic entity. In his post-Zarathustran phase, the "feminine" body blurs into the body of "woman"/women, whose otherness must be harnessed and ruthlessly destroyed, as it threatens to contaminate the super-"masculine" body of Nietzsche, the new Dionysus, with its effeminizing poison. Yet the body of the new Dionysus, in its dismemberment, resembles the crucified body of Christ, reifying, even in its attempted negation, the return of the "dead God."

---

6. Ansell-Pearson, "Who is the *Übermensch*? Truth, Time, and Woman in Nietzsche," 322.

The "feminine," initially aligned with the notion of "great health," because of its association with the power of birthing, undergoes a period of attempted assimilation into super-"masculinity." In the aftermath of the frustration of this attempted grafting, the "feminine" blurs into/ disappears/ is replaced by "woman"/ women, whom Nietzsche condemns as the most poisonous repository of resentment and the necrophiliac will against life. Yet what emerges as a consistent pattern, despite these reconfigurations of the "feminine"/ "woman" is that it is Nietzsche who suffers from the dis-ease of *ressentiment*. His inability to rebirth himself successfully through his disciples leads him to an increasingly radical and ruthless attempt to separate the supposedly "healthy" from the "sick," knowing that he, himself, is sick.

Thus, I have shown that although Nietzsche still uses the remythologizing strategies he had used in his pre-Zarathustran and Zarathustran phases, his remythologizing may be distinctively characterized as becoming: (1) increasingly pessimistic regarding the possibility of modernity's recovery from its decadence; (2) increasingly misogynistic, with decreasing references toward the "feminine" and more scathing remarks concerning "woman"; (3) increasingly exotericized, so as to enhance/hasten modernity's self-destruction; and (4) increasingly concerned with self-preservation.

Again, attention to how Nietzsche's reaction to the "feminine"/"woman" structures his emerging political philosophy has been crucial to the driving force of this inquiry. As I have shown, Nietzsche's anti-"feminine"/"woman" attitude deepens during his post-Zarathustran phase. For instance, in *Beyond Good and Evil*, he castigates the Sphinx and Circe as the poisonous goddesses to whom a sick age pays homage; in *Twilight of the Idols* (1888), Nietzsche gives all of Ariadne's powers of childbirth to Dionysus,[7] and relegates Ariadne to the realm of the "long eared"—the plebeian asses whose imperfection in hearing allegedly causes them to be resentful of the "short eared," among whom Nietzsche, the self-proclaimed "psychologist of the feminine," claims to possess the "shortest ears." His treatment of "woman," already negative in his pre-Zarathustran phase, grows even more markedly misogynistic. Thus, in *Beyond Good and Evil*, he informs his readers that woman's "great art is the lie, her highest concern is mere appearance and beauty"; "woman has much reason for shame, so much pedantry, superficiality, schoolmarmishness, petty presumption, petty licentiousness and immodesty lies concealed in woman"; and that "woman would not have a genius for finery if she did not have an instinct for a *secondary* role." In *Ecce Homo* (1888), he teaches that feminism fastens shut the door, preventing entrance into the "labyrinth of audacious insights." The political treatment of "woman" he advocates is ruthless. Citing the law of Manu and the so-called wisdom of the Greeks and their descendants, the orientals, he advocates the cruel slavery of "woman" in

---

7. Luce Irigaray makes a similar observation. Cf. Irigaray, *Marine Lover*, 117.

order to bring to a halt the sick "effeminization" of Europe. Crushing the most potent "descending line of life," "woman," and preserving himself (i.e., rebirthing himself through his future readers) become his all consuming concerns.

Thus has been my attempt at a genealogy of Nietzsche's developing political philosophy. As a "genealogy," it has sought not to arrive at a description of the "things" phenomenology holds to be the world, but rather to delineate the "*manner* in which 'things' are made into 'facts.'"[8] Such an approach is driven forward by attending to how Nietzsche's attitude to the "feminine" plots out in relation to his changing political vision. This Nietzschean use of Nietzschean genealogy has aimed at excavating how Nietzsche's gendered political mythology moves from (1) the use of myth as an ambiguous figuration of apparent polarities, to (2) employing myth as a life-sustaining "noble lie," and finally to a schizophrenic appeal to the need for a life-sustaining illusion, alongside which are the imperatives to cause the self-destruction of modernity and to preserve himself. This book has shown that in Nietzsche's developing politics, myths of the "feminine"—which are initially used as equals (alongside their "masculine" counterparts) as figurations of Nietzsche's antidote to the poison of modernity—are eventually robbed of the powers of birthing and creation, and increasingly silenced, resulting in a sterile and necrophiliac "phallic motherhood." In the genealogy of Nietzsche's aesthetico-political philosophy, the figure of the "feminine" increasingly grows into the figure of "woman," resulting in a progressively ruthless mytho-politics (masked as an antimythology) that attempts to eradicate both the "feminine" and "woman" in the narcissistic and Romantic dream of building a *polis* of (*Über*)men.

If it were not for Nietzsche's Romantic underpinnings, a topic that has remained a subterranean theme throughout this book,[9] one could conjecture that his attempt to repress the "feminine" was simply another of his strategies to make "Platonic" philosophy (as he understood it) implode—as it seems to be doing in contemporary philosophical discussions. It is this very propensity for self-destruction within Nietzsche's political philosophy that I have aimed to exploit and articulate, in my own critique of Nietzsche's account of modernity.

Ressentiment and the Death of the Author

One common problem I perceive among many interpreters of Nietzsche is their tendency to separate the issues of gender, politics, aesthetics, and myth in Nietzsche's

---

8. Strong, *Nietzsche*, 54.
9. This is a topic I treat in Caroline Joan S. Picart, "Nietzsche as Masked Romantic," *Journal of Aesthetics and Art Criticism*, 55 (Summer 1997): 273–91.

developing philosophy.[10] Yet all four are intextricably intertwined, although the dynamics that bind them are complex, enabling varying degrees of prominence or subtlety in the overall dynamic.[11] Detwiler similarly comments on the difficulties presented by attempting to isolate only passages overtly addressing Nietzsche's politics in isolation from the other areas on which Nietzsche remarks:

> Nietzsche's various literary styles lead to a highly digressive and disjointed mode of presentation. The political commentary is typically interwoven with a host of other concerns. . . . an exclusive focus on the political passages and on what unambiguously refers to them reveals a degree of consistency, but it tends to yield little more than an expanded checklist of Nietzsche's various positions on assorted issues.[12]

It is important to note as well that Nietzsche's increasingly misogynistic and fatalistic philosophy, characteristic of his post-Zarathustran period, comes into play as he begins to separate these four elements from each other. His post-Zarathustran writings, shrill with denunciations of the "effeminization" of Europe, no longer bear the rich interplay of aesthetics, politics, and mythology that characterizes his earlier phase, where both "masculine" and "feminine" figures function as masks for his principal philosophical doctrines. It appears that the more overtly destructive Nietzsche's philosophy becomes, as it appears in its formulation in *Twilight of the Idols*, the more crudely "political" it appears, seemingly devoid of any appeal to an aesthetic. Correspondingly, Nietzsche also appears, at this stage, to downplay significantly the role that mythology had in his earlier texts, and to replace the "duality/duplicity" of the "masculine" and "feminine" mythic figures in his earlier writings with the rigid demarcations of the "feminine long eared" versus the "masculine short eared." Nietzsche's attempt to separate (perhaps exoterically) these four realms from each other ironically leads to a destabilization of his own authority. The voice that we hear in the final phases of his post-Zarathustran period is steeped in hysterics, the lust for destruction, in tandem with the paradoxical desire for self-preservation and defensive narcissism. It is a voice that screams for authority, and seems less authoritative the louder it screams. As Ansell-Pearson notes in *Nietzsche Contra Rousseau*:

---

10. Stambaugh's *The Other Nietzsche* is a clear example of both the strengths and limitations of an approach that shears Nietzsche's aesthetics away from his politics. Joan Stambaugh, *The Other Nietzsche* (Albany: State University of New York Press, 1994).

11. Despite its unabashedly being "neither user-friendly nor necessarily Marxist," Waite's *Nietzsche's Corps/e* similarly attempts to trace connections binding Nietzsche's aesthetics and politics in relation to "technoculture." Geoff Waite, *Nietzsche's Corps/e: Aesthetics, Politics, Prophecy, or the Spectacular Technoculture of Everyday Life* (Durham: Duke University Press, 1996).

12. Bruce Detwiler, *Nietzsche and the Politics of Aristocratic Radicalism* (Chicago: University of Chicago Press, 1990), 9–10.

In Nietzsche's vision we do not find any redemption at all, but only the eternal return of the struggle between the will to power of the strong and the weak, of masters and slaves, of the justice that claims to be beyond resentment, and the resentment that masquerades as justice.[13]

This brings us to one of the subterranean questions that has been a factor in the formulation of this study. In what does the notion of "authority" inhere in Nietzsche's writings, and how does it attempt to operate? In one of his most famous essays, Michel Foucault asks "What is an Author?" He then articulates a good number of questions that have come to mold our contemporary ways of inquiring and thinking. It is important to note that the question of the function of the author is born only in a world in which the gods have been murdered; Foucault's article would not have been possible without Nietzsche's speculations on the self and its relation to the gods. Indeed, in some respects the question of the author is a subset of the larger question of the authority of God: What function did God's authority serve in our civilization, and what happens when He is stripped of that authority? Insofar as the notion of author-ity was originally aligned with speaking for, being a vessel of, or speaking instead/place of the original Author, God, is there any tenable notion of authority in a world in which God has been declared dead?

Viewed in one way, it seems that if God the Author is dead, then the author is dead; the location within the social space through which our discourse can be effectively authorized then seems to dissolve into nothingness. Within this schema, when the author disappears, so does her authority. When books become simply texts, they no longer carry the weight they had when the author's name on the title page provided them with a special status. A recurrent problem emerges. The texts of Nietzsche, as well as the texts of those who consider themselves Nietzsche's intellectual heirs—various types of cultural critics—are caught in a bind: they are principally attempts at undercutting traditional concepts of authority, while simultaneously trying to preserve some notion of authority.

James Hans phrases the dilemma eloquently:

> If the self is dead and the author is dead, and we no longer resemble those fetishized products of an earlier age, the problem of authority has not gone away simply because we have declared the self and the author to be dead. So Foucault is making his task too easy here. It is one thing to say "What matter who's speaking?" when the question reflects on the issues of the fetishization of the self and authority; it is another thing to say "What matter who's

---

13. Keith Ansell-Pearson, *Nietzsche Contra Rousseau: A Study of Nietzsche's Moral and Political Thought* (Cambridge: Cambridge University Press, 1991), 230.

speaking?" when the question concerns how our discourse could conceivably circulate in a society in which no one fetishized authors anymore.[14]

Yet despite our pretensions to a post-Authorial world, there is a certain sense in which the A/author has never died, much like the old god whom the ugliest man could reawaken in the farcical mass of the ass, in the fourth part of Nietzsche's *Zarathustra*. For as Hans points out, "surely a writer like Derrida could make a comfortable living by touring the United States and giving talks on the dissolution of authority and the end of the ontotheological world of discourse; surely a writer like Derrida (and Foucault while he was still alive) has become a major source of authority" (5–6).

Unlike Hans, who shares enough of the delusion of post-Authorialism to claim that important works can clearly exist outside of the A/author-function, and cites current scientific discourse as proof of the robustness of this statement, I contend that, in certain very distinct ways, the temptation to A/authorialism still persists in the commerce of today's texts. Even the seemingly anonymous production of a scientific fact, the very proof Hans points to as evidence of our post-A/authorial age, is bogus. Have not the names of figures like Darwin and Einstein become just as fetishized/deified?[15] If one were to base one's reasoning upon the observation that the production of a scientific fact depends, to a large extent, upon the exoterization of an esoteric doctrine—i.e., a popularization of specialized scientific knowledge, thereby rendering simultaneously magical and everyday a certain contention about the nature of the world and reality, similar to the way a religion simultaneously sacralizes and secularizes the world—the persistent fetishization of the A/author, even in science, would be hard to argue against. And if even the authorial power vested in individual names, accorded with the status of scientific super-stardom by both the scientific community and the larger public, were denied, there is still the question of how to explain the Authority that Science is imbued with, as a faceless God through whom the promise of the revelation of nature's secrets is invoked.

For me, the crucial question is *not* "[H]ow is authority conferred once God is dead, once everything is interpretation, once there is no self or author to ground and authenticate an utterance?"[16] as Hans phrases it. Rather for me, it is crucial that we inquire into how it is that some notion of "authority" can be preserved or continues

---

14. James Hans, *Contextual Authority and Aesthetic Truth* (Albany: State University of New York Press, 1992), 5.

15. The issue, in my view, is not whether Einstein or Darwin were pure "originals" or simply grand "synthesizers" of pre-existing ideas because I believe the answer is a hybrid of these two options. But rather, the issue is whether the shadow of the Author persists in the way the (supposedly non-Authorial) images of science and scientific fact are generated and operate in society.

16. Hans, *Contextual Authority*, 7.

to operate effectively in spite of the persistent reawakenings of Nietzsche's "old God"-Author. To slip into the categories of Hans's formulation of the problem is to fall, headlong, into the traditional deadlock that has animated the hostilities separating the various stripes of "conservatives" from their "liberal" opponents regarding the problem of authority. As Hans himself characterizes these warring positions, conservatives commonly argue that the horrible vacuum created by Nietzsche's pronouncement that "God is dead" is not a livable "truth"; thus, they argue that there must be grounds for authority, or else the will to power (and chaos and nihilism) is all there is (9). He goes on to sketch the fundamental features of the arguments of the left against the aforementioned contentions by the right.

> The liberals in turn would argue for the utter hopelessness of the conservative position in the late twentieth century, and they would do so with equal *moral* fervor: first, the conservative position is obviously thoroughly discredited by everything the West has learned in the past four hundred years; second, as a result, no one in good conscience could declare that there is any real mode of authorization to be had anymore. . . .
> Even worse, inasmuch as we know the former modes of authorization were used to usurp the power of others, we must recognize that *any* attempt to ground the forms of authorization will end up in the unfair oppression of the other in terms of which the ground will inevitably be defined. (9)

Naturally, so as not to seem to oversimplify these positions, there are various types of conservatives. The standards that serve as the "ground," the haven to which one can escape to flee the horror of the vision of the death of God, are not always the same. Sometimes, these standards spring from a Judeo-Christian structure of absolutes; at other times, they proceed from more generally humanistic grounds. Yet regardless of the specific source of these absolutes, a belief in their necessity is paramount for the conservatives. There may be differentiated, along rough, general lines, a "strong" and a "weak" position in this context. The strong position asserts that such grounding values do indeed exist and are demonstrable. The weak position claims that societies cannot exist without a belief in absolutes, even if the disseminators of them do not necessarily believe in these absolutes. Hans cites Leo Strauss's position as an example of this second, "more clearly elitist" type: "it bears certain similarities to Nietzsche's argument that the herd cannot bear very much reality and that it is therefore the goal of the strong to keep from them the knowledge that would devastate their lives." Even if my own genealogy of Nietzsche's philosophy is highly influenced by Strauss's methods of reading Nietzsche's deliberately crafted "art of interpretation," I, along with Hans (10), regard this persistent pretension to aristocracy (particularly along its increasingly rigid demarcation of the "masculine"/"few"/"noble" from the "feminine"/"many"/"plebeian") as a manifestation of the persistent decadence Nietzsche struggled with and decried throughout his work. In other words, I think Strauss's methodology for reading Nietzsche's politics is a more accurate one, particularly if one were to keep Nietzsche's historical embeddedness in Romanticism in mind. However, I do not think the Nietzsche that results from such an interpretation is one that should be deified, emulated, or treated as a prophet of Truth. Instead, I believe that Nietzsche's very own "malicious" art of interpretation should be applied to him with caution.

Hans states how he believes that the left has reified many of the inadequacies of the persistent A/authorial paradigm through its inversion, though retention, of the elitist categories of "good" and "evil" characteristic of the right in the wake of the supposed death of God.

> We have many studies on how, say, the *feminine*—that is, the *good*—within this or that writer has been previously ignored, just as we have many studies on how the male—that is, the *bad*—within a writer reflects the distortions of the West; and we have a good number of studies that show how the West distorted the third world and Islamic culture and Eastern cultures and Irish culture; but we don't have many serious appraisals of the very rich mixture Western culture is. There are glorifications, and there are denunciations, but not very much in the middle way at all. . . . Under the banners of "openness" and "tolerance" and "non-difference" and the like, one tends to find only a different kind of closedness, intolerance, and redifferentiation. . . . (15)

This is indeed a serious charge, for if there is nothing in between the Scylla and Charybdis of the so-called "right" and "left"-wing interpretations of Nietzsche's politics, the search for modes of legitimation *beyond* the traditional forms of A/authorization is null and void. But that is precisely where I take issue with how to proceed constructively with this dilemma. Perhaps it is less a matter of searching for a ground of legitimation *beyond,* or *neutral* toward, the eternal return of the A/author, and more a matter of channeling our efforts toward a creative and suspicious loosening and expansion from within these structures.

In order to characterize more concretely what I mean by this "loosening" and "expansion," allow me to begin with an observation that Hans and I share.

> [T]he death of God and the dissolution of self and the author had such monumental ramifications that we lost sight of the fact that the original site of the sacred was indeed the aesthetic.

Nietzsche, the writer who did most to establish the altered nature of our discourse and to delineate the effects of the changes, was also the last one seriously to recognize that the Death of God did not mean the death of the aesthetic as well. Instead, it allowed us to see that the sacred derived from the aesthetic rather than the other way around, prompted us to recognize the ways in which authority underlying our discourse was always *aesthetic* in nature rather than grounded in the sacred disposition of the subject or of God. (44)

What results is a return to the links binding aesthetics and politics. Also, invisibly fortifying the two is the structure of myth as gendered in the concrete image-ination of the flows of power and the beautiful. Hans charges Foucault with wanting to deal purely with the politics of discourse, and not the aesthetics of it; thus, Hans argues, it is "inevitable" that Foucault turns away from the aesthetic nature of language. He charges Derrida (at least in Derrida's earliest writings) with the opposite transgression. For Hans, Derrida revels so much in the "joyous affirmation of the freeplay of the world in the older aesthetic sense—that is, as an affirmation that exists more or less in a void, apart from any socius or experiential context that would allow that affirmation to establish a different set of values *in the world*"—that he overlooks the aesthetic connection of language to the pragmatic regulation of the flows of discourse.[17]

One of Hans's principal aims appears to be the domestication of the "political" in service of the "aesthetic." Hence, he reasons that whereas all aesthetic events have interests involved in them, they are not exclusively driven by self-interest, as is the case with the unbridled will to power. He characterizes an aesthetic situation to be one "in which the boundaries between 'self' and 'other,' or 'world,' have loosened precisely because the demand to sustain the self and its fictions is not in question." By declaring the world itself to be an aesthetic place, Hans claims that Nietzsche effectively undercut the more traditional Kantian offshoots that suggested the aesthetic was a place detached from the real. What emerges, in Hans's view, is the irrepressible preeminence of the aesthetic over the political, and a perceptible blind spot in Foucault's philosophy.

Although I am sympathetic to much of what Hans has expressed, I find myself disagreeing with him that the "aesthetic" realm utterly subsumes the "political." A more honest account seems to be that the two are primordially intertwined—with neither necessarily superior to the other, perhaps analogous to Nietzsche's initial vision of the interaction between Apollinian and Dionysian forces in *Birth*. The political and the aesthetic interact with each other in a complex fashion, involving mythic and gendered manifestations.

---

17. Hans limits his critique of Derrida's aesthetics to his early texts; he does not mention Derrida's deconstruction of institutions, which, naturally, have an overt political bent.

It turns out that Hans's desire to elevate the aesthetic realm to a status prior to the political realm is aligned with an ethical motive: "the aesthetic is the one regularly recurring way we have of locating an authority that is at least *potentially* beyond the self-interests of the will to power" (48–49). In other words, if the aesthetic were truly prior to the political, then the monsters of nihilism and chaos can be potentially held at bay—at least in principle. Yet, I argue that as operative within Nietzsche's philosophy, the realms of politics and aesthetics intertwine in a manner that belies the subordination of one to the other; in fact, it appears, based on Nietzsche's example, that it is when either politics or aesthetics is markedly subordinated to the other that either a crude, fatalistic politics, or a nostalgic, Romantic aesthetics emerges, neither of which adequately engages the persistent issue of A/authorization.

Yet another important issue married to the eternal return of the A/author is the problem of *ressentiment*, which drives Nietzsche's increasingly misogynistic and fatalistic philosophy. Part of the reason why Nietzsche feels great nausea over the rabble, and especially "woman"/the "feminine" is because they remind him all too much of his own sicknesses as a son of modernity. He must keep away from them—and especially harness "woman"/the "feminine" because one of the greatest dangers facing him is the possibility of succumbing to the nausea that would force him to see that he, despite his ability to glimpse the vision of the *Übermensch*, is no different from the rabble and vermin in most human respects. Maintaining the myth of "otherness" requires enormous effort. Above all, this perpetually looming encounter with his own mortality would compel Nietzsche to admit that the one thing he shares most with the rabble is that he, too, is driven by *ressentiment*, regardless of his acute knowledge of its destructiveness. And because Nietzsche is always close to this nausea within himself over himself, he can do no more than displace his resentment back to the rabble, and especially "woman"/the "feminine," thereby momentarily fleeing from it and yet guaranteeing its more powerful resurgence in his life as the guilt that results from his inability to overcome his own *ressentiment* comes back to haunt him.

Despite the fundamental points along which my account diverges from Hans's, I believe he provides a powerful analysis of how Nietzsche's persistent will-to-resentment, a reification of the persistent problem of the A/author, results in a dis-eased aesthetic built around bodily differentiations between health and sickness, which is one of the principal pairs of dualistic tropes recurrently refigured in Nietzsche's developing politics.

> The *need* for constant purification through swimming and bathing and splashing suggests that Nietzsche is not quite as comfortable as his body as he would lead us to believe, would suggest further that in trying to scrub off of himself the common air he shares with the rabble, he is trying to wash away his mortality. The linkage between the need to wash and the difficulties he

has in even being *around* general humanity cannot be mistaken, and the nausea is just beneath the surface here. (165)

Yet the issue of *ressentiment* does not stay a problem confined purely to the genesis of Nietzsche's philosophy. Its greater philosophical significance lies in it spilling over to seep into the very ground we ourselves stand upon. As Waite remarks:

> Required is the untimely attempt to grasp, to settle accounts with the uncanny phenomena of the endlessly attractive-repulsive adversary and paranoia that is Nietzsche's corps/e: that is, the living corpus of a dead man's work and the living corps of people it informs, incarnates, embodies, incorporates. . . . Nietzsche's may be the fundamental "hauntology" of our times.[18]

Ressentiment, as Nietzsche recognized it, springs from our all-too-human *un*willingness to accept the circumstances of our lives,[19] and the anxiety of forever living in the shadow of an Author one has declared dead. Consequently, there is the desire for revenge, which often manifests itself in the vindictive desire to create a scapegoat—an other upon whom one may dump the sins of one's mortality, which, in Nietzsche's case, achieves its most concentrated form in the collapsed figures of "woman"/the "feminine" in his post-Zarathustran phase. This desire for revenge is the opposite of one of Nietzsche's most compelling ideals: the vision of the human being who is strong enough to embrace fully and joyfully his or her fate.

Perhaps it is from Nietzsche's utterance of the *amor fati* that some sort of break from the tyranny of the will-to-resentment and the eternal return of the Author may be partially achieved. For if we always fall back upon some notion of "authority" to take stock of our lives, and if we have found that all previous forms of "A/authority" are either incomplete or masked expressions of one kind of self-interest or another, then perhaps there is no more appropriate gauge for our future aspirations than this "love of fate." However, this "fate" is one that is as much embraced as it is actively (re)created along aesthetic, political, mythic, and gendered strands, which interweave to form a complex fabric—a fabric we, "feminine" and "masculine," take full responsibility for weaving.

In other words, another way of reconceiving the constructive aspect of Nietzsche's response to the hidden selfishness of the so-called "descending" or life-denying sources of A/authority, is to focus on pained awareness of the degree to which *ressentiment* has been a primary sculpting force of human action in the world. Hans leaps

---

18. Waite, *Nietzsche's Corps/e*, 8.
19. Nietzsche propagates the doctrine of *amor fati* but is unable to live up to it—a root of the *ressentiment* that fuels his increasingly misogynistic politics and aesthetics.

joyfully toward a more optimistic conclusion than I would, based on these premises. He states: "Instead of guaranteeing the return of the repressed resentment through the guilty discipline of hiding the interests of the self, Nietzsche's version of self-interest asserts that there are forms of self-interest that are also *others*' interests, and that as joyful expressions of what is, they manage therefore also to do justice to the nature of the world."[20]

In contrast, I argue that although the grounds for authorization are ultimately rooted in this ability to interpret, and reconstruct, along mythic and gendered lines, a politics and aesthetics appropriate to our perpetual struggle with the continued R/resurrection of the A/author, I do not believe there is a realistic sense in which we can be certain that the selfishness necessary for affirming life necessarily sublates into a selfishness that is also in others' interests. The beast of the will-to-power never lurks far from the glorious vision of the coming of the *Übermensch*; the self-endowed authority of the "psychologist of the Eternally feminine" is conferred only through the damnation of "woman." Politics and aesthetics, equally prodigal, treacherous and surging with vitality, lie locked in an apparent embrace, which allows them neither to draw too close, nor to be radically separated. The results of an embrace that is too close, or an attempt at totally divorcing the two are the same—either an aesthetic that is maniacally driven by a politic, or an aesthetic blind to its political motivations, or a politics ruthlessly devoted to the aestheticization of its brutality.

If Hans is right that "any way one chooses to look at the question of the 'Nietzschean' perspective, it comes down to the exuberant celebration of life in the midst of its tragedy" (145), I feel compelled to add that the nature of this embrace of life must lie rooted against the ever-looming temptation of resurrecting the A/authorial function, and the ever-present indulgence in *ressentiment*. In other words, if we are to learn from the genealogy of Nietzsche's writings, we must learn how to live with the lack of certitude that accompanies an awareness of "authority" as always tinged with the possibility of the return of the Authorial referent, even when it is denied. And with this ever-present possibility is the resentful temptation of splitting the "same" from the "other," the "few" from the "many," the "noble" from the "plebeian," the "short-eared" from the "long-eared," the "masculine"/"man" from the "feminine"/"woman"—as we have seen Nietzsche, the resentment-resenting, self-resenting man attempting to establish an authority devoid of the Authorial function, succumb to bitterly. As Ansell-Pearson eloquently phrases it:

> We must strive to create the new through a creation which does not forget or ignore the horrors and sufferings of the past, but redeems the past and all that was by recognizing that it is a condition of any future creative willing that it

20. Hans, *Contextual Authority*, 334–35.

must engage in a labour of self-overcoming, for only a buffoon thinks the past can be jumped over. . . . Nietzsche is right in pointing out that, in order to achieve an emancipatory, creative willing, it will be necessary to affirm the paradoxes associated with the task of self-overcoming by recognizing the tragic conditions of creative human existence.[21]

If, in some ways, the will-to-resentment and possibility of the recurrent reification of the Author are a feature of modern existence—which continues to nurture and poison us today—what is left? Perhaps a vision steeped less in the impossible dream of redemption and transcendence, characteristic of Nietzsche's pre-Zarathustran period, and even less, in blood-lust and destruction, characteristic of Nietzsche's post-Zarathustran period, but in a project of perpetual resistance and revisioning—against these twin temptations of Author-ship and resentment. Such a resistance, if it is to be realistic, must root itself in the dynamic contextual fluctuations of the interweaving issues of power, beauty, the sacred, and the gendered. Drawing from feminist thinkers like Donna Haraway, Susan Bordo, Bat-Ami Bar On, and bell hooks, Daniel Conway outlines some of the more promising epistemological aspects of Nietzsche's perspectivism.

> Let us be clear about the political costs of embracing [Nietzsche's] perspectivism: . . . we must abandon the quest for a privileged, epistemically pure, God's-eye perspective on the world. We need not disavow our cultural, genealogical or political preferences for certain perspectives, but we must be careful to situate these preferences within a discernible political agenda. The privilege of a particular perspective will derive entirely from its situation within the political agenda it expresses, and not from its internal coherence or privileged access to the real world.[22]

Moving Beyond *Ressentiment* and the "Feminine"

Marion Tapper astutely points out how some feminist practices, characterized by wholesale denunciations of men, patriarchy, sex, language, philosophy, and every aspect of Western discourse and society, are motivated by *ressentiment*, and have been

---

21. Ansell-Pearson, *Nietzsche Contra Rousseau*, 231.
22. Daniel Conway, *Nietzsche and the Political* (New York: Routledge, 1997), 132–33. See also Daniel Conway, "*Das Weib an sich*: The Slave Revolt in Epistemology," in *Nietzsche, Feminism, and Political Theory*, ed. Paul Patton (New York: Routledge, 1993), 110–29.

preoccupied with power as control. These approaches spawn twin dangers: of reinforcing rather than undercutting repressive techniques of surveillance, normalization, and control, and of being forgetful of, or repressing, other positive forms of the will to power, such as those concerned with self-formation and autonomy. Nevertheless, she succinctly outlines some more positive thrusts open to feminism. "Rather than seeking power over, women in the academies are trying to establish discursive spaces for the expression of feminine specificities, expressions that have been denied by the dominant patriarchal discourses and social and political structures."[23]

And indeed, Tapper's warning concerning the ever-lurking fall to *ressentiment* resounds well with the main themes of this book. Nevertheless, in addition to warning of dangers, an equally urgent task, for me, lies in the realm of attempting to wrestle with the specter of *ressentiment* and the Author in view of having uncovered these dynamic imbrications linking aesthetics, politics, and myth. Thus, for a brief glimpse of what a situated, gendered, and mythic revisioning of an aesthetic politics might look like, I preliminarily begin with the insights of Hélène Cixous and Trinh Minh-ha. Both women have struggled with concrete issues binding politics and aesthetics rooted in contexts of gender. Both display an acute sensitivity to the role myth plays in shaping the imaginative revisioning of society, along the fluctuating demarcations separating the empowered from the disempowered, the beautiful/healthy from the ugly/ diseased, and the "masculine"/ "man" from the "feminine"/ "woman." As such, they constitute vivid examples of where outlines of a genuinely post-Romantic, post-Nietzschean politico-aesthetic may partially lie.

Cixous's writing corpus questions the relations binding politics and writing, the dimensions and implications of sexual difference, possible interactions between philosophy and literature, and the tenability of an identity based on ethical, textual, and political difference from dominant social relations. In her readings of works of writers such as Joyce, Hoffmann, Kleist, and Lispector, her interests shift from a deconstructive commitment to the materiality of the signifier, to an exploration of subjectivity and sexuality, and then move toward the development of an alternative textual, political, and ethical economy which she describes as "feminine." "Sorties"[24] draws attention to traditional oppositions such as "culture/nature," "head/heart," "form/matter," "speaking/writing," and attempts to trace their relationship to the opposition between "man" and "woman." Again and again, the critique she mounts against these rigid oppositions amounts to more than an argument against dualism, but rather to a political and philosophical rejection of the dialectical relation between

---

23. Marion Tapper, "*Ressentiment* and Power: Some Reflections on Feminist Practices," in *Nietzsche, Feminism, and Political Theory*, ed. Paul Patton (New York: Routledge, 1993), 141.

24. Hélène Cixous, "Sorties," trans. B. Wing, in *The Newly Born Woman* (Manchester: Manchester Universiy Press, 1986), 63–132.

each of these "couples," which elevates one term of the opposition necessarily at the other's expense. Shiach summarizes a few important points regarding the nature of Cixous's attack upon these traditional philosophical binaries.

> Cixous does not invent these systems of oppositions: she reads them off a series of literary, mythical, and philosophical texts, finding their purest articulation in Hegel's *Phenomenology of the Spirit.* The danger, for Cixous, in such philosophical and social categories, lies in their absolute dependence on strategies of power and exclusion. Each couple is based on the repression of one of its terms, yet both terms are locked together in a violent conflict. Without 'nature,' 'culture' is meaningless, yet culture must continually struggle to negate nature, to dominate and control it, with obviously deadly results.[25]

What is objectionable about these dialectical structures for Cixous, is that they also dominate the shaping of subjectivity, and consequently, of sexual difference. Cixous uses Hegel's "master/slave" dialectic as a paradigm of a type of subjectivity that is both limited and destructive: "a subjectivity that experiences itself only when it makes its law, its strength, its mastery felt."[26] Here, subjectivity requires the recognition of an Other, from whom the individual differentiates him- or herself. Yet this encounter is experienced as threatening, and the Other is immediately repressed, so that the subject can return to the security and certainty of self-knowledge—a critique that certainly resonates with Nietzsche's increasingly desperate attempts to harness the mythic figures of the "feminine"/"woman" and transplant their powers into his super-"masculine" mythic counterpart, Zarathustra.

Cixous argues that woman within a patriarchal social and cultural formation becomes figured or represented, as the Other—necessary to the constitution and recognition of identity, but always threatening to it. Sexual difference thus becomes locked into a structure of power, where difference, or otherness, is tolerated only when it is repressed; in Nietzsche's case, the attempt at repression eventually becomes so extreme that it leads to the attempt either to demonize or totally obliterate this otherness, as his post-Zarathustran writings reveal.

In general, Cixous's strategies for dismantling and revisioning these intertwined hierarchized structures of philosophical and political thought, and of cultural representations, may be roughly classified into two categories. The first step results in a deconstructive reading, which is presented as a critique of the narrative of origins, of the "Dawn of Phallocentrism." This reading/rewriting of the invisible history of philosophy, politics, and representation is intended to question the naturalness or

---

25. Morag Shiach, *Hélène Cixous: A Politics of Writing* (New York: Routledge, 1991), 7.
26. Cixous, "Sorties," 80.

inevitability of such structural hierarchies. The second step involves an exploration of the subversive, and the political, possibilities of a writing practice that deliberately sets itself up as a foil to such cultural categorization. Cixous calls this type of writing practice as "feminine."

Cixous's work is of particular interest to me as she consciously works at revealing the links binding the fluid constructions of myth alongside its political and aesthetic transformations. For instance, in her deconstructive readings of the *Oresteia*, she aims, like Irigaray, whose method has greatly influenced mine, to recapture what is repressed in this patriarchal myth of origins—to give voice to the hidden violence, the excess, and the justified murder of the Mother/Woman of excess and passion that play a crucial role in the establishment of patriarchy. Another example illustrating Cixous's striking use of mythology in line with her deconstructive thrust is her analysis of the politics of gender at work in Kleist's *Penthesilea*. Cixous details the unsettling of economies of war caused by the passionate love of Achilles and Penthesilea, and unflinchingly follows the development of their relationship through its catastrophic end: Penthesilea consumes the flesh of the fallen Achilles prior to killing herself. For Cixous, such a violent ending is but the inevitable consequence of the patriarchal economy of opposition, resentment, and war.

In terms of her more constructive bent, her attempt to explore a distinctively "feminine" writing, Cixous both describes and attempts a type of writing that transgresses and extends the boundaries of traditional narrative structures, and attempts to create subjectivities that are plural and shifting. She urges that when women begin to write as women, they must remain in critical collaboration with the languages and narratives they inherit and inhabit. They must invent new beginnings, detach themselves from the fixed categories and identities they have been pressed into, explore the "third body," which is encircled by neither the "inside" nor the "outside" but fluidly constitutes the space between.[27]

Cixous upholds that it is only via such an experimentation that women can challenge the culturally produced category of "woman" (which, in her case, seems to be the same as the blurring of the "feminine"/"woman" characteristic of Nietzsche's post-Zarathustran phase). The figure of "woman" is a representation, projected by the Law of the Father, policed through exclusion and censure as well as through modes of thought based on hierarchy and opposition. It is via writing, Cixous argues, that women can explore other identifications, other images. They can rediscover some of what has been unexpressed, or actively repressed—and to some extent, break free of or destabilize through constant reconfiguration the patriarchal mytho-politics. Ultimately, she argues for the possibility of sustaining a "bisexuality" in opposition

---

27. *Le Troisieme Corps* is also the title of a novel by Cixous, published in 1970.

to the "masculine"-"feminine" duality that has tyrannized the categories of philosophy. Such a bisexuality, she hastens to add, does not constitute a denial of sexual difference, but is an attempt at a lived recognition of plurality, of the individual subject, male or female. The bisexuality Cixous advocates[28] is theoretically open to all subjects who dare to attempt escape from the subjective and social effects of the patriarchal/modern/Romantic structures of desire that have contoured the formation of much of the history of philosophy, and is especially evident in the case of the post-Zarathustran Nietzsche.[29]

Hélène Cixous's scorn for the search for a neutral language is directed mainly at the immense majority of a "species of women scribblers"—a faceless majority whose technique is indistinguishable from masculine writing, and who either hide their womanhood or regurgitate patriarchal representations of "woman." To one characterization of bisexuality conceived of as fusion or erasure, Cixous opposes *an other bisexuality*, that of "the discovery in itself, individually, of the presence, diversely manifest and insistent according to each man or woman, of both sexes, non-exclusion of difference nor of sex, and from this 'permission' that one gives oneself, multiplication of the effects of the inscription of desire, on all parts of my body and the other body."[30]

Shiach describes one of Cixous's works that, for her, illustrates the more constructive, rather than deconstructive side of Cixous's political aesthetic.

---

28. Naturally, Cixous's position has not escaped critique, even and especially from feminists. For instance, Stanton's basic anxiety is that Cixous is returning to a metaphysics of identity and presence. The use of metaphor itself, she argues, alludes to an economy of similitude rather than one of difference. Cixous's choice of the maternal as the strategic point of engagement with the politics of sexual difference, however, raises particular issues for Stanton, threatening as it does to return to the certainties of biology and the "naturalness" of motherhood. Cf. Donna C. Stanton, "Difference on Trial: A Critique of the Maternal Metaphor in Cixous, Irigaray, and Kristeva," in *The Poetics of Gender*, ed. N. K. Miller (New York: Columbia University Press, 1986), 157–82.

29. It is interesting that Margaret Fuller's mythic "sacred marriage" within individuals predates, to some extent, Cixous's notion of "bisexuality." Briefly summarized, Fuller argues that men have a "Vulcan" ("masculine") and an "Apollo" ("feminine") side; women have the qualities of a "Minerva" ("masculine") and a "Muse" ("feminine") side. What is striking to me is that Fuller's schema enables men and women to possess "masculine" and "feminine" traits which are qualitatively different from each other because they draw from different gendered mythic figures. Such an approach potentially obviates the objection that "bisexuality" actually encourages the homogenization of gendered entities. Yet the weakness of Fuller's approach appears to be its appeal to a form of mythic transcendentalism—ignoring issues of multiculturalism and the construction of sexuality. What ultimately emerges in Fuller, in terms of political practice, is an appeal to a neutral, transcultural, perhaps even ahistorical foundation beyond "masculinity" and "femininity"—something that neither Cixous nor I would believe to be an effective response to the problem of genuine postmodernity. Cf. Margaret Fuller, "Woman in the Nineteenth Century," in *The Essential Margaret Fuller*, ed. J. Steele (Piscataway: Rutgers University Press, 1992).

30. Cixous, "The Laugh of the Medusa."

In *Le Livre Promethea*, Cixous succeeds in creating a novel that dramatizes many of her convictions about the transformative potential of a feminine economy. Her allusive use of myth facilitates this process, since it allows her to call on the resources of the dominant culture without being trapped within it. Milton, Dante, Shelley, Ariosto, and the Bible offer her narratives and images which she combines within a collage of voices that subvert their authority while acknowledging their intellectual and emotional power.[31]

Like Cixous, Trinh Minh-ha, a Vietnamese-American filmmaker and feminist critic, launches a parallel attack against patriarchal dualisms, and addresses the need to re-conceive and pluralize the notion of "subjectivity" along not only gendered but also cross-cultural lines. She writes:

> In the heterogeneity of the feminist struggle and its plurivocal subjects, the impossibility of defining once and for all the condition of being sexualized as feminine and racialized as colored does not result from a lack of determination, but rather, from an inescapable awareness of the sterility of the unitary subject and its monolithic constructs.[32]

Minh-ha also draws attention to the close conjunction between the realms of power and aesthetics in her critique of ideological representation. The function of an ideology in power is to re-create the world in its own image—to re-present the world as wholly unified. Prevailing regimes of representation, insofar as they share in the Master's Law of the center versus the marginal, must be disrupted at their foundations, and not simply reversed within an economy of the S/same. The risk of the return of the A/author and the cycling of the circle of resentment is ever-present, regardless of whether one is at the Center or in the margins. "The risk of reproducing totalitarianism is always present and one would have to confront, in whatever capacity one has, the controversial values likely to be taken on faith as universal truths by one's own culture/s" (19).

For even the notion of Center versus margins is a vestige of patriarchal dualism. There is only a Center insofar as there are margins against which it can define itself; margins as margins point toward a Center against which they measure themselves and aim to claim for themselves. To break out or at least loosen this bind, Minh-ha advocates a different kind of vocabulary or representation. What is necessary, according to her, is "to see through the revolving door of all rationalizations and to meet head on the truth of that struggle *between fictions*" (6).

---

31. Shiach, *Hélène Cixous*, 100.
32. Trinh Minh-ha, *When the Moon Waxes Red: Representation, Gender, and Cultural Politics* (New York: Routledge, 1991), 6.

What results is an insightful account of the interplay between aesthetics and politics. If art is understood as a form of (re)production—a perpetual commerce of myths—then a crucial issue facing liberation movements is not that of liquidating art in its not-quite-correct, ungovernable dimension, but rather, that of confronting the limits of Centralized knowledge. That is, a principal task in reconfiguring the Modern/resentful relationships between politics and aesthetics is simultaneously to demystify and politicize the artistic experience.

> When the textual and the political neither separate themselves from one another nor simply collapse into a single qualifier, the practice of representation can, similarly, neither be taken for granted, nor merely dismissed as being ideologically reactionary. By putting representation under scrutiny, textual theory-practice has more likely helped to upset rooted ideologies by bringing the mechanics of their workings to the fore. (42)

Like Cixous, Minh-ha returns to the structure of narrative (which functions at the heart of Cixous's characterization of "feminine writing") as a means of at least loosening the master-slave dialectic. For Minh-ha, s/he who speaks, speaks *to/through* the tale as s/he begins telling and retelling it; s/he does not speak *about* it. "Speaking about" is complicit in the conservation of the resentful systems of binary opposition ("subject"/"object," "I"/"It," "We"/"They") upon which territorialized knowledge depends. Speaking about, rather than speaking to/through secures for the speaker a position of mastery: the Same appropriates, owns, and demarcates sovereign territory as it advances while the other is relegated to the sphere of acquisition that the Same talks about.

Replacing speaking about with speaking to/through is possible for Minh-ha because narration (similar to Cixous's "writing") is a form of mediation, where the story and its telling are essentially adaptive. A narration can never be a passive reflection of reality; yet at the same time, it must always be "truthful" if it is to unwind compellingly and beautifully. "Truth" here, however, is not attained through the resentful dualism between truth and lie. As Minh-ha eloquently phrases it:

> Perhaps, when it is a question of both the lie and its truth, and the truth and its lie (if "lie" is what you think a "beautiful language" and a "fantastic story" are), this doubling back which enables the tale to designate itself, leads us necessarily to the deepest interiority (peculiar to the tradition of Western thought), but also to the "outside" (speech as speech) in which the speaking subject dis/appears. I am useless, useful. The boundaries of truth and lie are thus multiplied, reversed, and displaced without rendering meaningless either the notion of the lie or that of truth. (13–14)

The issue of authority, as aligned with the issue of reflexivity, consequently diversifies against this backdrop of the fabric formed from the intertwining of the realms of the artistic and the political. For if reflexivity can be reconceived as radically plural in scope, then "reflexivity is thus not a mere question of *rect*ifying and *just*ifying (*Subject*ifying)" (48). What is instead put into play are self-generating links between different forms of reflexivity, and thus, different forms of authority, enabling a brief yet distinct splintering of the spectre of Authority. Thus, a subject who points to him/her/itself is subject-in-process; a work that displays its own formal properties or its own constitution as work can unsettle one's sense of identity. The all-too-familiar distinction between the Same and the Other can be loose-ened since the latter is no longer kept in a recognizable relation of dependence, derivation, or appropriation. The process of self-constitution is less redemptive than it is marked by resistance—a process in which the self vacillates and loses its assurance.

In reply to the recurring question of how the Same-Other dualism may be reconfigured, Minh-ha has one suggestion: to let "difference" replace "conflict." By "difference," she means a state of becoming that is not necessarily set in opposition against "sameness," nor synonymous with "separateness." In other words, a type of "difference" does not necessarily lead to the yawning gap of separatism that enables the Center/Same and the marginal/other to set themselves against each other.

> There are differences as well as similarities within the concept of difference. One can further say that difference is not what makes conflicts. It is beyond and alongside conflict . . . many of us still hold onto the concept of difference not as a tool of creativity—to question multiple forms of repression and dominance—but as a tool of segregation—to exert power on the basis [of] racial and sexual essences. The apartheid-type of difference. (150)

Unlike Cixous, who writes with words, Minh-ha "writes" with filmic images and sound. Among her artistic trademarks are her unorthodox uses of silence and the veil. She acknowledges that the "feminization" of silence and the veil poses the danger of inscribing the "feminine" as absence, lapse, and blank that could be interpreted as "inadequacy" in the attempt to reject the importance of the act of enunciation. On the other hand, she aligns herself with the political aims necessitating the placement of women on the side of negativity (Kristeva), and the location of work in "undertones" (Irigaray) in the broad-based feminist attempt to undermine patriarchal/ resentful systems of values. What Minh-ha attempts to do, which does have Nietzschean underpinnings, is to revalue silence and the act of veiling or unveiling as expressions of power, rather than of lack, of "woman"/the"feminine"/women.

> Silence is so commonly set in opposition with speech. Silence as a will not to say or a will to unsay, a language of its own, has barely been explored.
> ... If the act of unveiling has a liberating potential, so does the act of veiling. It all depends on the context in which such an act is carried out, or more precisely, on how and where women see dominance. Difference should neither be defined by the dominant sex nor by the dominant culture. So that when women decide to lift the veil, one can say that they do so in defiance of their men's oppressive right to their bodies; but when they decide to keep or to put back on the veil they once took off, they may do so to reappropriate their space or to claim anew difference, in defiance of genderless hegemonic standardization. (150–51)

Another compelling feature I find in Minh-ha's work is her drawing from the mythologies of various cultures. Unlike Nietzsche and Cixous who predominantly appropriate and rewrite/retell Greek myths, Minh-ha draws from Chinese, Japanese, Vietnamese, American Indian, and African myths, resulting in a rich, multicultural critique of the Greek-centered Western tradition of dualisms. As an example of how Minh-ha skillfully integrates myth into her politico-aesthetic aims, I cite her reference to the Chinese myths of Moon-Queen Chang E who swallows the pill of immortality, the hare which throws itself into the magical fire to feed Buddha, and the Sun-King who comes to visit his wife Chang E on the fifteenth day of every moon—as the precursors to the Apollo landing on the moon. These myths pre-existed and continue to persist alongside the scientific and Western-based myths of the soon to be completed colonization of the "new moon." While the promise of the scientific dream of moon conquest has not been kept, the "old moon" continues to hover above the earth, resisting the logocentric assumptions of the West. The war of fictions is ongoing, and Minh-ha uses the figure of the "old moon" as one of her weapons.

> In the renewed terrain of struggle and of deterritorialized subjectivities, no moon-lovers can really claim possession of the soft light that illuminates towns, villages, forests, and fields. *The same moon that rises over the ocean lands in tea water. The wind that cools the waters scatters the moons like rabbits in a meadow.* . . . The one moon is seen in all waters; and the many-one moon is enjoyed or bawled at on a quiet night by people everywhere—possessors and dispossessed. (3)

Within this cross-cultural and gendered politico-aesthetic, therefore, to make a claim for multi-culturalism is not to advocate the juxtaposition-opposition of several cultures whose frontiers remain impermeable, nor is it to subscribe to a complacent "melting pot" concept that would seek to level all differences, thus enabling the return of the all too Nietzschean spectres of Author and *ressentiment*. It lies, instead, in an intercultural acceptance and active exploration of risks, unexpected detours, and the complexities of binding break and closure. A philosophy of the future, if it is to try to overcome its roots in resentment and the persistence of modern A/authority requires that such boundaries be ceaselessly called into question, undermined, modified, and reinscribed. Nietzsche's recurrent tropes of sickness versus health must, in my view, be revalued as entailing gradations of sickness/resentment as intertwined with health/the vigilant resistance to resentment. A politico-aesthetic of transformation, rather than obliteration-redemption must, in my opinion, critically approach, question, and rewrite its mythic, gendered, and cultural foundations and manifestations. Such a critical inquiry should be animated by the search for different approaches to politico-aesthetic experience(s), different ways of relating to them without categorizing/fixing them in the deadly dualisms Nietzsche struggled against, yet did not manage to free himself from.

Closing Remarks

Although there are some aspects of Levine's reading of Nietzsche with which I do not agree, such as his statement that "Nietzsche's account of the 'Eternal Feminine' is a hymn of praise and a self-description, hidden amid diversionary comments about women as cooks and so on,"[33] I do think his differentiation between a strictly "modern" paradigm and a genuinely "post-modern" paradigm is useful, in terms of trying to grapple with the concrete issues of multiculturalism, gender, and power that face us in the wake of the ever-looming possibility of the eternal return of the A/author and of *ressentiment*.

Levine effectively uses figures to differentiate between what he calls the "Modern"/ apparently postmodern position and the genuinely "post-modern" position. The Modern Paradigm characterizes the revolt against reason—which Levine views as the most pronounced feature of what he dismisses—as "so-called 'postmodern' thought." The principal objection Levine mounts against it is that is does appear to be "a truly *post-*modern development; it is merely a moment of renunciation, a declaration of revolt, a recognition of modernity's contradictions, beyond which nothing comprehensible lies" (188).

33. Peter Levine, *Nietzsche and the Modern Crisis of the Humanities* (Albany: State University of New York Press, 1995), 135.

To gesture toward an alternative vision, Levine points to two observations—that there is diversity *within* cultures, and the crucial determining factors in our lives also cut *across* cultural lines. "Cultures" represent useful categories in which to locate people who share similar characteristics in some tangible manner. But these categories can be (re)configured in many ways, and the resulting pattern is not a series of sharply delimited and juxtaposed islands, but a tangled and crisscrossing web.

While I agree with Levine that this is a clear formulation of some of the problems we face as an age grappling with the shadow of Nietzsche's resentful and A/authorial philosophy, I disagree that gender, class, religion, sexual orientation, ethnic identity, and language all fall neatly and homogenously into the umbrella schema of the "cultural." With the nonconfrontation of the complex interaction binding nature and culture(s) in Levine's vision of postmodernity, the solution becomes merely a matter of making certain no single "category" (gender, class, religion . . .) becomes "privileged." Although Levine does acknowledge that "the line between the natural and the cultural is difficult to draw, to say the least" (191), he makes no sustained effort to address that issue across concrete instances involving differences across genders, myths, classes, religions, and so on.

I agree with Levine that a truly postmodern philosophy must abandon the notion of a universal "human nature" as the ultimate precondition for genuine communication, and instead assume a complex web of differences that binds and separates us to varying degrees. But I also think that such a post-Nietzschean philosophy must locate itself within the prevailing socio-politico-economic conditions. As a philosophy dedicated to the ongoing resistance against (rather than redemption from) the vicious return of *ressentiment*, I believe it must locate itself, not in Levine's abstract and neutral (ad)vantage point, but in concrete practices of representation, re-presence-ing, overturning, reshaping the shifting contours of politics and aesthetics. To me, that entails a commitment to trying to understand and participate in the broader framework of the political and ethical struggles of the marginalized—in a still primarily patriarchal, neocolonial world. It also requires the aims of trying to preserve cultural diversity in the face of homogenization, and of attempting to resist the deadly cynicism of subjective and social domination—which is but another reification of the ever-lurking will-to-resentment that possessed Nietzsche, and continues to haunt us today. To illustrate concretely how I see myself beginning to enter into the complex interplay of politics, aesthetics, myth, and gender across a multicultural spectrum, as both a philosopher and an artist, I wish to present one of the pen and ink sketches I have worked on and displayed in various exhibitions during the nine-year period I have been shuttling across the Philippines, England, South Korea, and the United States. It is but one sketch among others, but I take it to be paradigmatic of a direction I envisage myself moving toward.

The title of the piece is "Nurturance?" The drawing's central image is that of an aborigine mother bending down to feed the young of a wild boar, which leans, from the viewer's point of view, upon her left thigh as it suckles from her left breast. Upon her upraised right knee, she straddles a child, whose face is turned away. The mother's hand supports the back of the child, as the child's arm reaches out for one of the necklaces dangling from its mother's neck.

The image is ambiguous and often elicits conflicting interpretations. One viewed it as the image of *caritas*—the total, unselfish generosity with which a mother gives herself to all who are vulnerable and in need. Yet another viewed it as an image of rivaling oppositions, as it appears that the woman's act of suckling the wild boar deprives the child of the care and attention necessary to give her other breast to that child whose visible back, elbow, and legs seem in between nestling within and struggling against the mother's embrace. This viewer also drew attention to the fact that the mother's right breast appears diminutive compared to the left one, which swells with ripeness from the young boar's lips.

Yet another viewer pointed out the fact that the mother's gesture gently supports the child, while the grip with which she supports the suckling boar is much tighter and more restrictive. Ultimately, as the larger social setting is that of a primitive tribe in a wilderness, the question of what the woman intends to do with the boar later comes up—nurture it as a pet, set it free when it is mature enough to fend for itself, or eventually prepare it as a meal for her family.

Yet another viewer came up to me, claiming to see the outlines of a hidden self-portrait of myself in this drawing. For him, the left side, with its image of the suckling boar, signifies my Filipino background, with its tropicality; its spontaneous fusion with nature. The right side, to him, was emblematic of the Western-inspired conflicting aspirations both to career and motherhood, and its tendency to disjoin me from my Filipino background.

Notwithstanding the exoticizing/Orientalizing tendencies of some of the responses this particular drawing has elicited, the ambiguity of the image is particularly appealing to me, as it illustrates how the recurrence of the Same-other distinction (and thus, the will-to-resentment) reifies itself in the most subtle forms, across cultural and gendered lines. The drawing was an attempt to address or at least to put to question several issues that have repeatedly surfaced in my experiences as a perpetual insider-outsider to both Eastern and Western cultures. What does it mean to be characterized as a "Filipino" woman—a woman whose mother tongue was English and whose name reveals my lack of racial purity, particularly within the context of the Philippines, a country whose history is marred by successive foreign conquests? What does it entail, having the label "Filipino" emblazoned across my very being—a label applied, with ease, to overseas maids and factory workers; to dancers and prostitutes;

Looking Back, Looking Forward 177

"Nurturance?" by the author

to mail-order brides; to the opulent and corrupt Marcoses; to the image of a tropical paradise? What does it mean, longing for and being suspicious of, the gender roles inscribed in the Catholic tradition I have been raised in? What realms of being/becoming are allowed by looking "Asian" to non-Asians and "not-quite-Asian" to Asians? What mechanisms of power are in play for one who is shaped by both East and West, in language, values, and experiences?

The title of the piece, "Nurturance?," flows from two springs. First, it draws from one of the most distinctive mythic motifs that inhabits the Filipino imagination, as expressed in its literature, films, and visual and plastic arts. That myth is of *Ina*, the immortal image of Mother as eternal fount of life; source of milk, blood and heat; the ultimate bastion of protection and nurturance within an environment where minor demons, like *dwendes* (cantankerous dwarfs living underground), *tikbalangs* (horselike creatures capable of aerial flight and deeds of malice), and *aswangs* (female vampires who look like innocent country lasses or irresistable beauty queens by day), inhabit the ant hills, trees, and caves one meets everyday. Second, it problematizes the political effectiveness of this aestheticized myth, particularly against the backdrop of the persisting neocolonial condition of the Philippines as a Third World country. "Nurturance," particularly within the context of a neocolonialism—a colonialism that continues to exist, not because of overt military conquest, but because of a thorough-going colonializing mentality, along with an invisible politico-economic stranglehold upon the supposedly liberated "former" colony—is a double-edged sword. The myth of *Ina* becomes protean, used to suit various ideological ends: to perpetuate the myth of the benevolent West as well as the helpless and blameless East, resulting in tyrannies of enclosure and exclusion. The complex and ambiguous interplay of culture and nature, or savagery and civility, which may be glimpsed in the woman's grasp upon the wild boar suckling her breast, often leads to rivaling wills to resentment, with the outsider dismissing the insider as "primitive" and the insider labeling the outsider as *peke* (literally, "fake" or "artificial"—metaphorically, "someone who has forgotten how to live genuinely").

Furthermore, the drawing is done using a predominantly pointillistic technique, employing various gradations of black dots of different sizes, to simulate the chiaroscuro of a shard of light breaking upon the woman's shoulder, as well as the shadows that soften and define the swelling curve of the woman's breast, and the rotundity of the child's belly against the crook of its arm pressed against the woman's other breast. From afar, it looks like a black and white photograph, as the pinpoints of ink and white spaces mingle to give the illusion of straight, unbroken lines and a grainy texture characteristic of some types of film. And indeed, simply from afar, devoid of context, the drawing is as if it were a snapshot taken by an anthropologist studying the practices of a primitive tribe, or perhaps a tourist stumbling upon what seems like a bizarre scene worth taking a snapshot of. Yet if the viewer were to draw closer, the "snapshotish" character of the drawing—its seeming enclosure within the realms of anthropological dissection or touristic consumerism—dissolves into a mass of dots and white spaces that disruptively mimes the outlines of a problematic rather than a resolution.

Caught within the interstices of being cross-cultural and female, "Nurturance?" is, to me, an image that captures the power and beauty of that dangerous, nostalgic longing for the archetypal, ancestral home: a vision that often hardens into a political desire for absolute enclosure within a constructed notion of racial purity (another reification of the Authorial temptation), and of clear, dividing lines between what is within (Same) as opposed to what is without (other) (yet another manifestation of *ressentiment*).

Naturally, this image must be located within the boundaries of a larger project, if it is to rise above the merely individual and incidental. For now, I envisage myself continuing to explore how my interests in philosophy and art may converge to address concrete issues of artistic representation that have political, gendered, and mythic dimensions. This ongoing project, as far as I can frame it at this stage, aims to explore the subtle reifications of *ressentiment* that may be glimpsed through the arduous attempts to maintain the various tyrannical dualisms characteristic of the modern/Romantic period, which continue to operate today. Such an excavation of the modes of construction, deconstruction, and reconstruction of the Same-other divide aims to understand better how the notion of "resistance" (as opposed to "redemption" or "salvation") may be concretely approximated in what may be termed the "politics of spectatorship"—a politics that is often invisibly at work not only in gazing at art gallery paintings or museum pieces, but also in the everyday realm of television advertisements and popular culture. Ultimately, this ongoing project aims to move toward developing what may be termed an "ocular politics"—a politics of the gaze. Such a perspective frames and reframes questions such as: What mechanisms of empowerment and disempowerment are at play when one is categorized as an exotic "other" to cultures one is both part of and apart from? What enables the act of gazing to become an expression of power, particularly within the context of tourism? What myths are at work in the war of fictions re-presenting the "masculine" and "feminine" across various cultures, and how do these myths function to reify a politics and aesthetics of resentment?

While this project is certainly far from flawlessly conceptualized, it does confront the problem of the persistence of the "Modern" stance that Levine describes, which may be characterized as but another version of the twin problems of *ressentiment* and the possible reawakening(s) of the Author. What I would prefer to do, as a philosopher-artist who is also a woman and of mixed ancestry, is to resist Levine's abstract and neutral stance, and to get involved in actively and vigilantly reconfiguring the fluctuating boundaries of the political, aesthetic, mythic, and gendered web that differentially encloses each of us. I believe that it is only when questions of philosophy are grounded in concrete, everyday experiences and cross-cultural and gendered figure-ations of power and beauty, that philosophy can genuinely aspire to the title, "post-Modern." Only then can such a philosophy of the future move toward a realistic and workable notion of "resistance" against the residual poison of *ressentiment*. Yet such a project can be embraced only within the shadow of the possible return(s) of the A/author, and the renunciation of the dream of redemption. Like Kleist, we find that the front gate to the garden of Eden is shut; the only way in (if we can ever regain it or if it is even a question of regaining something we have lost) is through the back door—whose "backness" we must revalue in order to splinter the all too Modern dualism of "front"-"back-ness."

Bibliography

Ackerman, Robert John. *Nietzsche: A Frenzied Look*. Amherst: University of Massachusetts Press, 1990.
Ainley, Alison. "'Ideal Selfishness': Nietzsche's Metaphor of Maternity." In *Exceedingly Nietzsche*, edited by David Farrell Krell and David Wood. New York: Routledge, 1988.
Alighieri, Dante. *The Divine Comedy*. Translated by Carlyle-Wicksteed. New York: Random House, 1950.
Andreas-Salomé, Lou. *Nietzsche*. Edited by Siegfried Mandel. Redding Ridge, Conn.: Black Swan Books, 1988.
Ansell-Pearson, Keith. *Nietzsche Contra Rousseau: A Study of Nietzsche's Moral and Political Thought*. Cambridge: Cambridge University Press, 1991.
———. "Who is the *Übermensch*? Truth, Time, and Woman in Nietzsche." *Journal of the History of Ideas* 53 (April–June 1992): 301–31.
———. "Woman and Political Theory." In *Nietzsche, Feminism, and Political Theory*, edited by Paul Patton. New York: Routledge, 1993.
Blondel, Eric. *Nietzsche: The Body and Culture: Philosophy as a Philological Genealogy*. Translated by Sean Hand. Stanford: Stanford University Press, 1991.
Braidotti, Rosi. *Patterns of Dissonance: A Study of Women in Contemporary Philosophy*. Translated by Elizabeth Guild. Cambridge: Polity, 1991.
Burgard, Peter J. Introduction to *Nietzsche and the Feminine*, edited by Peter J. Burgard. Charlottesville: University Press of Virginia, 1994.
Butler, Judith. "Bodies that Matter." In *Engaging with Irigaray: Feminist Philosophy and European Thought*, edited by Carolyn Burke, Naomi Schor, and Margaret Whitford. New York: Columbia University Press, 1994.
Cixous, Hélène. "The Laugh of the Medusa," translated by Keith Cohen and Paula Cohen. In *New French Feminisms*, edited by I. de Courtivron and E. Marks. New York: Shocken Books, 1981.
———. "Sorties," translated by B. Wing. In *The Newly Born Woman*. Manchester: Manchester University Press, 1986.

Conway, Daniel. "*Das Weib an sich*: The Slave Revolt in Epistemology." In *Nietzsche, Feminism, and Political Theory*, edited by Paul Patton. New York: Routledge, 1993.
———. *Nietzsche and the Political*. New York: Routledge, 1997.
———. *Nietzsche's Dangerous Game: Philosophy in the Twilight of the Idols*. Cambridge: Cambridge University Press, 1997.
Cornell, Drucilla. *Beyond Accommodation: Ethical Feminism, Deconstruction, and the Law*. New York: Routledge, 1991.
Dannhauser, Werner. "Friedrich Nietzsche." In *History of Political Philosophy*, 3d. ed., edited by Leo Strauss and Joseph Cropsey. Chicago: University of Chicago Press, 1987.
———. "Spiritedness in *Thus Spoke Zarathustra*." In *Understanding the Political Spirit: Philosophical Investigations from Socrates to Nietzsche*, edited by Catherine Zuckert. New Haven: Yale University Press, 1988.
de Man, Paul. *Allegories of Reading*. New Haven: Yale University Press, 1979.
Derrida, Jacques. *Spurs: Nietzsche's Styles*. Translated by Barbara Harlow. Chicago: University of Chicago Press, 1979.
Detwiler, Bruce. *Nietzsche and the Politics of Aristocratic Radicalism*. Chicago: University of Chicago Press, 1990.
Diethe, Carol. "Lou Andreas-Salomé and Female Sexuality at the Turn of the Century." In *German Women Writers 1900–1993*, edited by Brian Keith-Smith. Lampeter: Mellen, 1993.
———. "Nietzsche and the Early German Feminists." *Journal of Nietzsche Studies* 12 (Autumn 1996): 69–81.
———. *Nietzsche's Women: Beyond the Whip*. Berlin: de Gruyter, 1996.
Diprose, Rosalyn. "Nietzsche, Ethics, and Sexual Difference." *Radical Philosophy* 52 (Summer 1989): 27–32.
Eden, Robert. *Political Leadership and Nihilism: A Study of Weber and Nietzsche*. Tampa: University Presses of Florida, 1983.
Euripides. *The Bacchae and Other Plays*. Translated by Philip Vellacott. New York: Penguin Books, 1973.
Fuller, Margaret. "Woman in the Nineteenth Century." In *The Essential Margaret Fuller*, edited by J. Steele. Piscataway: Rutgers University Press, 1992.
Graybeal, Jean. *Language and "The Feminine" in Nietzsche and Heidegger*. Bloomington: Indiana University Press, 1990.
Grosz, Elizabeth. "Derrida, Irigaray, and Deconstruction." *Intervention* 20 (1986): 70–81.
Habib, Lawrence. "Nietzsche on Woman." *Southern Journal of Philosophy* 19 (Fall 1981): 333–46.
Hamilton, Edith. *Mythology*. New York: Penguin, 1982.
Hans, James. *Contextual Authority and Aesthetic Truth*. Albany: State University of New York Press, 1992.
Irigaray, Luce. *Marine Lover of Friedrich Nietzsche*. Translated by Gillian Gill. New York: Columbia University Press, 1991.
———. "Female Genealogies," translated by Luisa Muraro. In *Engaging With Irigaray: Feminist Philosophy and European Thought*, edited by Carolyn Burke, Naomi Schor, and Margaret Whitford. New York: Columbia University Press, 1994.
Jardine, Alice. *Gynesis: Configurations of Woman and Modernity*. Ithaca: Cornell University Press, 1985.
Johnson, Kathleen B. Introduction to *Dissemination*, by Jacques Derrida. Chicago: University of Chicago Press, 1981.
Kaufmann, Walter. "Nietzsche and the Seven Sirens." *Partisan Review* (May–June 1952).
———. *Nietzsche: Philosopher, Psychologist, Antichrist*. 3d. ed. Princeton: Princeton University Press, 1968.

Kennedy, Ellen, and Susan Mendus, eds. *Women in Western Political Philosophy*. New York: St. Martin's Press, 1987.
Kerenyi, Carl. *Dionysos: Archetypal Image of Indestructible Life*. Translated by R. Manheim. Bollingen Series 65, 2. New Jersey: Princeton University Press, 1976.
Keuls, Eva C. *The Reign of the Phallus: Sexual Politics in Ancient Athens*. Berkeley and Los Angeles: University of California Press, 1985.
Koelb, Clayton. "Castration Envy: Nietzsche and the Figure of Woman." In *Nietzsche and the Feminine*, edited by Peter J. Burgard. Charlottesville: University Press of Virginia, 1994.
Kofman, Sarah. "Baubo: Theological Perversion and Fetishism." In *Nietzsche's New Seas*, edited by M. A. Gillespie and T. B. Strong. Chicago: University of Chicago Press, 1988.
———. *Nietzsche and Metaphor*. Translated by Duncan Large. Stanford: Stanford University Press, 1993.
———. "A Fantastical Genealogy: Nietzsche's Family Romance." In *Nietzsche and the Feminine*, edited by Peter J. Burgard. Charlottesville: University Press of Virginia, 1994.
Krell, David Farrell. *Postponements: Woman, Sensuality, and Death in Nietzsche*. Bloomington: Indiana University Press, 1986.
———. "To the Orange Grove at the Edge of the Sea: Remarks on Luce Irigaray's *Amante marine*." In *Nietzsche and the Feminine*, edited by Peter Burgard. Charlottesville: University Press of Virginia, 1994.
Lampert, Laurence. *Leo Strauss and Nietzsche*. Chicago: University of Chicago Press, 1996.
Le Bris, Michel. *Romantics and Romanticism*. New York: Rizzoli International Publications, 1981.
Levine, Peter. *Nietzsche and the Modern Crisis of the Humanities*. Albany: State University of New York Press, 1995.
Loraux, Nicole. *Tragic Ways of Killing a Woman*. Translated by Anthony Forster. Cambridge: Harvard University Press, 1987.
———. *The Experiences of Tiresias: The Feminine and the Greek Man*. Translated by Paula Wissing. Princeton: Princeton University Press, 1995.
Lungstrum, Janet. "Nietzsche Writing Woman/Woman Writing Nietzsche: The Sexual Dialectic of Palingenesis." In *Nietzsche and the Feminine*, edited by Peter Burgard. Charlottesville: University Press of Virginia, 1994.
Mandel, Siegfried. Introduction to *Nietzsche*, by Lou Andreas-Salomé. Redding Ridge, Conn.: Black Swan Books, 1988.
Mann, Thomas. *Death in Venice and Seven Other Stories*. Translated by H. T. Lowe-Porter. New York: Vintage Books, 1936.
———. *The Magic Mountain*. Translated by H. T. Lowe-Porter. New York: Vintage Books, 1969.
Martin, Biddy. *Woman and Modernity: The (Life)styles of Lou Andreas-Salome*. New York: Cornell University Press, 1991.
Middleton, Christopher, ed. *Selected Letters of Friedrich Nietzsche*. Vol. 8. Chicago: University of Chicago Press, 1969.
Minh-ha, Trinh. *When the Moon Waxes Red: Representation, Gender, and Cultural Politics*. New York: Routledge, 1991.
Moi, Toril. *Sexual/Textual Politics: Feminist Literary Theory*. London: Methuen, 1985.
Nietzsche, Friedrich. *Thus Spoke Zarathustra: A Book for All and None*. Translated by Walter Kaufmann. New York: Viking Penguin, 1966.
———. "Attempt at a Self-Criticism." In *The Birth of Tragedy and the Case of Wagner*. Translated by Walter Kaufmann. New York: Random House, 1967.
———. *The Birth of Tragedy and The Case of Wagner*. Translated by Walter Kaufmann. New York: Random House, 1967.

———. *Nietzsche Werke: Kritische Gesamtausgabe: Menschliches, Allzumenschliches I; Nachgelassene Fragmente 1876 bis Winter 1877–1878*. Edited by Giorgio Colli and Mazzino Montinari. Berlin: de Gruyter, 1967.
———. *Also Sprach Zarathustra: Ein Buch für Alle und Keinen*. In *Nietzsche Werke: Kritische Gesamtausgabe*, edited by Giorgio Colli and Mazzino Montinari. Berlin: de Gruyter, 1968.
———. *Jenseits von Gut und Böse: Einer Philosophie der Zukunft*. In *Nietzsche Werke: Kritische Gesamtausgabe*, edited by Giorgio Colli and Mazzino Montinari. Berlin: de Gruyter, 1968.
———. *Ecce Homo*. In *Nietzsche Werke: Kritische Gesamtausgabe*, edited by Giorgio Colli and Mazzino Montinari. Berlin: de Gruyter, 1969.
———. *Götzen-Dämmerung*. In *Nietzsche Werke: Kritische Gesamtausgabe*, edited by Giorgio Colli and Mazzino Montinari. Berlin: de Gruyter, 1969.
———. *The Gay Science*. Translated by Walter Kaufmann. New York: Vintage, 1974.
———. *Human, All Too Human II*. Translated by Paul V. Cohn. New York: Gordon Press, 1974.
———. *The Joyful Wisdom*. Translated by Thomas Common. New York: Gordon Press, 1974.
———. *Twilight of the Idols*. Translated by Anthony Ludovici. New York: Gordon Press, 1974.
———. *Sämtliche Werke: Die Geburt der Tragödie; Unzeitgemasse Betrachtungen 1–4; Nachgelassene Schriften 1870–1873*. Edited by Giorgio Colli and Mazzino Montinari. Berlin: de Gruyter, 1988.
———. *Sämtliche Werke: Kritische Studienausgabe: Morgenrote; Idyllen aus Messina; Die Fröhliche Wissenschaft*. Edited by Giorgio Colli and Mazzino Montinari. Berlin: de Gruyter, 1988.
———. "*Versuch einer Selbstkritik.*" In *Sämtliche Werke: Die Geburt der Tragödie; Unzeitgemasse Betrachtungen 1–4; Nachgelassene Schriften 1870–1873*, edited by Giorgio Colli and Mazzino Montinari. Berlin: de Gruyter, 1988.
———. *Beyond Good and Evil: Prelude to a Philosophy of the Future*. Translated by Walter Kaufmann. New York: Vintage Books, 1989.
———. *Ecce Homo*. In *On the Genealogy of Morals and Ecce Homo*, translated by Walter Kaufmann. New York: Random House, 1989.
———. *Human, All Too Human*. Translated by R. J. Hollingdale. Cambridge: Cambridge University Press, 1994.
Nye, Andrea. *Feminist Theory and the Philosophies of Man*. London: Croom Helm, 1988.
Okhamafe, Imafedia. "Heidegger's Nietzsche and Nietzsche's Play: The Questions of Wo(man), Christianity, Nihilism, and Humanism." *Soundings* 71 (Winter 1988): 533–53.
Okonta, Ike. *Nietzsche: The Politics of Power*. New York: Peter Lang, 1992.
Oliver, Kelly. "Woman as Truth in Nietzsche's Writings." *Social Theory and Practice* 10 (Summer 1984): 185–99.
———. "Nietzsche's 'Woman': The Poststructuralist Attempt to do Away with Women." *Radical Philosophy* 48 (Spring 1988): 25–29.
———. "Nietzsche's Abjection." In *Nietzsche and the Feminine*, edited by Peter Burgard. Charlottesville: University Press of Virginia, 1994.
———. *Womanizing Nietzsche: Philosophy's Relation to the "Feminine."* New York: Routledge, 1995.
Oppel, Frances. "Irigaray with Nietzsche." In *Nietzsche, Feminism, and Political Theory*, edited by Paul Patton. New York: Routledge, 1993.
Ormiston, Gayle. "Traces of Derrida: Nietzsche's Image of Woman." *Philosophy Today* 28 (Summer 1984): 178–88.
Owen, David. *Nietzsche, Politics, and Modernity: A Critique of Liberal Reason*. London: Sage Publications, 1995.

Patens, Erik. "Traces of Derrida, 'Woman,' and Politics: A Reading of Spurs." *Philosophy Today* 33 (Winter 1989): 291–301.
Pautrat, Bernard. "Nietzsche Medused." In *Looking After Nietzsche*, edited by L. Richels. Albany: State University of New York Press, 1990.
Peters, H. F. *Zarathustra's Sister: The Case of Elisabeth and Friedrich Nietzsche*. New York: Crown Publishers, 1977.
Picart, Caroline Joan S. "Nietzsche as Masked Romantic." *Journal of Aesthetics and Art Criticism* 55 (Summer 1997): 273–91.
———. *Thomas Mann and Friedrich Nietzsche: Eroticism, Death, Music, and Laughter*. Dordrecht, Netherlands: Rodopi/Kluwer Academic Press, forthcoming.
Pinsent, John. *Greek Mythology*. Yugoslavia: Newnes Books, 1983.
Pippin, Robert. "Irony and Affirmation in Nietzsche's *Thus Spoke Zarathustra*." In *Nietzsche's New Seas*, edited by M. A. Gillespie and T. B. Strong. Chicago: University of Chicago Press, 1988.
Reinach, Salomon. *Cultes, mythes, religion*. Vol. 4. Paris: Leroux, 1912.
Rosen, Stanley. "Plato's Myth of the Reversed Cosmos." In *The Quarrel Between Philosophy and Poetry*. New York: Routledge, 1993.
———. *The Mask of Enlightenment: Nietzsche's Zarathustra*. Cambridge: Cambridge University Press, 1995.
Sallis, John. *Crossings: Nietzsche and the Space of Tragedy*. Chicago: University of Chicago Press, 1991.
Schutte, Ofelia. *Beyond Nihilism: Nietzsche Without Masks*. Chicago: University of Chicago Press, 1984.
———. "Nietzsche on Gender Difference: A Critique." *Newsletter on Feminism and Philosophy* (1990).
Seery, John. *Political Returns: Irony in Politics and Theory from Plato to the Antinuclear Movement*. Boulder: Westview Press, 1990.
Shapiro, Gary. *Alcyone: Nietzsche on Gifts, Noise, and Women*. Albany: State University of New York Press, 1991.
Shiach, Morag. *Hélène Cixous: A Politics of Writing*. New York: Routledge, 1991.
Singer, Linda. "Nietzschean Mythologies: The Inversion of Value and War Against Women." *Soundings* 66 (1983): 281–95.
Spivak, Gayatri Chakravorty. "Feminism and Deconstruction, Again: Negotiating with Unacknowledged Masculinism." In *Between Feminism and Psychoanalysis*, edited by Teresa Brennan. New York: Routledge, 1989.
Stambaugh, Joan. *The Other Nietzsche*. Albany: State University of New York Press, 1994.
Stanton, Donna C. "Difference on Trial: A Critique of the Maternal Metaphor in Cixous, Irigaray, and Kristeva." In *The Poetics of Gender*, edited by N. K. Miller. New York: Columbia University Press, 1986.
Starrett, Shari Neller. "Nietzsche, Women, and Relationships of Strength." *Southwest Philosophical Review* 6 (January 1990): 73–79.
Stassinopoulos, A., and R. Beny. *The Gods of Greece*. New York: Harry N. Abrams, 1983.
Staten, Henry. *Nietzsche's Voice*. Ithaca: Cornell University Press, 1990.
———. "The Birth of Tragedy Reconstructed." *Studies in Romanticism* 29 (Spring 1990): 9–38.
Stewart, Walter K. "My Sister and I: The Disputed Nietzsche." In *My Sister and I*, edited by Stuart Swezey and Brian King. Los Angeles: AMOK, 1990.
Strauss, Leo. *The City and Man*. Chicago: Rand McNally, 1964.
Strong, Tracy B. *Friedrich Nietzsche and the Politics of Transfiguration*. Berkeley and Los Angeles: University of California Press, 1975.

———. "Nietzsche's Political Aesthetics." In *Nietzsche's New Seas*, edited by Michael Gillespie and Tracy Strong. Chicago: University of Chicago Press, 1988.

Tapper, Marion. "*Ressentiment* and Power: Some Reflections on Feminist Practices." In *Nietzsche, Feminism, and Political Theory*, edited by Paul Patton. New York: Routledge, 1993.

Taylor, Seth. *Left-Wing Nietzscheans: The Politics of German Expressionism 1910–1920*. Berlin: de Gruyter, 1990.

Theisen, Bianca. "Rhythms of Oblivion." In *Nietzsche and the Feminine*, edited by Peter Burgard. Charlottesville: University Press of Virginia, 1994.

Thiele, Leslie Paul. *Friedrich Nietzsche and the Politics of the Soul: A Study of Heroic Individualism*. Princeton: Princeton University Press, 1990.

Thomas, R. Hinton. *Nietzsche in German Politics and Society 1890–1918*. Manchester: Manchester University Press, 1983.

Visker, Rudi. *Michel Foucault: Genealogy as Critique*. Translated by Chris Turner. New York: Verso, 1995.

Waite, Geoff. *Nietzsche's Corps/e: Aesthetics, Politics, Prophecy, or the Spectacular Technoculture of Everyday Life*. Durham: Duke University Press, 1996.

Wallace, Mark. Introduction to *Figuring the Sacred: Religion, Narrative, and Imagination*, by Paul Ricoeur, translated by David Pellauer. Minneapolis: Fortress Press, 1995.

Weed, Elizabeth. "The Question of Style." In *Engaging with Irigaray: Feminist Philosophy and European Thought*, edited by Carolyn Burke, Naomi Schor, and Margaret Whitford. New York: Columbia University Press, 1994.

Whitford, Margaret. *Luce Irigaray: Philosophy in the Feminine*. New York: Routledge, 1991.

———. "Reading Irigaray in the Nineties." In *Engaging with Irigaray: Feminist Philosophy and European Thought*, edited by Carolyn Burke, Naomi Schor, and Margaret Whitford. New York: Columbia University Press, 1994.

Index

abjection, 32, 36, 38, 111, 127
Achilles, 48, 54, 168. *See also* Cixous, Hélène; free spirit; Homer; Kleist, Heinrich von; *Penthesilea*
Ackerman, Robert John, 2, 24
Adam(ic), 73, 87
adder. *See* animal(s)
Aeschylus, 40, 44, 53, 69. *See also* Euripides
aesthetics, 6, 8, 10–11, 13, 16–17, 19, 23, 26, 148, 155–56, 161–62, 163, 164, 166, 170, 172, 178, 180
    aesthetico-moral. *See* aesthetico-moral [*under* moral(ity)]
    aesthetico-political. *See* politico/aesthetico
afterlife. *See* life
against life. *See* life
age/era. *See* sick(ness)
agon, 31, 44, 122
Ainley, Alison, 23
Ajax, 61. See also *der Frevel*; Prometheus
Alcibiades, 118. *See also* Caesar; da Vinci, Leonardo
aletheia, 46. *See also* truth
Alexander, 112. *See also* Caesar; Napoleon; Wagner, Richard

Alexandrian, 47
Alighieri, Dante. *See* Dante
alter ego, 98, 99, 102, 109–10
amor fati, 83, 100, 110, 128, 129, 141, 146, 151, 163. *See also* eternal return
amoral(ity). *See* moral(ity)
Andreas-Salomé, Lou, 11–13, 18–19, 98
animal(s), 29, 63, 68, 73, 74, 76, 77, 84–86, 89–90, 117–18, 133, 134. *See also* Dionysus
    adder, 103, 106
    animal heritage, 68
    animality, 85
    animal world, 74, 77
    ass, 30, 90, 96, 102–3, 110, 137–39, 142, 152, 154, 158. *See also* (jack)ass-eared [*under* ears]; ugliest man [*under* "man"/"men"]
    bird, 104, 106. *See also* "woman"/"women"
    boar, 176, 178
    cat, 104, 106. *See also* "woman"/"women"
    cow, 58, 90, 104, 106, 118, 125, 134, 135; Motley Cow, 90, 95. *See also* "woman"/"women"

animal(s) *(continued)*
  crab, 136. *See also* moral(ity)
  eagle, 86, 90, 103, 104, 106. *See also* Dionysus
  fire-hound, 106. *See also* Zarathustra
  goat, 43
  herd animal, 117–18, 134. *See also* herd
  horned kid, 93, 153
  lion, 86, 88, 92, 107
  lioness, 107, 152. *See also* feminine
  parasite, 22, 50, 52, 62–63, 66, 76, 105, 121, 134, 144, 147; "woman-as-parasite," 22, 62
  serpent, 82, 89–90, 96, 103, 106, 109. *See also* Dionysus
  sheep, 71
  snake, 81, 84–86, 89, 103. *See also* Dionysus; eagle (*above*)
  social animal, 73
  tarantula, 107, 110, 152. *See also* feminine
  vermin, 7, 8, 112, 134, 144, 147, 162; "woman-as-vermin," 7. *See also* "woman"/"women"; mother; sister
Ansell-Pearson, Keith, 2, 20, 28, 82, 83, 91, 92, 101, 153, 156–57, 164–65
anthropomorphism, 4, 7, 40, 41, 48, 58–59, 60, 63–64, 66, 67, 70, 147, 150. *See also* personification; figure(s)
anti-Christ(ian). *See* Christian(s)
antidemocratic. *See* democracy
antifeminist. *See* feminist
antimythic. *See* mythic
antimythology. *See* mythology
anti-Romantic(ism). *See* Romantic(ism)
Antigone, 41, 44, 45, 70, 150. *See also* Cassandra
Aphrodite, 5, 48, 52, 53, 76. *See also* free spirit
apocalypse(-tic), 105, 106, 133, 136, 153
apolitical. *See* political
Apollo, 5, 6, 8, 40, 41–46, 48, 54, 60, 65–66, 67, 72, 76, 82, 83, 94–96, 102, 106, 108, 112, 119–20, 121, 143, 146, 148, 149–50, 151, 153, 169, 173. *See also* art; Artemis; Athena; Dionysus; Hyperboreans; Zeus
Apollinian, 42–45, 65–66, 67, 69, 120, 147, 150, 153, 161
appearance, 42–43, 45, 55, 64, 65–67, 68, 73, 117, 132, 149, 154. *See also* art
Archilochus, 41, 44, 46, 76, 150. *See also* Homer
Argus, 58, 72, 77, 150. *See also* Io
Ariadne, 15, 18, 85, 115, 138, 139, 154. *See also* Dionysus; ears; Zeus
Ariosto, Lodovico, 170
art, 3, 7, 17, 18, 40, 42–45, 48, 54, 55, 56, 60–61, 64–65, 67, 68, 69–70, 71, 73, 74, 76, 77–78, 81, 98, 102, 104, 117, 118, 119–20, 125, 132, 143, 154, 171, 179. *See also* appearance; life; nature
art of interpretation, 4, 20, 141, 148, 151, 159, 160
Artemis, 82. *See also* Apollo; Athena
artist, 3, 11, 45, 54, 64, 66, 68, 73, 74, 120, 125, 137, 147, 175. *See also* philosopher; scientist [*under* science]
  artist-scientist, 72–75, 77. *See also* scientist [*under* science]
  male artist, 18. *See also* male
  sick/imperfect artist(s), 55, 71, 76. *See also* sick(ness)
Aryan, 46, 135. *See also* Fall
ascending lines of life. *See* life
ascent, 73, 84–85, 88, 106, 121, 126, 127, 128, 134, 137, 144
ascetic(ism), 49, 61, 122. *See also* Christian(s); fettered spirit [*under* fettered]; priest; saint; "woman"/"women"
Asclepius, 121–22. *See also* Socrates
ass. *See* animal(s)
ass-eared. *See* ear
Athena, 15, 56, 82, 84, 87. *See also* Apollo; Artemis; Zeus
Athens, 1, 17, 121–22
Athenian, 17, 51, 95, 122
Attic
  Attic tragedy, 43–44, 53, 69

New Attic Comedy, 46. *See also* Euripides
author, 10, 20, 27, 37, 98, 126, 129,
    157–60, 162–65, 166, 170, 174, 179,
    180. *See also* authority; God; science
authorial, 97–99, 158, 160, 164, 175, 179
authorship, 9, 28, 165
authority, 9, 10, 22, 25, 26, 28, 29, 36, 38,
    65, 70, 84, 128, 143, 156–59,
    161–64, 170, 172, 174

Bachofen, J. J., 90
bad, 118, 119, 125, 160. *See also* evil; good;
    master morality, slave morality
    [*under* moral(ity)]
Bar On, Bat-Ami, 165
Baubô(n), 6, 8, 22, 24–25, 40, 78, 108,
    150. *See also* Demeter; Gaia; Medusa;
    Persephone
Beethoven, Ludwig von, 59. *See also* German
    Virtue
Bellephoron, 24
Beny, R., 84
Bible, 170
    biblical, 62, 93
bird catchers, 115
birth(ing), 5, 9, 15, 16, 17, 20–21, 24, 30,
    33–34, 43, 46, 56, 58, 61, 65–66,
    71–72, 74, 81–83, 86, 88–92, 93–95,
    97, 101, 102, 103, 107, 108, 109–10,
    112, 116, 118, 141, 150–55. *See also*
    midwife(ry); motherhood; partheno-
    genesis; power of birthing [*under*
    power]; pregnancy; rebirth
    "childbirth," 74, 95, 134, 154
    thigh birth, 15, 84, 94–95, 141. *See also*
        Dionysus; Zeus
bisexuality. *See* sexuality
Blondel, Eric, 26, 30, 148
body/bodies, 9, 10, 15, 26, 30, 34, 36, 49,
    66, 70, 94, 139, 140, 151, 153, 162,
    168–69, 173
Bordo, Susan, 165
Braidotti, Rosi, 35
Buddha, 173

Burckhardt, 17
Burgard, Peter, 1, 3, 8, 10, 17, 18, 23, 36
Burke, Carolyn, 21, 35, 151
Butler, Judith, 151

Caesar, 112, 118. *See also* Alcibiades;
    Alexander; da Vinci, Leonardo;
    Napoleon; Wagner, Richard
Calderon, 56
Cassandra, 7, 41, 44, 45, 150. *See also*
    Antigone
caste system, 121, 134. *See also* Chandala;
    law of the knife; law of Manu; Sudra
Castorp, Hans, 39, 44
castration, 3, 22, 34, 37, 122
centaur, 48, 54. *See also* free spirit
Chandala, 134–35, 137, 145. *See also* caste
    system; law of the knife; law of Manu;
    Sudra
Chang E, 173
chaos, 21, 72, 102, 107, 152, 159, 162
    Chaos, 67
child, 5, 24, 36, 39, 65, 67, 69, 72, 84–86,
    87, 91–92, 98, 103, 106, 108, 112,
    116, 139, 146, 176, 178. *See also*
    Zarathustra
    child-begetting, 69
    child-Dionysus, 87
    child-god, 82
childbearing, 152. *See also* birth; pregnancy
childbirth. *See* birth
childish, 50, 69
childlike, 88, 91
children, 44, 50, 87, 91–92, 106, 108,
    114, 116, 134
Chios, 101
Christ, 45, 54–55, 59, 71, 95, 106, 126,
    153. *See also* decadence; democracy;
    fettered spirit [*under* fettered]; God;
    herd; modern(ity); pity; plebeian; slave
    morality [*under* moral(ity)]; strong
    [*under* strength]; weak;
    "woman"/"women"
anti-Christ(ian). *See under* Christian(s)

Christ *(continued)*
  Christlike, 84
  death of Christ, 55
Christian(s), 40, 49, 53, 55, 61, 71, 75–77,
    83, 84, 85, 87, 88, 89, 90, 93, 97,
    104, 105, 106, 107, 108, 109, 117,
    118, 119, 120, 122–24, 128, 129,
    131, 135, 137, 138, 139, 141, 143,
    149, 159
  anti-Christ(ian), 9, 86, 93, 95, 97, 98,
    105, 106, 126
  Christian God, 61, 90, 104–5, 109
  Christian morality, 53, 77, 122, 123
  non-Christian, 84, 88
Christianity, 49, 54–55, 60–63, 71, 74, 75,
    77, 87, 103, 107, 108, 114, 120,
    121–22, 135, 140, 144, 145, 149
  Christianization, 143–144
Cicero, 138
Circe, 114, 115, 125, 145, 154. *See also*
    Sphinx
citizen(s), 29, 31
  citizenship, 1, 56
Cixous, Hélène, 11, 16, 37, 166–73. *See
  also* bisexuality; feminine writing
  [*under* feminine]; Kleist, Heinrich von;
  Minh-ha, Trinh
Colli, Giorgio, 42, 48, 84, 85, 88, 91, 92,
    94, 96, 100, 101, 104, 105, 108, 111,
    114, 120, 127
Common, Thomas, 2, 41, 59, 148
convalescence, 49, 96, 103, 104, 110, 126,
    128, 140, 143–44, 146, 152. *See also*
    decadence; disease; health(iness)
  convalescent-healer, 140
Conway, Daniel, 19, 95, 165
Cornaro/Cornarism, 119, 123, 143. *See also*
    dietitian-psychologist [*under* diet]
Corneille, Pierre, 129
Cornell, Drucilla, 35
Criton, 52
cross-cultural. *See* cultural
cult(s), 43, 68, 88, 90, 95
culture, 3, 4, 8, 15, 16, 17, 26, 27, 30,
    43, 48, 49, 54, 56, 60, 69, 70, 73, 77,
    81, 83, 99, 111, 114, 117, 118, 122,
    129, 135, 136, 141, 149, 160,
    166–67, 170, 173, 175–79
  cultured, 55
cultural, 32, 165, 167–68, 174, 175–76
  cross-cultural, 170, 173, 179–80
  cultural analysis, 3
  cultural critics, 157
  transcultural, 169
Cyclops, 59, 115
  Cyclopean, 59–60

dance, 60, 86, 107, 110, 136
  dancer(s), 29, 97, 176
  dancing, 44, 66, 87, 92, 136
  dancing song, 92
  knife dance, 86
dandy, 57, 83, 96, 97, 99, 100, 101, 151.
    See also David; Romantic(ism)
danger(s), 30, 67, 70, 75, 91, 92, 97, 118,
    129, 137, 138, 142, 162, 166, 167,
    172. *See also* "man"/"men"; play;
    "woman"/"women"
  dangerous, 9, 19, 52, 63, 69, 91, 92, 112,
    117, 118, 131, 134, 138, 149, 179
Dannhauser, Werner, 28, 29, 30, 148, 151
Dante (Alighieri), 71, 170
Danto, Arthur, 28
Darwin, Charles; Darwinian, 120, 158
David, 96
da Vinci, Leonardo, 118. *See also* Alcibiades;
    Caesar
death, 24, 25, 32, 36, 42, 47, 53, 55, 58,
    61, 69, 71, 81, 84, 85, 87, 93, 99,
    100–101, 103, 110, 121, 122, 152,
    155, 161. *See also* will
  death mask, 81
  death of Christ. *See* Christ
  death of God. *See* God
  death of Socrates. *See* Socrates
  death of tragedy. *See* tragedy
  death throes, 30, 83, 101, 113, 123
  death-rattle, 87

deathly, 82, 101
Death in Venice. See Mann, Thomas
Death of Sardanapalus. See Delacroix, Eugene
decadence, 7, 9, 19, 29, 30, 38, 40, 41, 44, 46, 48, 52–63, 68, 69, 73, 75–77, 79, 83, 99, 102, 106, 109, 110, 113, 115, 116, 117, 120–29, 132–37, 139, 140–44, 149, 152, 154, 160. *See also* Christianity; convalescence; disease; health(iness); herd; impotence; modern(ity); vitality
decline, 4, 128
deconstruction, 11, 26, 35, 81, 161, 179. *See also* decadence; reconstruction
Delacroix, Eugene, 83, 101
  Death of Sardanapalus, 101
  Massacre at Chios, 101
Deleuze, Gilles, 28
de Man, Paul, 29
Demeter, 7, 24–25, 39, 40, 66–67, 72, 76, 147–48, 150. *See also* Baubô(n); Dionysus; Eleusinian; Gaia; Iaachos; Medusa; Persephone/Proserpine; Mother Goddess
democracy, 31, 37, 99, 116, 144. *See also* Christianity; modern(ity)
democratic, 40, 87, 90, 97, 117–18, 119, 135, 140, 143; antidemocratic, 31
democratization, 143, 144
demon(s), 54, 67, 178
  demonic, 87
demoness, 107
demythologize. *See* mythologize
der Frevel. See sin
Derrida, Jacques, 2, 4, 16, 18, 24, 34–37, 91–92, 148, 158, 161
descending lines of life. *See* life
descent
  i.e., journey downward, 6, 19, 23, 24, 25, 61, 71, 85, 86, 88, 94, 99, 113, 121, 126–27, 137, 153, 163
  i.e., lineage, 84, 109, 124, 126–27
Detwiler, Bruce, 156
devil, 56

devolving, 4, 5, 20, 33, 38, 130, 147. *See also* evolving
die Sunde. See sin
diet, 117, 123, 140
  dietitian-psychologist, 123. *See also* Cornaro/Cornarism
Diethe, Carol, 13
dietitian-psychologist. *See* diet
difference, 36, 147, 166–67, 169, 172–74
  gender difference, 1–2
  nondifference, 160
  sexual difference, 166, 167, 169
Dionysus, 5, 6, 8, 15, 24, 25, 30, 39, 40–46, 48, 65–67, 72, 76, 78, 83–88, 90, 92–96, 100, 102, 107, 108, 112, 115, 119, 120, 121, 126, 138, 141–44, 146, 148–51, 153–54
  Dionysian, 42–46, 48, 60, 65–67, 69, 86, 89, 90, 93–95, 97, 120, 139, 146, 147, 150, 153, 161; Dionysian cult, 90, 95
Diprose, Rosalyn, 2
dis-ease, 5, 30, 82, 102, 110, 132–33, 142, 154, 162
disease, 4, 8, 10, 19, 32, 61, 65, 70, 73, 79, 89, 96, 114, 117, 120–22, 128, 129, 134, 147, 166. *See also* convalescence; decadence; health(iness); impotence; vitality
disempowerment. *See* empowerment
dismemberment, 9, 39, 65–67, 85, 95, 96, 143, 151, 153. *See also* art; Dionysus; nature
Doppelgänger, 140. *See also* Socrates
duality, 42, 43, 93, 126–27, 150, 156, 169
duplicity, 42, 156

ears
  hyperborean-eared, 102, 110, 137–38
  (jack)ass-eared, 102–3, 110, 138–39, 142
  long-eared, 20, 105, 110, 138–39, 146, 154, 156, 164. *See also* Ariadne
  Odysseus's blocked ears, 115, 120, 139
  short-eared, 20, 110, 139, 154, 156, 164
  small(est) ears, 64, 105, 139, 142–44, 146

Eden, 136, 180. *See also* Adam(ic); Fall
Eden, Robert, 47, 96
education, 51, 62, 69–70, 79, 91, 136, 149
ego, 58, 123. *See also* alter ego
Electra, 70
Eleusis, 24
Eleusinian, 25, 66. *See also* Demeter; Persephone
embody (–ied) (–ies), 5, 6, 10, 25, 26, 30, 31, 36, 40, 45, 65, 127, 148, 163
Emerson, Ralph Waldo, 17, 64. *See also* prose-poetry [*under* poetry]
empowerment/disempowerment, 5, 18–19, 25–26, 105, 148, 152, 166, 179. *See also* power
  re-empowerment, 9
  self-empowerment, 18
Epicurus, 71
Er, 21
era/age. *See* sick(ness)
Eris
  good, 52, 53, 70, 76
  terrible, 53
eros, 106. *See also* Apollo; art; Dionysus; love
Eros, 42, 55
erotic, 43, 45, 47, 63, 69, 76, 101, 122
  eroticism, 18
esoteric, 5, 9, 20, 26, 27, 98–99, 102, 113, 126, 142, 143, 151, 152, 158. *See also* exoteric; Strauss, Leo
Eternal Feminine. *See* feminine
eternal return/recurrence, 4, 7–11, 18, 25, 32–34, 36, 37, 81–83, 88–89, 93, 100, 103–4, 107, 110, 112, 116, 127, 146, 150–51, 153, 157, 160, 162–63, 174. See also *amor fati*
eternally generating. *See* regeneration
eternity, 8, 58, 82, 89, 90, 92, 93, 101, 128, 152
Euripides/Euripidean, 39, 40, 42, 46, 48, 53, 69. *See also* Aeschylus; New Attic Comedy
Europe, 59, 73, 75, 132, 143, 144, 145, 155, 156

European, 23, 60, 73, 83, 133, 144
evil, 46, 52, 64, 115, 119, 139, 143, 146, 149, 160. *See also* bad; good; moral(ity)
evil spirits, 124
evolving, 4, 5, 9, 20, 25, 32, 68–75, 109, 130, 147, 151, 152. *See also* devolving
exoteric, 27, 99, 102–3, 113, 126, 142–43, 152, 154, 156, 158. *See also* esoteric; Strauss, Leo
exotic(ism), 83, 176, 179. *See also* Oriental

Fall, 16, 21, 46, 87, 166, 168. *See also* Adam(ic); Aryan; Semitic; sin
fascist, 23, 31
"father," 8, 15, 31, 36, 44, 45, 50, 64, 67, 70, 77, 82, 83, 96, 108, 110, 111, 112, 126–27, 141, 143, 146, 151, 168. *See also* mother; sister
father of the philosophers, 116, 118, 130, 143
Law of the Father, 168
Faust, 12, 40, 48, 56
female, 1, 17, 18, 21, 22, 25, 32, 50, 68, 73, 74, 81, 90, 91, 92, 101, 104, 107, 113, 124, 125, 131–35, 138, 139, 145, 146, 169, 178, 179. *See also* feminine; "man"/"men"; masculine; maternal; "woman"/"women"; virtue
feminine, 2–12, 16–23, 25–26, 28, 30, 31–34, 82, 83, 85, 90–94, 97, 99, 102, 104–7, 109, 113, 115–18, 125, 128, 131–33, 135, 138–40, 142, 143, 145–56, 160, 162–64, 166–70, 172, 179
Eternal Feminine, 71, 139, 140, 146, 164
feminine mother. *See* mother
feminine writing, 166–68, 171
"feminine/woman," 2, 4, 5, 9, 10, 17–19, 32, 38, 76–77, 99, 112–13, 132, 135, 142, 145, 147, 150, 154, 164, 167–68, 172
feminine as opposed to woman, 52, 149
femininity, 11, 26, 139, 150, 169

feminism, 1, 2, 18, 23, 26, 36, 113, 133, 139, 147, 154, 166
feminist, 2, 10, 16, 18–19, 22, 31, 35, 37, 139, 140, 165, 169–70, 172; antifeminist, 2
feminized men. *See* "man"/"men"
fettered, 48, 53, 59, 75
fettered spirit, 48–49, 50–52, 54, 69–70, 76–77. *See also* free spirit
unfettered, 54. *See also* free
fiction(s), 10, 112, 123, 161, 173, 179
figuration(s), 3, 4, 9, 18, 38, 81, 155, 180. *See also* transfiguration
figure(s), 3–9, 15, 17–18, 20, 22, 24–26, 28–29, 33–35, 37, 39–42, 44, 45, 48, 52–55, 57–59, 64, 66, 67, 70–73, 76–78, 81–87, 89, 90, 91, 94–97, 99, 101–3, 106–8, 110, 112–15, 119–21, 125, 138, 140, 142–46, 148–53, 155, 156, 163, 167–69, 173–74, 180
Forster, Anthony, 17
Förster-Nietzsche, Elizabeth, 8, 13, 28, 148. *See also* sister
Foucault, Michel, 9, 28, 157, 158, 161
frau, 5, 7, 51, 58, 71
free, 53, 55, 75, 136
free spirit, 48–49, 52–54, 58, 69–70, 73, 75, 77, 116, 124, 128, 149
free will. *See* will
frenzy, 28, 44, 119, 120. *See also* Dionysus; madness
Fuller, Margaret, 169

Gaia, 7, 66, 67, 147, 148, 150. *See also* Demeter
Gast, Peter, 12
gender, 1, 2, 7–8, 11, 15, 17–18, 20, 26, 31, 36–38, 41, 78, 90, 147–48, 151, 152, 155, 166, 168, 174–75, 178. *See also* sex
gender difference. *See* difference
gendered, 6, 8, 10, 11, 16, 17, 20, 25, 26, 28, 31, 38, 40, 42, 48, 64, 148, 149, 150, 155, 161, 163, 164, 165, 166, 169, 170, 173, 174, 176, 179, 180
genealogy, 2, 4, 7, 9, 10, 13, 15–17, 19, 21, 22, 25, 26, 30, 32–34, 36–38, 74, 112, 113, 117, 125–26, 130, 142, 147–49, 155, 159, 164–65
generative power. *See* power
genesis, 85–86, 90, 93, 130, 163
Genesis, Book of, 93, 124. *See also* Bible
German, 7, 13, 23, 111, 117, 125, 127, 129, 143, 146, 149
German art, 76
German music, 64
German Romanticism. 64, 84
German Virtue. *See* virtue
non-German, 129, 143, 146
Germany, 13, 76, 129, 136
Gersdorff, Carl von, 12
God, 6, 31, 49, 55, 61, 63, 71, 78, 90, 116, 124, 147, 153, 157–61. *See also* god; goddess
death of God, 6, 61, 99, 102, 158, 159, 160, 161
God as Author, 157, 159. *See also* author
old God, 90, 110, 158, 159. *See also* new god [*under* god]
god, 43, 44, 58, 60, 61, 67, 76, 82, 84, 85, 88, 90, 93–96, 98, 99, 100, 102, 104, 105, 109, 115, 121, 141, 152. *See also* God
godlike, 68, 96, 151
gods, 5, 15, 28, 41, 42, 82, 94, 150, 157
new god, 46. *See also* old God [*under* God]
goddess, 5, 24, 31, 39, 53, 59, 64, 66, 78, 84, 94, 114, 115, 154. *See also* God
naked/nude goddess, 46, 48, 78. *See also* science; truth
Goethe, Johann Wolfgang von, 56, 71
"good," 54, 118–19, 143, 149, 160. *See also* bad; evil; master morality, slave morality [*under* moral(ity)]
good nature, 68, 139
Graces, 63, 64, 76. *See also* Pleasantness
Graybeal, Jean, 26, 31–32, 34, 141
Great Mother. *See* mother

194   Index

Greek, 9, 17, 27, 42–44, 46, 49, 53, 61, 66, 67, 70, 84, 121, 133, 141, 173. *See also* Athens; Attic; wisdom
anti-Greek, 121
Greek art, 43–44
Greek culture, 8, 17, 27, 70, 141
"Greek deities," 5, 7, 147. *See also individual names of deities*; god
Greek language, 25, 46, 150
Greek mythology. *See* mythology
Greek poetry. *See* poetry
Greek politics/political life, 6, 17, 29. *See also* politics
Greek tragedy. *See* tragedy
Greeks, 17, 55, 60, 61, 75, 76, 78, 121, 145, 151
Greek world, 42
Grosz, Elizabeth, 35
Guild, Elizabeth, 35
gynecocratic, 15, 21

Habib, Lawrence, 2
Hades, 24, 25, 42, 67, 71, 84, 88, 94. *See also* Dionysus; underworld
halcyon, 20, 26, 98
Hamilton, Edith, 58
Hamlet, 40, 48
Hans, James, 157–64
happiness, 50, 57–61, 64, 76, 100, 101, 104, 106, 118, 121–23, 144, 149. *See also* virtue
Haraway, Donna, 165
Hayman, Ronald, 13
health(iness), 4, 7–11, 16, 19, 32, 47, 49, 60, 65–67, 68, 70–71, 75, 77, 95, 101, 109, 111, 114, 120, 122, 126, 128, 140, 143–44, 148–50, 154, 162, 174. *See also* convalescence; decadence; disease; impotence; pathos of distance; sick(ness); vitality
healthy, 9, 43, 45, 53, 59, 67, 115, 120, 123, 125, 126, 128, 134, 135, 140, 142–44, 146, 149, 154, 166
unhealthiness, 7, 55, 63, 76, 110, 150

Hegel, Wilhelm Friedrich, 167. *See also* master/slave dialectic
Heidegger, Martin, 2, 22, 26, 28, 31, 32
Helen, 5, 22, 40, 41, 43, 45, 76, 150
Hellenic, 43, 47
Hera, 8, 58, 84. *See also* Dionysus; Semele; Zeus
herd, 9, 71, 73, 103, 116–18, 134, 144, 159. *See also* Christianity; decadence; herd [*under* animal(s)]; slave morality [*under* moral(ity)]
herd morality. *See* moral(ity)
higher man/men. *See* "man"/"men"
Hipta-Rhea, 94
history, 5, 7, 9, 15, 16, 21, 22, 27, 33, 40, 44, 47, 50, 59, 60, 65, 90, 121, 130, 133, 134, 147, 148, 151, 160, 167, 169, 176. *See also* mytho/history
Hitler, Adolph, 28, 134
homeopathic, 35, 49
Homer, 41, 44, 48, 54, 56, 69, 71, 76, 150. *See also* Achilles; Archilochus; fettered spirit
homosexuality. *See* sexuality
hooks, bell, 165
hope, 16, 20, 52, 53, 76, 124. *See also* Midas; Pandora; Silenus
humor, 78, 114, 138. *See also* laughter
hybrid, 84, 98, 117–18, 133, 135, 137, 143–45, 158
hyperbole, 6, 24, 88
Hyperboreans, 94–95, 103–4, 110, 137, 138, 142. *See also* Apollo; Dionysus; ears
hyperborean, 44, 128, 146
hysteria, 131
hysterical, 9, 83, 103, 152
hysterical pregnancy. *See* pregancy

Iaachos, 24. *See also* Demeter; Dionysus
ignoble. *See* nobility
ignoble/slavish man. *See* "man"/"men"
image. *See* symbolic image
immoral(ist). *See* moral(ity)
impotence, 4, 5, 7, 19, 26, 32, 33, 38, 132,

149. *See also* decadence; disease; health(iness); vitality
Ina, 178
infection, 8, 10, 22, 26, 49, 69, 103, 116, 118, 135, 145
inoculation, 7, 10, 19, 26, 69, 142
Io, 58, 59, 77, 150. *See also* Argus
Irigaray, Luce, 10, 15, 16, 18, 21–22, 24, 26, 31, 33–35, 81–83, 101, 148, 151, 154, 168, 169, 172. *See also* lover
irony, 12, 19, 27–28, 106. *See also* mask
ironic, 4, 27–28, 31, 33, 37, 53, 62, 63, 115, 131, 133, 152

jackass. *See* animal(s), ass; ears, (jack)ass-eared
Janus, 48, 54, 67, 71. *See also* free spirit
Jardine, Alice, 18, 24
Jocasta, 115
John, Book of, 55. *See also* Bible
Johnson, Kathleen, 16

Kant, Immanuel, 59, 97, 161. *See also* German Virtue [*under* virtue]
Kaufmann, Walter, 12–13, 23, 28, 41–42, 44, 66, 84, 85, 88, 91, 92, 95, 96, 98, 100, 101, 104, 105, 108, 114, 126, 127
Kennedy, Ellen, 56, 57
Kerenyi, Carl, 85, 86, 88, 90, 93, 94–95
Keuls, Eva, 15, 17, 84
Kleist, Heinrich von, 166, 168, 180
  Penthesilea, 168. *See also* Achilles; Cixous, Hélène
knife dance. *See* dance
knife, law of. *See* law of the knife
knowledge, 48, 55, 58, 63, 73, 91, 99, 114, 138, 158, 159, 162, 171. *See also* poetry, Pleasantness
  self-knowledge, 28, 40, 58, 73, 150, 167
Koelb, Clayton, 3
Kofman, Sarah, 8, 11, 24–25, 36, 39, 40, 52, 78, 111–12, 126, 127, 148, 150
koilia, 25. *See also* Baubô
Krell, David Farrell, 2, 10, 15, 16, 20, 22, 23

Kristeva, Julia, 26, 31–32, 36–37, 148, 169, 172
Kronos, 8, 47, 94. *See also* Zeus

ladder of life. *See* life
Lampert, Lawrence, 27
Landor, Walter Savage, 64. *See also* prose-poetry [*under* poetry]
last men/smallest men. *See* "man"/"men"
laughter, 24, 55–56, 73, 74, 86, 87, 89, 97, 103, 106, 108, 138. *See also* humor
law of Manu, 121, 128–29, 134–35, 138, 143, 144, 154. *See also* caste system; Chandala; law of the knife; Sudra
Law of the Center, 170
Law of the Father. *See* father
law of the knife, 134. *See also* caste system; Chandala; law of Manu; Sudra
Law of the Sexes, 62, 149
Le Bris, Michel, 100
Leopardi, Giacomo, 64. *See also* prose-poetry [*under* poetry]
Levine, Peter, 174, 175, 179
Levy, Oscar, 12–13. See also *My Sister and I* [*under* Nietzsche, Friedrich]
lie(s), 10, 17, 26, 29, 30, 40, 54, 56, 61, 65, 68, 104, 108, 110, 132, 149, 151, 154, 171. *See also* truth
life, 3, 8, 21, 25, 27, 29, 40, 43, 47–49, 56, 58, 60, 64–66, 68, 71–76, 81, 85, 90, 92, 93, 95, 101–3, 106, 107, 109, 110, 116, 120–23, 128, 143, 147, 149–53, 164, 178. *See also* art; nature; will; zöe
  afterlife, 21
  against life, 61, 87, 122, 154
  ascending lines of life, 121, 123, 133–35, 138, 142–44
  descending lines of life, 119, 121–22, 124–25, 133–35, 144, 155
  ladder of life, 127. *See also* ascending/descending lines of life (*above*)
  life-denying, 163

life *(continued)*
  life-disabling, 61
  life-giving, 4
  life-invigorating, 103
  life-sustaining, 29, 30, 69, 104, 151, 153, 155
  life-threatening, 60, 73
  yes-to-life, 112, 127, 146
little, 8, 64, 78, 85, 90, 92, 104, 105, 106, 145, 152. *See also* "woman"/"women"
long-eared. *See* ear
Loraux, Nicole, 1, 22
Lorde, Audre, 10, 147
love, 8, 44, 45, 50–53, 55, 56, 59, 62, 63, 69, 74, 77, 92, 93, 96, 104, 108, 111–12, 119, 124, 128, 131, 132, 135, 138, 139, 146, 147, 168. *See also* sexual love
  self-love, 108
love of fate. *See amor fati*
lover's discourse, 33
lovers. *See also* Irigaray, Luce
  i.e., romantic partners, 81, 85
  i.e., admirers of things, 46, 114, 129, 173
Lungstrum, Janet, 18, 19

macroscopic, 11, 19, 38. *See also* microscopic
Madame de Guyon, 131
Madame de Lambert, 133
Madame de Stael, 117, 125, 132
madness
  i.e., Dionysian frenzy, 44, 90, 96
  i.e., psychological illness, 6, 7, 12, 60, 99, 126, 127, 153
Maenad/mainas, 44, 67, 93. *See also* Dionysus; Thyiades/thyein
male mother. *See* mother
"man"/"men," 25, 50–53, 55–56, 62–63, 70, 91–92, 104–6, 124–25, 129, 132, 135, 139, 149, 166. *See also* danger; play; "woman"/"women"
  feminized men, 57, 116, 117, 125, 135, 145
  higher man/men, 30, 34, 93, 96, 100, 103, 109–10, 112, 151–52

ignoble/slavish man, 51
last men/smallest men, 102, 127, 133, 138
manly, 56–57, 63, 79, 135. *See also* masculine; manly love, 62–63; manly morality, 119; manly virtues (*see* virtues)
married men, 52. *See also* marriage
noble man, 7, 9, 46, 51, 102, 103, 105, 113, 118, 119, 121, 128, 133, 136, 138, 139, 142, 143, 144, 145, 146, 160, 164
"old man," 57, 116
softer men, 135, 143
ugliest man, 90, 93, 98, 110, 158. *See also* animal(s); ass
unbred man, 134, 135
Mandel, Siegfried, 11, 12
Mann, Thomas, 12, 39, 42, 44, 81
  Death in Venice, 42, 81
marriage, 50–52, 55, 57, 63, 69, 76, 85, 92, 108, 109, 119, 169
Martin, Biddy, 13
masculine, 3, 4, 8–11, 17, 19, 20, 25, 37, 40, 42, 43, 46, 53, 58, 61, 63–67, 69, 70, 72, 74, 77–78, 85, 91–92, 94, 97, 102, 105, 107, 115–18, 140, 145, 148, 150–51, 153, 155, 156, 160, 163–64, 166, 169, 179. *See also* female; feminine; feminist; "man"/"men"; virtue
masculine mother. *See* mother
masculinity, 11, 26, 106, 146, 150, 169
super-masculine, 72, 77, 94, 115, 116, 120, 153, 154, 167
mask(s), 5, 9, 20, 25, 28, 33, 38, 40, 41, 43–45, 49, 50, 52–54, 58–60, 64–67, 70, 72, 74, 76, 78, 83, 94, 98, 100, 102, 104–6, 108, 115, 118, 126, 130, 134, 140, 142, 149–50, 152–53, 156. *See also* irony
masked, 11, 18, 27, 79, 100, 104, 113, 155, 163
Massacre at Chios. *See* Delacroix
master morality. *See* moral(ity)

master-myth, 83, 108
master/slave dialectic, 11, 167, 171. *See also* Hegel, G. W. F.
maternal, 31, 33, 36–37, 50, 66–67, 74, 81–83, 91, 105, 107, 110, 127, 130, 146, 150, 153, 169. *See also* feminine
Medusa, 4, 6, 8, 22, 24, 25, 37, 67, 76, 108, 150, 169. *See also* Baubô; Demeter; Gaia; Persephone
Merimee, Prosper, 64. *See also* prose-poetry [*under* poetry]
metaphor, 39, 40, 65, 69, 121, 169, 178. *See also* figure; trope
microscopic, 11, 19, 38. *See also* macroscopic
Midas, 44, 45, 53. *See also* hope; Pandora; Silenus
Middleton, Christopher, 6
midwife(ry), 64, 75, 149. *See also* rebirth
Miller, N. K., 169
Milton, John, 170
Minh-ha, Trinh, 11, 16, 37, 170, 171, 172, 173. *See also* Cixous, Hélène; difference; silence; veil
minotaur, 85. *See also* Ariadne; Dionysus; Zeus
misogynist(ic), 1, 2, 3, 4, 5, 16, 19, 20, 22, 23, 26, 33, 34, 37, 38, 57, 63, 76, 113, 116, 119, 130, 131, 133, 138, 139, 140, 146, 149, 154, 156, 162, 163. *See also* "woman"/"women"
modern(ity), 4–7, 9–11, 17, 19, 20, 22, 26, 30–31, 33, 38, 40–41, 44, 46–50, 53, 54, 59–61, 63–66, 69, 70, 72–77, 79, 83, 86, 90, 93, 102–5, 107, 109, 110, 112–18, 120, 122–24, 126, 128, 130, 132–36, 138–45, 147, 149, 150–51, 153–55, 162, 165, 169, 171, 174, 179–80
Moi, Toril, 35
Moira, 45
Moliere, 129
Montaigne, Michel Eyquem de, 71, 129
Montinari, Mazzino, 42, 48, 84, 85, 88, 91, 92, 94, 96, 100, 101, 104, 105, 108, 111, 114, 120, 127
moon, 56, 82, 89, 173
Moon-Queen, 173
moral(ity), 9, 28, 59, 68, 72, 73, 99, 114, 118, 119, 123, 124, 130, 131, 132, 136, 143, 159. *See also* crab [*under* animal(s)]; Procrustes
aesthetico-moral, 83, 151
amoral(ity), 63, 97
herd morality, 116, 131. *See also* herd; herd [*under* animal(s)]
immoral, 131; immoralist, 59
master morality, 116, 118, 119, 144
slave morality, 116, 118, 119. *See also* ascetic; bad; Christian(s); evil; fettered spirit; good; herd; pity; plebeian; priest; saint; weak; "woman"/"women"
morals, 9, 47, 131
Moses, 89, 102
"mother," 7, 8, 10–11, 32–34, 36, 37, 39, 50–52, 66–67, 71–72, 74–75, 78, 81–82, 84–85, 88, 95, 101–2, 106, 108, 111–12, 116, 126–27, 129–30, 131, 141, 143, 146, 148, 150, 168, 176, 178. *See also* birth; birthing; father; Nietzsche, Franziska; sister; vermin [*under* animal(s)]
feminine mother, 36
Great Mother, 94
male/masculine mother, 3, 72, 74–75, 77, 84, 95, 103, 149, 151, 152. *See also* phallic mother (*below*)
mother earth, 34, 67
Mother Goddess, 31, 94. *See also* Demeter
mother-maiden, 72
mother nature, 15, 150
mother savior, 112
motherhood, 19, 34, 67, 108, 169, 176
motherly love, 50, 51, 74
phallic mother, 9, 19, 28, 32–34, 81, 83, 101–3, 109, 112, 151–52, 155. *See also* male/masculine mother (*above*)
wife-mother, 51, 115
warrior-mother, 83, 109

Motley Cow. *See* animal(s), cow
multicultural(ism), 11, 169, 173, 174, 175
Muraro, Luisa, 15, 21
music, 47, 48, 56, 60, 61, 62, 64, 65, 71, 73. *See also* Beethoven, Ludwig; dance; Romantic(ism); Socrates; Wagner, Richard
myth(s), 1, 3, 5–11, 15, 18, 20–23, 25–26, 29, 32, 36, 37, 41, 43, 47, 48, 52–54, 59–60, 65, 67, 81, 83–86, 88, 90, 92–95, 106, 115, 126, 147–49, 151–53, 155, 161, 162, 166, 168, 170–71, 173, 175, 178–79. *See also* history; nature; reversed cosmos; science; truth
mythologize, 59, 147, 153
 demythologize, 113, 125, 143
 remythologize, 95, 107, 112, 113, 115, 125, 143, 150, 154
mythology, 6, 8, 20, 21, 29, 34, 40, 58, 68, 76, 94, 104, 115, 120, 143, 153, 156, 168
 antimythology, 155
 "Greek mythology," 5, 8, 21, 24, 29, 42, 53, 58, 76, 81, 90, 94, 113, 115, 126, 142, 173
mytho-poetics, 21
mytho/history, 40, 47
mytho/politico
 mythic politics, 77, 93
 mytho-political, 8, 30, 33, 46, 155, 168
 political mythology, 30, 38, 83, 87, 151, 155
 politico-mythic, 6, 101, 107

naked goddess. *See* goddess
Napoleon Bonaparte, 112, 125, 132. *See also* Alexander; Caesar; Wagner, Richard
narcotic(s), 55, 60, 120
nature. *See also* art; Dionysus; dismemberment; life; myth; science
 i.e., essence, 4, 6, 10, 17, 29, 30, 36, 38, 42, 43, 45, 60, 62, 68, 76, 92, 94, 108, 148, 149, 158, 161, 164, 167
 i.e., human disposition, 19, 21, 51–52, 55–56, 62, 68–69, 75, 84, 91–92, 96, 123, 127, 129, 132–33, 139, 146, 149
 i.e., material world, 3–4, 7, 9, 15, 29, 40, 44–46, 55, 58–59, 62, 65–66, 73, 76–78, 97, 99, 115, 131, 139, 147, 150, 153, 158, 166–67, 175–76, 178
New Attic Comedy. *See* Attic
new god. *See* god
new psychologist. *See* psychologist
Nietzsche, Elizabeth. *See* Forster-Nietzsche, Elizabeth; sister
Nietzsche, Franziska, 8, 32, 148. *See also* mother
Nietzsche, Friedrich
 Beyond Good and Evil, 2, 5, 114, 117, 119, 125, 130, 139, 143–45, 153–54
 Birth of Tragedy, The, 5, 7, 17, 25, 40, 41, 42, 47, 53, 54, 60, 61, 63, 64–67, 68, 70, 73, 75–77, 95, 97, 108, 120, 136, 138, 148–49, 161
 Ecce Homo, 2, 5, 7, 8, 12, 13, 32, 98, 111, 112, 122, 125–26, 127, 128, 129, 130, 139, 141–44, 146, 148, 154. *See also* Pilate, sick noble
 Gay Science, The, 2, 5, 7, 8, 19, 23, 32, 34, 41, 59, 62, 63, 64, 72, 75–77, 108, 148–50
 Human, All Too Human, 5, 7, 8, 41, 48, 51, 53, 54, 57, 63, 64, 68–71, 75–77, 148–49
 Joyful Wisdom, The, 2, 41, 59, 72, 78, 148
 My Sister and I, 12–13
 "Nietzsche's life," 8, 12, 18–20, 25, 128–29, 162
 Thus Spoke Zarathustra, 1, 4–8, 15, 18, 28–29, 32, 33, 83–86, 88, 90–93, 96–97, 99, 100, 101, 104, 105, 106, 108, 111, 112, 116, 138, 141, 146, 151, 152, 158. *See also* Zarathustra, Zarathustran
 Twilight of the Idols, 5, 19, 119–20, 124–25, 130, 133–34, 137, 140, 143, 144, 145, 154, 156. *See also* physician

of modernity
Nietzchean, 3, 4, 18, 22, 26, 30, 31, 37, 38, 114, 124, 155, 164, 172, 174
post-Nietzschean, 10, 11, 37, 166, 175
nihilism, 6, 19–20, 28, 29, 40, 102, 103, 153, 159, 162. *See also* modern(ity); resentment
nobility, 8, 29, 30, 61, 76, 77, 83, 98, 99, 109, 112, 121, 128, 138, 140, 145, 146
  ignoble, 46, 102, 108, 116, 121; ignoble/slavish man (*see* "man"/"men"); ignoble soul, 118; ignoble women, 50–51
  noble lie, 6–7, 18, 20–21, 27–30, 83, 103–4, 148, 151–53, 155. *See also* rhetoric
  noble man. *See* "man"/"men"
non-Christian. *See* Christian(s)
nondifference. *See* difference
non-German. *See* German
non-Platonic. *See* Plato
nonpolitical. *See* apolitical; political
nude goddess. *See* goddess
nurturance, 40, 47, 88, 91, 93, 118, 128, 165, 178
Nurturance?. *See* Picart, Caroline Joan
Nye, Andrea, 35

Odysseus, 19, 46, 71, 115, 120, 139
Oedipus, 45–46, 64, 72, 107, 114–15, 120, 140. *See also* Prometheus
  Oedipus-Dionysus, 115
  Oedipus-Odysseus, 115
Okhamafe, Imafedia, 2
Okonta, Ike, 28
old God *See* God
old man. *See* "man"/"men"
old woman. *See* "woman"/"women"
Oliver, Kelly, 2, 11, 24, 32–33, 35–37
Olympian(s), 44, 67, 84
Oppel, Frances, 101
optimism, 4, 6, 19, 25, 29, 33, 41, 48, 102–3, 133, 136, 149–51, 164
Oresteia (Orestes), 21, 45, 168. *See also*

Cixous, Hélène
Oriental, 83, 133, 145, 154, 176. *See also* exotic(ism); wisdom
Ormiston, Gayle, 2
other-worldly. *See* world
overman. See *Übermensch*
Owen, David, 31

Pandora, 48, 52–53, 70, 76. *See also* fettered spirit; hope; Midas; Silenus
Parousia, 59
parthenogenesis, 9, 43. *See also* birthing; pregnancy
Pascal, Blaise, 71, 129
Patens, Erik, 2
pathos of distance, 28, 135, 146. *See also* health(iness); master morality [*under* morality]; vitality
Pautrat, Bernard, 4
Pellauer, David, 21
penis. *See* phallus
Penthesilea. *See* Kleist, Heinrich von
Persephone, 24, 25, 66, 67. *See also* Baubô; Demeter; Eleusinian; Gaia; Medusa
Persian Wars. *See* war
personification, 7, 25, 40–41, 43, 46, 58, 60, 64–66, 70, 76–77, 94, 108. *See also* anthropomorphism; figure
pessimism, 4–6, 33, 49, 65, 95, 97, 102–3, 113, 115, 122, 133, 138, 139, 151, 154
Peters, H. F., 13
phallic mother. *See* "mother"
phallicacy, 10
phallocentrism, 37, 167
phallocratic, 21. *See also* gynecocratic
phallogocentrism, 35, 151
phallus, 3, 25, 88. *See also* Baubô
philosophers
  father of the philosophers. *See* father
  philosopher-artist, 11, 179
  philosopher of the future, 116–19, 130, 143
  philosopher-lover, 138
  philosophico-political. *See* politico/philosophico

physician of modernity, 130, 134. See also
  Twilight of the Idols [*under* Nietzsche,
  Friedrich].
physiologist-psychologist, 129
Picart, Caroline Joan, 42, 79, 155
  Nurturance?, 176–79
Pilate, 54, 55, 126. See also *Ecce Homo*
  [*under* Nietzsche, Friedrich]
Pinsent, John, 84, 88, 95
Pippin, Robert, 28
pity, 61, 68, 96, 99, 100, 105, 114, 117,
  119, 145, 151. See also Christianity;
  philosopher of the future [*under*
  philosophers]; slave morality [*under*
  moral(ity)]
self-pity, 64
Plato, 20–21, 27–28, 40, 47, 71, 137, 148.
  See also Socrates
Platonic, 27–28, 33, 65, 87, 122, 124,
  155; non-Platonic, 34
Platonism, 20; reverse Platonism, 27
Republic, The, 21, 27–29
Statesman, The, 47, 148
play
  i.e., activity in pursuit of pleasure, 91–92,
    102, 146. See also danger;
    "man"/"men"; "woman"/"women"
  i.e., theatrical production, 40, 114;
    playful virtues (*see* virtues); woman as
    dangerous plaything (*see*
    "woman"/"women")
Pleasantness, 63–64, 76. See also graces;
  knowledge; poetry
plebeian, 7, 20, 46, 58, 68, 83, 98, 102–3,
  105, 111, 113, 118, 119, 121, 127,
  135, 137–40, 142, 144–45, 152, 154,
  160, 164. See also Christian(s); ears;
  slave morality [*under* moral(ity)];
  "woman"/"women"
poet, 54, 73, 110
poetry, 60, 63, 64. See also knowledge;
  mytho-poetics; Pleasantness
  Greek poetry, 44
  poetic, 22, 33, 34, 60, 72, 102, 117

prose-poetry, 64
polis, 5, 6, 20, 21, 28, 69, 97, 102, 133,
  139, 140, 141, 148, 150, 151, 155
political
  apolitical/nonpolitical, 28
  mytho-political. See mytho/politico
  political mythology. See mytho/politico
  political philosophy. See politico/
    philosophico (*below*)
  politico-mythic. See mytho/politico
  socio-political, 8, 17, 34, 57, 76, 175
politico/aesthetico
  aesthetico-political, 37, 40, 48, 67, 83,
    90, 150, 151, 155
  political aesthetic(s), 6–8, 10, 11, 16, 17,
    29, 66, 141, 149, 169
politico/philosophico
  philosophico-political, 36, 83
  political philosophy, 3, 5, 8–9, 16,
    19–20, 25–28, 32–33, 36, 40, 64, 69,
    78, 99, 128, 131, 138, 141–42, 144,
    147–48, 151–52, 154–55
politics, 3, 5–6, 8, 10, 11, 13, 15–20, 22,
  23, 26, 28, 29, 31, 32, 36, 37, 38, 41,
  47, 48, 62, 70, 77, 91, 93, 97, 99,
  115–17, 132, 139, 143, 147–56,
  160–69, 171, 175, 179. See also
  aesthetics; Greek; sexual politics
post-Nietzschean. See Nietzschean
post-Romantic(ism). See Romantic(ism)
post-Zarathustran. See Zarathustran
postmodern(ity), 10, 11, 18, 37, 169, 174,
  175, 180. See also modern(ity)
power, 3–4, 9, 11, 18–21, 25–26, 28, 29,
  30, 31, 37–39, 45, 46, 49, 59, 61, 65,
  73, 74, 77, 81, 82, 90, 91, 96, 97, 99,
  102, 105, 117, 119–21, 134, 141,
  149–51, 158, 159, 161, 165–67, 170,
  172, 174, 178–80. See also decadence;
  disease; empowerment/disempowerment;
  health(iness); impotence; vitality; will
  generative power, 5, 19, 149
  power of birthing, 5, 9, 21, 33, 65, 72,
    74, 77, 94, 152–154

procreative power(s), 95
regenerative power(s), 4, 5, 8, 26
reproductive power(s), 47, 66
pre-Zarathustran. *See* Zarathustran
pregnancy, 3, 15, 71, 74, 77, 84, 89, 91–92, 102–3, 107–8, 152. *See also* birth; parthenogenesis; "woman"/"women"
hysterical pregnancy, 9, 103, 152. *See also* hysteria
priest, 49, 58, 59, 72, 73, 78, 83, 105, 124, 151. *See also* ascetic; Christian(s); saint; slave morality [*under* moral(ity)]; "woman"/"women"
priestly, 105, 134
priestess, 49, 58, 76
procreative power(s). *See* power
Procrustes, 136. *See also* moral(ity)
Prometheus, 45, 46, 61, 63, 64. *See also* Ajax; *der Frevel*; Oedipus
prose-poetry. *See* poetry
Proserpine, 66, 67, 76
Proteus, 52
psychologist, 122
new psychologist, 130, 143. See also *Beyond Good and Evil* [*under* Nietzsche, Friedrich]
psychologist of modernity, 132, 133
psychologist of the feminine, 133, 139, 140, 146, 154, 164
psychology, 3, 32, 115, 123

Racine, 56, 129
Raphael, 45, 72
Transfiguration, 45
rausch. *See* frenzy
rebirth, 41, 43, 47, 66–67, 75, 77, 83, 85–87, 89, 94, 142–44, 151, 154–55. *See also* birth; midwife; recuperation
rebirth of tragedy. *See* tragedy
reconstruction, 9, 10, 26, 81, 145, 164, 179. *See also* deconstruction
re-creation, 11, 19, 40, 54, 73, 83, 93, 102, 109, 112, 170
recuperation, 38, 41, 65–66, 70, 113, 133,
153. *See also* rebirth
Rée, Paul, 54
re-empowerment. *See* empowerment
regeneration, 25, 32, 109, 111
eternally generating, 9, 25, 107
regenerative power(s). *See* power
Reinach, Saloman, 24
remythologize. *See* mythologize
reproductive power(s). *See* power
Republic, The. *See* Plato
resentment/*ressentiment*, 5, 10–11, 16, 19, 22, 33, 36–37, 57, 61, 64, 70, 81, 82, 87, 92, 101–3, 110, 126, 128–29, 142, 152, 154–55, 157, 162–66, 168, 170, 174, 175, 179, 180. *See also* modern(ity); nihilism; revenge; will
self-resenting, 164
resurrection, 20, 67, 85, 88, 90, 126, 135, 141, 148, 149, 164
revaluation, 5, 68, 73, 105, 128, 139, 143, 172, 174, 180
revenge, 9, 81, 103–4, 107, 119, 122, 125, 131–32, 135, 139, 145, 163. *See also* resentment/*ressentiment*
reverse Platonism. *See* Plato
reversed cosmos, 47, 65, 148. *See also* myth
Rhea, 85, 94
rhetoric, 3, 20, 98–99, 102–3, 109, 127, 135, 138, 143, 152. *See also* noble lie
Ricoeur, Paul, 21
Roman(s). *See* Rome
Romantic(ism), 5, 11, 18–19, 40, 49, 54, 60–62, 64, 68, 69, 71, 75, 77–79, 83, 84, 95–97, 99–101, 103–4, 107–8, 112, 128, 149, 155, 160, 162, 169, 179. *See also* dandy; David; Wagner, Richard; Schopenhauer, Arthur
anti-Romantic(ism), 73, 78
post-Romantic(ism), 166
Roman(s), 107, 137
Rome. *See* Stoic Rome
Rosen, Stanley, 91, 92, 102–3, 142, 148, 152
Rosenburg, Alfred, 28

Rosenthal, Maud, 12
Roth, Samuel, 12, 13
Rousseau, Jean Jacques, 59, 71, 125. *See also* German Virtue [*under* virtue]; Sand, George

sacrilege, 46, 61
saint, 49, 122, 126, 131. *See also* ascetic; Christian(s); fettered spirit; priest; slave morality [*under* moral(ity)]; "woman"/"women"
Sainte-Beuve, Charles Augustin, 125
Sallis, John, 41, 42
Salomé, Lou Andreas-. *See* Andreas-Salomé, Lou
Sand, George, 125. *See also* Rousseau, Jean Jacques
satyr(ic), 41, 43–45, 76, 114, 126, 150. *See also* Dionysus; Helen; shepherd; Silenus;
  satyr play, 114
Schiller, Johann, 66
Schopenhauer, Arthur, 6, 17, 49, 61, 65, 68, 71, 75, 95. *See also* Romantic(ism); Wagner, Richard
Schor, Naomi, 21, 35, 151
Schutte, Ofelia, 2, 24
science, 40, 46, 47, 50–51, 59, 60, 68–73, 77–78, 115, 158. *See also* author; myth; nature; truth
  scientific, 41, 46, 47, 48, 59, 65, 69, 72–73, 114, 158, 173
  scientist, 72–75, 77–78, 114, 149. *See also* artist
sea, 63, 82, 88, 95, 107. *See also* Irigaray, Luce
Seery, John, 71
self-empowerment. *See* empowerment/disempowerment
self-knowledge. *See* knowledge
self-love. *See* love
self-pity. *See* pity
self-resenting. *See* resentment/*ressentiment*
Semele, 15, 39, 84. *See also* Dionysus; Hera; Zeus

Semitic, 46. *See also* Aryan; Fall
seven, 92, 93
sex. *See also* gender
  i.e., coupling, 12, 90, 149, 165
  i.e., gender, 1, 7, 25, 42, 51, 62, 68, 70, 92, 94, 124, 139, 145, 149, 169, 172–73
sex organ(s), female, 25, 101. *See also* phallus
sexes, law of. *See* Law of the Sexes
sexual, 18, 42–44, 57, 67, 70, 76, 90
sexual difference. *See* difference
sexual identity, 18
sexual love, 90
sexual orientation, 175
sexual politics, 15
sexuality, 53, 65, 76, 166, 169
  bisexuality, 18–19, 77, 168–69. *See also* Cixous, Hélène
  homosexuality, 15
Shakespeare, William, 27
Shapiro, Gary, 9, 26
Shelley, Percy Bysshe, 170
shepherd, 44, 88, 89, 103. *See also* satyr; *Übermensch*
Shiach, Morag, 167, 169, 170
short-eared. *See* ear
sick(ness), 7, 9, 11, 16, 19, 48, 53, 55, 59, 60, 63, 65, 67, 71, 73, 75, 77, 95, 98, 106, 109, 113–14, 117, 120–21, 124, 128–29, 133–35, 140, 144, 146, 148–49, 150, 154–55, 162, 174
  sick age/era, 5, 69, 117, 120, 123, 135–36, 142–43, 145, 154
  sick noble, 130, 139. See also *Ecce Homo* [*under* Nietzsche, Friedrich]
silence(d), 18, 25, 33, 38, 39, 87, 88, 155, 172–73. *See also* Minh-ha, Trinh
Silenus, 44–45, 53, 76. *See also* Dionysus; Midas; satyr
sin, 46, 56, 61, 112, 116, 124
  der Frevel/die Sunde, 40, 46, 61
  original sin, 46, 123
  sinful, 61
  sins, 5, 9, 61, 140, 163
sing(ing)/song, 30, 39–40, 46, 92, 101,

103, 110
Sirens' song, 19, 59, 61, 115, 139
Singer, Linda, 2
Siren(s), 19, 59, 61, 107, 114–15, 139
sister, 7, 8, 11–12, 61, 63, 64, 76, 78, 82, 85, 88, 111–12, 127, 129, 146. *See also* father; Forster-Nietzsche, Elizabeth; mother; vermin [*under* animal(s)]
slave, 46, 61–62, 131, 167
slave morality. *See* moral(ity)
slave virtue. *See* virtue
slavery, 60, 89, 154
slaves, 119, 131, 133, 135, 137
slavish woman. *See* "woman"/"women"
smallest ears. *See* ear
social animal. *See* animal(s)
socio-political. *See* political
Socrates, 27–29, 40, 46–48, 52, 55, 65, 69, 121–22, 140–41. *See also* Asclepius; death; Doppelgänger; Plato
death of Socrates, 55, 122
softer men. *See* "man"/"men"
Sophocles, 44, 56
Sosipolis, 84, 86. *See also* Dionysus; Zeus
soul, 20, 50, 51, 58, 63, 70, 71, 72, 77, 78, 85, 87, 96, 105, 107, 116, 117, 118, 119, 138–40, 150, 151
spirit. *See* evil; fettered; free
Sphinx, 40, 114–15, 145, 154. *See also* Circe
Spinoza, Baruch, 71
Spivak, Gayatri Chakravorti, 24
Stambaugh, Joan, 22, 156
Stanton, Donna C., 169
Starrett, Shari Neller, 2
Stassinopoulos, A., 84
Statesman, The. See Plato
Staten, Henry, 24, 65
Steele, J., 169
Stewart, Walter, 13
Stoic Rome, 59. *See also* German Virtue [*under* virtue]
Strauss, Leo, 18, 20, 26, 27–30, 37, 142, 148, 151, 152, 159, 160. *See also*

esoteric; exoteric
strength, 6, 30, 34, 37, 50, 63, 69, 70, 102, 106, 119–20, 124, 130, 135, 156, 167
strong, 59, 62, 69, 86, 98, 118, 124, 128–29, 136, 140, 157, 159. *See also* master morality [*under* moral(ity)]; pathos of distance; war; warrior; weak(ness); will to power [*under* will]; vitality
Strong, Tracy B., 5, 6, 16–17, 24, 26, 28, 155
style(s), 15–16, 28, 34, 42, 96, 126, 137, 141, 142, 156
Sudra(s), 134. *See also* caste system; Chandala; law of the knife; law of Manu
Sun-King, 173
super-masculine. *See* masculine
superbeing. See *Übermensch*
superhuman, 112, 127. See also *Übermensch*
superman. See *Übermensch*
superstition, 59, 60, 68, 106
symbolic image, 65. *See also* Apollo; Dionysus
symptomatology, 3–6, 15, 20, 32, 34, 38, 111, 130

Tadzio, 42
Tapper, Marion, 165–66
Taylor, Seth, 23
tertium datur, 17
Theisen, Bianca, 17, 18
Theocritus, 56
Thiele, Leslie Paul, 20
thigh birth. *See* birth
this-worldly. *See* world
Thomas, R. Hinton, 13
Thyiades/theyein, 93
tragedy, 40, 43–44, 47, 65, 75–77, 114, 164
    Birth of Tragedy, The. See Nietzsche, Friedrich
    death of tragedy, 46
    Greek tragedy, 44, 46, 53, 76
    rebirth of tragedy, 46–47, 64, 75, 77
transcultural. *See* cultural
transfiguration, 17, 45, 58, 88, 120. *See also* figuration

Transfiguration. See Raphael
trieteris, 93. *See also* Dionysus
trope, 3–4, 7, 16, 34, 40, 59, 66, 75–76, 82, 120, 128, 143–44, 162, 174. *See also* figure; metaphor
Truth (as woman), 28, 61, 78, 145, 150, 160
truth, 3, 10, 16, 17, 21, 26, 28, 29, 33, 40, 46, 48, 54, 61, 65, 68, 73, 92, 114, 116, 126, 132, 149, 159, 170, 171. *See* also *aletheia*; lie; myth; science; will
truths, 29, 108, 131, 170
twilight of the idols, 6, 113, 119

Über-figure, 102, 108
Übermensch, 2, 9, 12, 16, 20, 28–30, 32–33, 81, 83, 86, 88–90, 92–93, 95–97, 101–3, 106–10, 112, 118, 126, 128, 133–34, 138, 141, 151–53, 155, 162, 164. *See also* shepherd
ugliest man. *See* "man"/"men"
uglification, 132, 145. *See also* "woman"/"women"
unbred man. *See* "man"/"men"
underworld, 24, 85, 106. *See also* descent; Hades; world; Zarathustra
unfettered. *See* fettered
unhealthiness. *See* health(iness); sick(ness)

veil. *See also* Minh-ha, Trinh
 i.e., garment or scrim, 172–73
 i.e., metaphorical concealment, 12, 68
virtue, 53, 62, 63, 68, 109, 121–23, 132, 135, 136. *See also* happiness
virtues, 29, 68, 102, 108, 119. *See also* happiness
 Christian, virtue(s), 124, 139
 effeminate virtues, 114
 German Virtue, 58, 59. *See also* Beethoven, Ludwig; Kant, Immanuel; Rousseau, Jean Jacques; Stoic Rome
 male/manly virtue(s), 53, 70, 102, 116, 125, 129, 145. *See also* feminine; male; masculine; "woman"/"women"

 master virtues, 119
 playful virtues, 119. *See also* danger; manly virtues (*above*); play
 slave virtue, 63
vitality, 4, 7–9, 21, 30, 40, 60, 61, 70, 74–76, 94, 101, 109, 128, 140, 147, 151, 153, 164. *See also* decadence; disease; health(iness); impotence, masculine; master morality [*under* moral(ity)]; pathos of distance; power; war; warrior

Wagner, Cosima, 7, 11, 13, 112, 129–30, 146, 148
Wagner, Richard, 17, 47, 49, 54, 57, 60–61, 65, 68, 71, 75, 112, 129. *See also* music; Alexander; Caesar; Napoleon; Romanticism; Schopenhauer, Arthur;
Wagnerian, 30, 71, 95, 125
Waite, Geoff, 156, 163
Wallace, Mark, 21
war, 17, 53, 64, 76, 91, 117, 118, 119, 129, 135, 144, 147, 168, 173, 179. *See also* health(iness); master morality [*under* moral(ity)]; strong [*under* strength]; vitality
Persian Wars, 95
warlike, 63, 119
warrior, 40, 47, 50, 63, 91, 92, 102, 104, 106, 108, 116, 134, 135. *See also* health(iness); master morality [*under* moral(ity)]; strong [*under* strength]; vitality
warrior-heir, 103
warrior-mother. *See* mother
warrior-woman, 93
weak(ness), 4, 30, 52, 59, 61–63, 69–70, 99, 109, 115, 117, 122, 129, 130, 134–37, 140, 143–44, 157, 159. *See also* Christianity; health(iness); slave morality [*under* moral(ity)]; strength
Weed, Elizabeth, 35
weib, 5, 7, 49, 51–52, 54–56, 58, 62, 71, 124, 125, 139. *See also*

"woman"/"women"
weibchen, 104
weiblich, 5, 7, 33, 46, 71, 74, 125, 139. See also feminine
well-being, 117, 121, 135, 144
whip, 1, 92
Whitford, Margaret, 21, 35, 151
whore, 106–7, 152
wife-mother. See mother
will, 34, 40, 43, 52, 56, 62, 74, 82, 104, 109, 115, 120, 122, 123, 136, 173
　free will, 124, 143
　will-to-death, 55, 61. See also death
　will-to-life, 95, 114. See also life
　will-to-Nothingness, 61
　will-to-power, 3, 8, 28, 32–33, 92, 98, 102–3, 110, 116, 119, 153, 157, 159, 161–62, 164, 166 See also power
　will-to-resentment, 36, 79, 147, 162–63, 165, 175–76, 178. See also resentment/*ressentiment*
　will-to-truth, 72, 74, 114, 145. See also truth
　will-to-untruth, 114
wisdom, 8, 21, 29, 44, 45, 72, 89, 90, 99, 104, 107, 126, 131, 152
　Greek wisdom, 60, 87, 145, 154. See also Greek
　Oriental wisdom, 133, 145, 154. See also Oriental
"woman"/"women," 3, 5, 7–8, 11, 17–19, 23, 25, 32, 36–37, 41, 49, 50–52, 54–58, 60, 62–63, 68, 70–72, 74–75, 77–79, 91–93, 104, 106–7, 124–25, 132–33, 139–40, 145–46, 149, 153–55, 162–63, 168. See also animal(s); ascetic; Christian(s); danger; feminine; feminist; fettered spirit; little; "man"/"men"; marriage; masculine; misogyny; play; plebeian; pregnancy; priest; slave morality [*under* moral(ity)]; uglification; virtue
　as dangerous plaything, 9, 91–92. See also danger; play
　clever woman, 50, 55, 139, 146
　noble woman, 51, 52, 62
　"old woman," 8, 39, 90–92, 106, 114, 131, 152
　perfect woman, 50, 62, 124
　slavish woman, 51, 63, 104, 106, 119, 133, 135, 145, 154
　woman as opposed to feminine, 5, 51, 113
　woman-as-parasite. See parasite [*under* animal(s)]
　woman-as-vermin. See vermin [*under* animal(s)]
　woman/feminine. See feminine/woman
womanish, 57, 62, 71, 105, 117
womanly, 7, 22, 51, 54, 57, 59, 61, 72, 131, 134–35, 145; womanly love, 50–51, 62–63; womanly virtue, 62, 114
womb, 3–4, 15, 48, 72, 82, 84, 93, 101, 153
womb envy, 3, 15, 82, 101, 110
world, 3, 4, 6, 17, 21, 34, 40, 45, 47, 54, 66, 72–73, 74, 81, 82, 93, 100, 101, 120, 145, 155, 157, 158, 161, 163–64, 165, 170, 175
　animal world. See animal(s)
　Greek world. See Greek
　new world order, 9
　other-worldly, 122
　scientific world. See scientific
　Third World, 160, 178
　this-worldly, 97, 122
　true world, 124, 145
　world-affirming, 116
　world-destiny, 55
　world-weary, 105

Yes to life. See life. See also *amor fati*; will-to-life

Zarathustra, 6, 28, 30, 82–100, 102, 103, 106–10, 152–153, 167. See also child; fire-hound, snake [*under* animal(s)]
Zarathustran, 5, 9, 19, 20, 29, 32, 41, 81, 116, 133, 141, 150, 153–54
　post-Zarathustran, 2, 5–7, 9, 19–20,

Zarathustran *(continued)*
    28–30, 34, 41, 111, 113, 125, 130,
    140–44, 148, 150, 152–54, 156, 163,
    165, 167–69
  pre-Zarathustran, 2, 5–7, 9, 19, 20, 25,
    29, 32, 34, 39, 40, 41, 45, 48, 64, 75,
    78, 79, 107, 113, 116, 141, 148–50,
    153–54, 165

Zeus, 6, 8, 15, 47, 52–53, 58, 64, 67, 76,
    82, 84, 94, 95, 143
  Zeus-Athena, 56, 84
  Zeus-Dionysus, 84–86, 88–89, 92–94
  Zeus-Dionysus-Apollo, 5, 8, 72, 83, 94,
    96, 102, 108, 112, 146, 151, 153
  Zeus-Dionysus-Zarathustra, 94
zöe, 85. *See also* life

www.ingramcontent.com/pod-product-compliance
Lightning Source LLC
Chambersburg PA
CBHW031550300426
44111CB00006BA/257